D1084516

EURODÉLICES

PASTRIES

EURODÉLICES

PASTRIES

DINE WITH EUROPE'S MASTER CHEFS

KÖNEMANN

Acknowledgements

We want to thank the following persons, restaurants and companies for their contribution to this book:

Ancienne Manufacture Royale, Aixe-sur-Vienne; Baccarat, Paris; Chomette Favor, Grigny; Christofle, Paris; Cristalleries de Saint-Louis, Paris; Grand Marnier, Paris; Groupe Cidelcem, Marne-la-Vallée; Haviland, Limoges; Jean-Louis Coquet, Paris; José Houel, Paris; Lalique, Paris; Les maisons de Cartier, Paris; Maîtres cuisiniers de France, Paris; Philippe Deshoulières, Paris; Porcelaines Bernardaud, Paris; Porcelaine Lafarge, Paris; Puiforcat Orfèvre, Paris; Robert Haviland et C. Parlon, Limoges; Société Caviar Petrossian, Paris; Villeroy & Boch, Garges-les-Gonesse; Wedgwood Dexam-International, Coye-la-Forêt.

A special thank you goes to: Lucien Barçon, Georges Laffon, Clément Lausecker, Michel Pasquet, Jean Pibourdin, Pierre Roche, Jacques Sylvestre and Pierre Fonteyne.

Difficulty of a recipe

✶   easy

✶✶   advanced

✶✶✶   difficult

Photos: Studio Lucien Loeb, Maren Detering

© Fabien Bellhasen and Daniel Rouche

© 1998 for the English-language edition
Könemann Verlagsgesellschaft mbH
Bonner Str. 126, D - 50968 Köln

Translation from German: Fiona Hulse
Coordinator for the English-language edition: Tammi Reichel
English-language editor: Tammi Reichel
Jacket design: Peter Feierabend
Series project manager: Bettina Kaufmann
Assistant: Stephan Küffner
Typesetting: Goodfellow & Egan
Proofreading: Jacqueline Dobbyne
Production manager: Detlev Schaper
Assistant: Nicola Leurs
Reproduction: Reproservice Werner Pees
Printing and binding: Leefung Asco Printing Co., Ltd.

Printed in China

ISBN 3-8290-1131-8

10 9 8 7 6 5 4 3

Contents

Foreword

The Eurodélices series brings a selection of European haute cuisine right into your kitchen. Almost 100 professional chefs, many of them recipients of multiple awards and distinctions, associated with renowned restaurants in 17 countries throughout Europe, joined forces to create this unique series. Here they divulge their best and their favorite recipes for unsurpassed hot and cold appetizers, fish and meat entrees, desserts, and pastry specialties.

The series as a whole, consisting of six volumes with over 1,900 pages, is not only an essential collection for gourmet cooks, but also a fascinating document of European culture that goes far beyond short-lived culinary trends. In a fascinating way, Eurodélices explores the common roots of the different "arts of cooking" that have developed in various geographic locations, as well as their abundant variety.

For eating is much more than the fulfillment of a basic bodily need; cooking is often elevated to the level of an art, especially in association with parties and celebrations of all kinds, in private life and in the public sphere. Young couples plan their futures over a special dinner at an elegant restaurant, partners gather at table to launch new business ventures, heads of state are wined and dined. Every conceivable celebration involves food, from weddings to funerals, from intimacies shared over coffee and cake to Sunday dinners to Passover and Thanksgiving feasts.

We often have our first contact with the cultures of other lands, whether nearby or across an ocean, through their food. Precisely because the various contributing chefs are rooted in their distinct traditions, some flavors and combinations will be new to North American readers, and occasionally ingredients are called for that may be unfamiliar or even difficult to locate. The texts accompanying each recipe help elucidate and, wherever possible, suggest substitutes for ingredients that are not readily available in North America. A glossary is also included to explain terms that may not be obvious, listing some ingredients.

Because precision is often crucial to the success of recipes of this caliber, a few words regarding measurements and conversions are in order. In Europe, it is customary to use metric units of liquid volume or weight, that is, milliliters or grams. Every household has a kitchen scale and solid ingredients are weighed, rather than measured by volume. Converting milliliters to fluid cups and grams to ounces is straightforward, if not always neat. More problematic are ingredients given in grams that North Americans measure by volume, in tablespoons and cups. Throughout the Eurodélices series, the original metric measurement follows the North American equivalent. The conversions are painstakingly accurate up to 100 ml and 100 g (which necessitates some awkward-looking amounts). Thereafter, they are more neatly, and thus less accurately, rounded off. As with all recipes, measurements are approximate for many ingredients, and a wide variety of factors ranging from temperature and humidity to accuracy of kitchen implements to the way food is sold will affect the amount actually used. If the reader wants to recreate the recipes as given, however, the use of a kitchen scale is strongly recommended.

The unique collection of around 750 recipes contained in Eurodélices aims to excite its readers' curiosity. Classic dishes, which have been enjoyed for generations and thus form the foundations of modern cookery, are liberally presented. But there are also new and surprising pleasures, familiar foods prepared in novel ways, as well as culinary delights composed of ingredients from far away places that we experience for the first time. Allow yourself to be inspired by the European master chefs to try and, perhaps, try again.

Riesling

Preparation time: 45 minutes
Cooking time: 30 minutes
Difficulty: ★★★

Serves 8

Viennese sponge cake, short pastry, marzipan
mixture: (see basic recipes)

For the Riesling cream:
3¹/₂ tbsp / 50 ml Riesling wine
3¹/₂ tbsp / 50 g superfine sugar
3 egg yolks
3 sheets of gelatin
4 tsp / 20 ml pear schnapps
³/₄ cup / 175 ml cream, whipped

For the topping:
3 Williams pears

For the syrup:
2 tbsp / 30 g superfine sugar
²/₃ cup / 150 ml Riesling wine
juice of ¹/₂ lemon

For the coating:
1 oz / 25 g milk chocolate, melted

For the jelly:
2 tbsp / 30 g superfine sugar
³/₄ cup / 200 ml pear juice
1 tbsp agar

For the apricot glaze:
1 tbsp / 25 g apricot jam

Adolf Andersen has a few things in common with his name-sake Hans Christian Andersen, creator of "The Little Mermaid." Both are certainly inventive and have an extremely deft touch when it comes to making their ideas manifest. And, just as the author made the imaginary seem real, Adolf Andersen feels it is important to preserve the natural flavor and quality of the ingredients he uses, making the real seem heavenly.

Once upon a time, there was a gentle little fruit from England, soon available all over Europe and much in demand because it stayed firm when cooked and went very well with alcohol. It was the Williams pear. In this recipe, it is paired with a marzipan mixture, which must be very fresh and tender even though it consists almost entirely of marzipan and contains neither sugar nor eggs.

The marzipan mixture is easy to work with. Like the Riesling cream, it is important to infuse it with air, but neither mixture should be stirred too long or it will collapse when baked or cooked.

In this recipe, Adolf Andersen replaces gelatin with agar, a gelling agent produced from a certain marine algae, which produces a somewhat jelly-like result when cooked. In the Far East, especially in Japan, agar is very widely used. You will be pleased with the result; in a way, it provides the final touch for the Riesling Fairy Tale, just like that old ending, "and they lived happily ever after ..."

1. To make the Riesling cream, bring the wine and sugar to a boil, then whisk with the egg yolks until foamy; remove from the heat and continue to beat. Before the foamy mixture has completely cooled, add the gelatin, which has been soaked in water and carefully drained. Allow to cool. Add the pear schnapps and carefully fold in the stiffly whipped cream. Prepare the Viennese sponge cake and the short pastry.

2. Place the marzipan mixture in a pastry bag with a large tip and pipe rings with a diameter of 12 in / 26 cm onto baking paper. The mixture must be quite stiff or it will lose shape and flatten during baking. Bake for 12–15 minutes at 320 °F / 160 °C until golden brown. Peel the pears, quarter them and add to the boiling syrup. Remove from the heat. Allow the pears to cool in the syrup until they are soft but still firm. Drain and rinse with cold water.

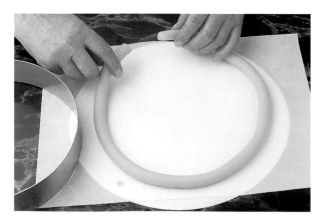

Fairy Tale

3. Cut out a short pastry base with a diameter of 12 in / 26 cm, prick several times with a fork and bake for 20 minutes at 320 °F / 160 °C. Spread the melted milk chocolate on it, and place three macaroon rings on top. Halve the Viennese sponge cake, and cut one of the sponge cake bases in half again. Place the thickest layer of sponge cake inside the rings and cover with Riesling cream (leave ¹/₂ in/1 cm free around the edge); repeat. Cover with the last base, and garnish with Riesling cream.

4. To make the jelly, add the sugar and agar to the pear juice, and boil for three minutes while stirring constantly. Cut the pear quarters into thin slices and arrange on the cake in the form of a fan. Cover with the jelly and refrigerate for two hours. Before serving, brush the macaroon sides with the hot apricot jam.

Raspberry

Preparation time: 1 hour
Cooking time: 30 minutes
Difficulty: *

Serves 8

Viennese sponge cake, short pastry:
   (see basic recipes)

For the raspberry cream:
1²/₃ cups / 400 ml cream
¹/₂ cup, 1 tbsp / 140 g sugar
1 tsp freshly squeezed lemon juice
6 sheets of gelatin
10¹/₂ oz / 300 g raspberries

For the coating:
1³/₄ oz / 50 g milk chocolate, melted

To garnish:
small raspberries
³/₄ cup / 200 ml cream
2 tsp sugar
1 sheet of gelatin

Raspberries, already familiar in ancient times, were known as the "bush of Ida" (after the mountain of that name on the island of Crete, where they originated). In northern Europe, they are used relatively rarely for cakes. But this recipe, which brings out the full velvety flavor of the raspberries, is sure to go down well anywhere.

When you prepare the raspberry cream, there are a few things you can do to preserve both the bright color and high vitamin content of the raspberries. Use only unblemished raspberries, preferably without washing them, and dab them clean using paper towels. The cream can also be prepared when raspberries are in season and kept in the freezer for a real treat in winter.

Raspberries should not be stirred too long or too vigorously if their flavor is to be fully retained. Adolf Andersen sticks to the principles of his grandfather, also a pastry chef. In his view, it is better to use more raspberries than cream and to use as little sugar as possible. If you keep to these guidelines, you will not be disappointed.

This cake is a little like a fruit mousse and can be made in many other flavor varieties. In the Andersen *konditorei* (pastry shop) it was long made using strawberries. If you use generous amounts of wild strawberries, the results will be difficult to surpass.

1. Make the Viennese sponge cake according to the basic recipe, folding the flour into the foamy egg mixture as shown below. After it has thoroughly cooled (and preferably rested overnight), slice the sponge cake horizontally into two layers. Prepare the short pastry and roll it out to a thickness of ¹/₄ in / 3 mm. Cut out a base with a diameter of 13 in / 28 cm, prick several times with a fork and bake for 20 minutes at 320 °F / 160 °C.

2. To make the raspberry cream, beat the cream until stiff. Coarsely puree the raspberries with the sugar and lemon juice. Dissolve the soaked and thoroughly drained gelatin in a double boiler, and add to the raspberry puree. Fold in a quarter of the whipped cream to blend, then fold in the remaining cream.

Cream Torte

3. For the garnish, whip the cream until stiff, add the sugar and stiffen with the dissolved gelatin. Place the short pastry in a cake ring and coat it with melted milk chocolate. Place a $\frac{1}{2}$ in / 1 cm thick layer of Viennese sponge cake on top. Cover with half of the raspberry cream, and top with a second, slightly smaller sponge cake layer. Cover with the remaining raspberry cream, leaving a $\frac{1}{4}$ in / 5 mm space around the edge. Fill the cake ring with whipped cream. Refrigerate for three hours.

4. Remove the cake ring from the torte. Garnish the top by piping dollops of cream around the perimeter of the torte, and place a raspberry on top of each.

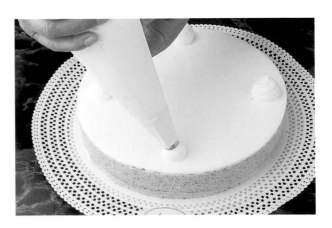

Preparation time: 1 hour 30 minutes
Cooking time: 1 hour 30 minutes
Difficulty: ★★★

Serves 8

For the chocolate glaze:
3¹/₂ oz / 100 g milk chocolate coating
4 tsp / 20 ml sugar syrup
4 tbsp condensed milk
1 tbsp / 20 g honey
Caracas sponge cake, Sacher sponge cake,
  Baumkuchen (see basic recipes)

Cream for garnishing:
6¹/₂ tbsp / 100 g butter

4¹/₂ tbsp / 50 g confectioners' sugar
1 egg
¹/₂ oz / 15 g bittersweet chocolate

For the ganache:
7 oz / 200 g bittersweet chocolate
1¹/₄ cups / 300 ml cream
6¹/₂ tbsp / 100 g butter
³/₄ cup / 200 g sugar
2 egg yolks
4¹/₂ tbsp / 70 ml lemon juice, freshly squeezed

For the coating:
2¹/₂ oz / 75 g bittersweet chocolate

For the marzipan topping:
5¹/₄ oz / 150 g marzipan
3 tbsp / 30 g confectioners' sugar

In the Middle Ages the Hanseatic League was a powerful association of more than one hundred and fifty north German towns that banded together to promote their trade interests. Hamburg, along with Bremen and Lübeck, was one of its most important members and to this day retains a special administrative status derived from its role as a Hansastadt. Hamburg is now one of three German cities that is also a state (something like Washington D.C.) and, uniquely, is ruled by a senate; hence this cake is also called "Senator's Torte."

Hansa torte is a rich combination of several elements. It is filled with ganache, which does not achieve its full effect until it is combined with certain types of sponge cake; for example, the Caracas sponge cake, made using marzipan and a praline

paste, and the *baumkuchen*, which is composed of a number of different layers. The latter is a German specialty found throughout Germany around Christmas. It is baked in a cylindrical form and then sliced horizontally, just as tree trunks are. A certain degree of skill is required to make it. One could also substitute chocolate-covered sponge cake or ladyfingers for the *baumkuchen*. Surprisingly, a variation on the *baumkuchen* is even found in the Pyrenees, perhaps a legacy of the Visigoths on one of their numerous raids.

But there can be no compromising with the ganache, which must be smooth and creamy, not too firm. Using a marzipan made with Italian almonds, which have a higher moisture content, makes the marzipan smoother.

1. To make the chocolate glazing, melt the milk chocolate coating in a double boiler with the sugar syrup (30 °Beaumé), honey and condensed milk, heating it to 100–105 °F / 38–40 °C. Bake the Caracas and Sacher sponge bases. For the garnishing cream, melt the chocolate in a double boiler, and beat the egg and confectioners' sugar until foamy. Cream the butter, then fold in the cooled beaten egg mixture and melted chocolate.

2. Begin the ganache a day in advance by bringing the cream to a boil with the butter and sugar. Set aside. The following day, whisk the egg yolks with part of the cream, then mix everything together and heat until the cream starts to thicken. Remove from the heat, fold in the finely chopped chocolate and the freshly squeezed lemon juice. Refrigerate until needed.

Torte

3. On a cake plate, place the Caracas sponge base inside a cake ring and cover with a quarter of the ganache. Place the Sacher sponge cake on top, centered, and surround with halved baumkuchen rings. Cover with the remaining ganache cream. Press down firmly to eliminate air pockets, and smooth off the surface. Refrigerate for two hours. Invert onto a cake lid, and spread melted chocolate onto the base. Allow to set, then invert again onto a cooling rack.

4. Roll out the marzipan and cover the cake with it. Reheat the chocolate glaze, pour onto the center of the cake and smooth over the top and sides with a spatula. Allow to cool. Pipe chocolate flowers onto waxed paper. Using the garnishing cream, make small balls of the size of a quail's egg and arrange around the sides of the top. Finally place a chocolate flower on top of each dollop of cream.

Preparation time: 1 hour
Cooking time: 30 minutes
Difficulty: ✶

Serves 8

short pastry, Viennese sponge cake:
  (see basic recipes)

For the hazelnut cream:
1 cup, 3 tbsp / 160 g hazelnuts, roasted and ground
4 sheets of gelatin
2¹/₂ cups / 600 ml cream
3 tbsp / 50 g sugar
¹/₂ vanilla bean

For the coating:
1³/₄ oz / 50 g milk chocolate

For the topping:
14 oz / 400 g marzipan
confectioners' sugar (for rolling out)

To garnish:
6¹/₂ tbsp / 100 ml cream
1 tbsp sugar
walnuts

Johann Georg Niederegger, founder of the Niederegger marzipan company in Lübeck, played a major part in distributing marzipan throughout Europe at the beginning of the 19th century. Though the man himself has by now been largely forgotten, his company remains the preeminent manufacturer of quality marzipan, and it is impossible to miss the variety of forms in which marzipan is available – animals, baskets, figures, cigars, balls and many other things – in Lübeck, the former "queen of the Hansa cities."

According to Adolf Andersen, it is particularly important to choose the hazelnuts for this recipe carefully; hazelnuts from Piedmont, for example, work very well. Since they are roasted inside their shells, no harm comes to their delicate flavor. High levels of phosphorus, calcium, and potassium also make up for their relatively low sugar content.

Devote equal attention to the marzipan mixture, which should be relatively light and not too dense. Also, if it is overheated it will become too firm. Avoid questionable artificial colors.

Andersen is clearly fond of using this easily molded material and sculpts entire menageries out of marzipan. You can get a further sense of the active gastronomic traditions in northern Germany by reading *Buddenbrooks*, one of the most famous works of Thomas Mann, who received the Nobel Prize for Literature in 1929 and was himself born in Lübeck.

1. To make the short pastry, knead all the ingredients except for the flour using the kneading hook on an electric mixer until a smooth dough has been produced. Add the flour gradually and knead thoroughly. Wrap the dough in a cloth and refrigerate overnight. Roll it out and cut out a round base with a diameter of 12 in / 26 cm, prick several times with a fork and bake for 20 minutes at 320 °F / 160 °C.

2. Roast the hazelnuts for the hazelnut cream in the oven, then grind them in a blender or food processor. Soak the gelatin in cold water. Whip the cream until stiff, and fold in the nuts. Add the sugar, vanilla pulp, and dissolved gelatin and combine everything thoroughly.

Hazelnut Torte

3. Cut the Viennese sponge cake into two layers, one ¹/₂ in / 1 cm thick and the other a little thinner. Melt the milk chocolate, coat the short pastry base with it, and place the thicker sponge cake base on top. Assemble inside a cake ring. Spread half of the cream on to the Viennese sponge. Cut off a ¹/₂ in / 1 cm strip all the way around the thinner sponge base and place it in the ring. Spread the remaining cream on top. Refrigerate for two hours.

4. Roll out the marzipan on confectioners' sugar. Take the cake out of the ring and cover with the rolled out marzipan. Firm down with your hands; cut off the excess, and press the edge into place so that no tears or folds appear. Garnish the cake with dollops of whipped cream, placing half a walnut on each.

Schöppenstedt

Preparation time: 1 hour
Cooking time: 30 minutes
Difficulty: ★★★

Serves 8

short pastry, vanilla cream: (see basic recipes)

For the Schöppenstedt sponge cake:
1/3 cup / 40 g flour
1/3 cup / 40 g cornstarch
1/4 cup / 30 g cocoa powder
4 1/2 tbsp / 50 g finely ground almonds
3 1/2 oz / 100 g marzipan
4 eggs, separated
2 pinches of salt
1 tsp cinnamon
7 1/2 tbsp / 110 g superfine sugar

For the chocolate cream:
1 1/4 cups / 300 ml milk
2 1/2 tbsp / 40 g superfine sugar
1 pinch of salt
1 egg yolk

3 tbsp / 20 g cornstarch
2 tbsp cocoa powder

For the Schöppenstedt cream:
3 sheets of gelatin
1 3/4 oz / 50 g nut nougat
2 tbsp milk
1 1/2 cups / 350 ml cream

For the coating:
1 3/4 oz / 50 g milk chocolate

To garnish:
3 1/2 oz / 100 g milk chocolate

During his apprenticeship in Braunschweig and at the nearby confectionery school, which has produced a whole stream of contemporary master bakers, Adolf Andersen learned how to create cakes and tortes. He also learned the principles that guide his craft to this day. Andersen uses an extensive repertoire of creams, flavored with various aromas or enriched with dairy cream, as well as various types of cake bases including dough and sponge cake mixtures, to produce a highly creative and almost unlimited range of delicious baked goods.

It is not always easy to coordinate the various stages of work when producing a complicated torte, and certain basic rules must be observed.

The cream for the filling needs to be ready at the same time as the sponge cake base and spread on it right away, as most cream fillings stick very poorly once they have cooled. If another layer is not placed on top of the cream immediately, cover it with plastic wrap so that a skin or crust does not form.

The basis of the Schöppenstedt cream is nut nougat, which, due to its high cocoa content, has a much stronger flavor than the milk chocolate used for the coating and garnish. Before removing the cake from the cake ring, freeze it for a while so that it reaches the right consistency.

1. For the Schöppenstedt sponge cake, sift the flour with the cornstarch and cocoa, and stir in the almonds. Mix the marzipan with the egg yolks, salt and cinnamon until creamy. Beat the egg whites and sugar until stiff, fold a quarter into the marzipan mixture, and then fold in the remainder using a wooden spatula. Finally blend in the flour. Pour the mixture into a 8 in / 20 cm cake ring set on a baking sheet lined with baking paper. Bake for 18–20 minutes at 320 °F / 160 °C.

2. Slice the sponge cake horizontally twice, producing three bases. Bake a short pastry base with a diameter of 13 in / 28 cm. To make chocolate flakes, melt the chocolate in a double boiler, spread on to a plate and allow to set. Use a metal spatula to scrape off flakes. For the chocolate cream, bring 1 cup / 250 ml milk to a boil with the sugar and salt. Beat the egg yolk with the remaining milk, cornstarch, and cocoa powder, stir into the boiling milk and thicken like a custard.

Torte

3. To make the Schöppenstedt cream, soak the gelatin in cold water. Melt the nougat in a double boiler, add the squeezed out gelatin and lukewarm milk, and stir until smooth. Whip the cream until stiff and fold a quarter of it into the cooled nougat mixture. Using a wooden spatula, carefully fold in the remaining whipped cream. Prepare the vanilla cream according to the basic recipe.

4. Spread the melted milk chocolate on to the short pastry and top with the sponge base. Cover with hot vanilla cream, place a second sponge cake base on it and cover with hot chocolate cream. Top with the final layer of sponge cake, leaving a ¹/₂ in / 1 cm strip for the Schöppenstedt cream. Refrigerate for two–three hours. Spread the cream on top and refrigerate. Take the torte out of the ring and garnish with chocolate flakes.

Hamburg

Preparation time: 1 hour
Cooking time: 15 minutes
Difficulty: ★★★

Serves 8

For the sponge cake:
7³/₄ oz / 220 g marzipan
2 tbsp water
6 egg yolks
1 tsp ground cinnamon
3 egg whites

¹/₄ cup / 65 g superfine sugar
6¹/₂ tbsp / 50 g flour
¹/₂ cup / 60 g cocoa powder
4 tbsp sponge cake crumbs
buttercream (see basic recipes):
1³/₄ oz / 50 g semi-sweet chocolate
5 tsp / 25 ml rum
5 tsp / 25 ml arrack

To garnish:
30–35 thin wafers of chocolate

Adolf Andersen's creations are available only in Hamburg, either in his own *konditorei* or in one of its numerous branches, in order to maintain perfect quality control and to prevent the cakes having to be transported in any way.

For this cake to be worthy of the name of this important Hansa town, an exceptional degree of skill and the ability to achieve subtle nuances of flavor are required; these are produced mainly through the combination of two contrasting spirits, rum and arrack. Various sorts of arrack are available; a brandy with an aniseed flavor, it was originally made in India using sugar-cane molasses or rice and eventually from grapes, palm juice or dates (the latter is now the most widely available, produced in Iraq or Lebanon).

The buttercream, with a fat content of about 40% ("French buttercream"), has to be flavored with the rum and arrack right away. The cream should have a light consistency (since the butter and eggs are beaten separately until foamy), but still be sufficiently smooth.

The chocolate wafers garnishing the completely assembled torte at the end should be handled with special care. Place them on to a firm, preferably transparent base and arrange them by size, using a ruler, in such a way that a smooth, shining, almost reflective surface results – a real visual treat for the many fans of this cake.

1. For the sponge cake, mix the marzipan, water, egg yolks, and cinnamon until they form a smooth mixture. Beat the egg whites with the sugar until stiff. Fold half of the beaten egg whites into the marzipan mixture, then fold in the remaining beaten egg whites, flour, cocoa powder and the sifted sponge cake crumbs with a wooden spatula.

2. Place three cake rings with the same diameter on a baking sheet lined with baking paper. Pour the sponge cake mixture into them and bake for 10–12 minutes at 375 °F / 190 °C. Divide the buttercream into two portions, flavoring one half with the melted chocolate and rum, and the other with arrack.

Harbor Torte

3. Set a cake ring with a diameter of 13 in / 28 cm on a cake plate. Place a layer of sponge cake inside the ring, and spread it with some of the rum and chocolate cream. Place a second sponge layer on top and spread arrack cream on to it. Place the last layer on top upside down. Refrigerate for two hours. Take the torte out of the ring.

4. Stir the rest of each of the creams with a whisk until they are smooth. Fill the arrack cream into a pastry bag with a large tip (no. 8), and the rum and chocolate cream into a pastry bag with a medium-sized tip (no. 6). Pipe alternating straight lines of both creams on to the top of the torte. Press chocolate wafers against the sides of the cake.

Preparation time: 1 hour
Cooking time: 20 minutes
Difficulty: ★★

Serves 8

For the Caracas sponge cake:
2 oz / 60 g praline paste
1/2 cup / 60 g sifted flour
1 cup / 60 g sponge cake crumbs
2 1/4 oz / 70 g marzipan
7 egg yolks

1 pinch of salt
2/3 cup, 2 tbsp / 190 g sugar
7 egg whites
1/4 cup / 60 g butter, melted

For the buttercream:
4 eggs
3/4 cup / 200 g sugar
1 pinch of salt
2 cups / 500 g butter
6 1/2 tbsp / 100 ml Grand Marnier

Adolf Andersen created this delicious cake in honor of an architect's wedding. In fact, it could be argued that the art of creating harmonious, gentle pastry compositions has certain parallels with architecture. Make sure your mind is firmly focused on what you are doing when you select and precisely weigh your ingredients, work with them in a calm and focused way and assemble them to form a spectacular end result.

Given that there are 2 cups / 500 g of butter in the buttercream (to just 3/4 cup / 200 g sugar), it is clear that only an excellent butter with a delicate flavor should be used. Do not beat the cream for too long, no longer than 8 minutes in total, because doing so could make it lose its light consistency and perhaps even its flavor.

It is a good idea to prepare the Caracas sponge cake a day in advance, for it must be thoroughly baked and firm. If it becomes too firm, you can revive it by sealing it in a tin immediately after baking. The condensation from the steam it still contains will soften it.

Tastes vary, even regionally; Adolf Andersen has repeatedly found that whipped cream is preferred in northern Germany, while buttercream is very popular in southern Germany. Whichever he chooses, he applies very strict criteria to his choice of ingredients: only first-class ingredients are good enough for his superior concoctions.

1. For the Caracas sponge cake, combine the praline paste with the sifted flour and sponge cake crumbs. Beat the marzipan, egg yolks, salt, and 2 1/2 tbsp / 40 g of sugar with a whisk until smooth. Beat the egg whites until stiff with the remaining sugar. Fold a third of the beaten egg whites into the egg yolk mixture. Fold the remaining egg whites into the flour and praline mixture, and add the melted butter. Finally, gently blend in the egg yolk mixture, stirring just to combine.

2. Line a baking sheet (27 x 18 in / 60 x 40 cm) with baking paper, spread the sponge cake mixture on it with a spatula; and bake for 15 minutes at 340 °F / 170 °C. To make the buttercream, whisk the eggs with the sugar and salt until foamy in a double boiler at 100 °F / 37 °C. Remove from the double boiler and allow to cool completely while stirring. Cream the butter until it is light, then stir in the foamy egg mixture a little at a time.

in Caracas

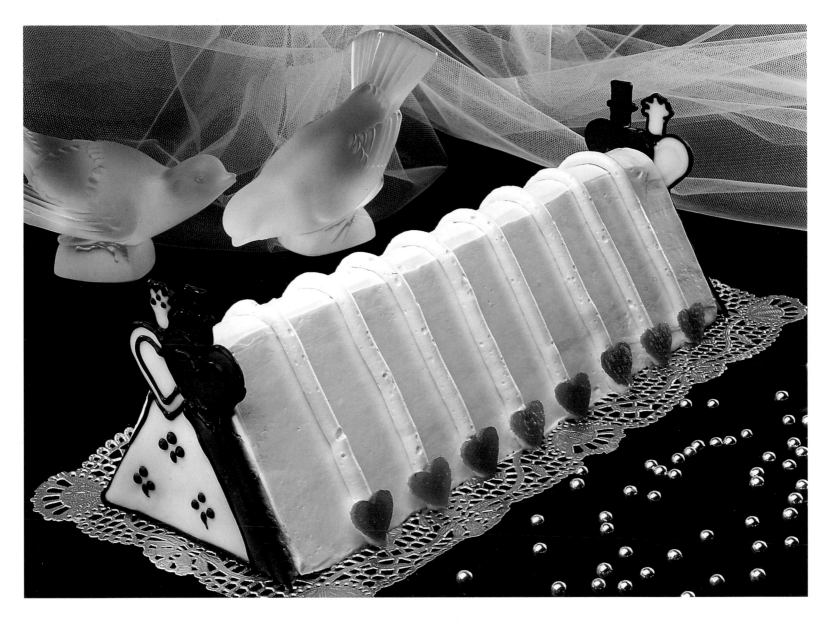

3. Place the sponge cake on a work surface. Flavor the buttercream with Grand Marnier and spread it on the sponge cake, coating the entire surface of the cake with an even, generous layer of cream.

4. Cut the sponge cake into strips 4, 3, 2³/₄, 2¹/₂, 2, 1¹/₂, and ³/₄ in (9, 7, 6, 5, 4, 3 and 1.5 cm) wide and place these on top of each other to form a triangular structure. Cover with buttercream, and mark the individual portions with piped lines of buttercream. Decorate as desired and refrigerate for two hours.

Preparation time: 40 minutes
Cooking time: 15 minutes
Difficulty: ★★

Serves 4

For the sponge cake:
¹/₄ cup / 30 g flour
¹/₄ cup / 30 g cornstarch
5 egg yolks
5 egg whites
5 tbsp / 75 g sugar

For the cream:
3 sheets of gelatin
1¹/₂ cups / 350 ml cream

2 egg yolks
2 tbsp sugar
¹/₂ vanilla bean

To garnish:
1 lb / 500 g strawberries or raspberries

For dusting:
confectioners' sugar

When you choose your strawberries, you should keep in mind that small, dark red berries with plenty of brown seeds are particularly aromatic and have the best flavor. Smaller strawberries are also easier to arrange in the "Strawberry Dream." Just as rules are flexible in dreams, raspberries or other seasonal fruits may be substituted.

Making the sponge cake bases framing the "Strawberry Dream" requires concentration. If you can, prepare the sponge cake a day in advance and do not forget to add the cornstarch,

which makes it easier to cut. Allow it to cool thoroughly before filling it with the cream and strawberries and covering it with another layer of sponge cake. All this must be done with the utmost gentleness, because even the slightest pressure could destroy the whole creation.

Create a special effect by cutting out a slice of the "Strawberry Dream" before serving, so that your guests can admire the layering of sponge cake, cream, and strawberries along the cut edge, a visual treat before they even taste the cake.

1. To make the sponge cake, sift the flour with the cornstarch. Whisk the egg yolks until creamy, and beat the egg whites with the sugar until stiff. Fold a third of the beaten egg whites into the egg yolks, then fold in the flour and cornstarch with a wooden spatula. Finally, carefully fold in the remaining egg whites.

2. Line a baking sheet with baking paper and, using a pastry bag with a large round tip (no. 9), pipe spirals of the sponge cake mixture to a diameter of 7 in / 16 cm on to it. Bake for 10–12 minutes at 355 °F / 180 °C. Allow to cool and peel off the paper.

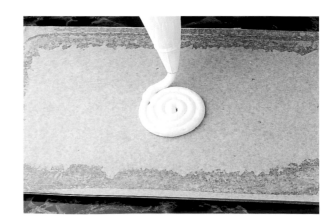

Dream

3. For the cream, soak the gelatin in cold water. Whip the cream until stiff. Whisk the egg yolks with the sugar and vanilla in a double boiler until foamy. Dissolve the gelatin and fold into the foamy mixture with a small amount of whipped cream, then fold in the remaining whipped cream. Place half of the sponge cake bases on a work surface, and arrange the strawberries on them.

4. Fill the cream into a pastry bag with a large tip (no. 10) and pipe onto the strawberries. Place a second sponge cake on top of the cream and press down gently. Refrigerate for two hours. Dust with confectioners' sugar before serving.

Mango

Preparation time: 45 minutes
Cooking time: 20 minutes
Difficulty: ✽✽

Serves 10

For the sponge cake:
6¹/₂ tbsp / 50 g flour
6 tbsp / 40 g cocoa powder
1³/₄ oz / 50 g bittersweet chocolate
6 egg whites
³/₄ cup / 175 g superfine sugar

For the mango buttercream:
2 mangoes
2 eggs
³/₄ cup, 1 tbsp / 200 g superfine sugar
1 cup / 250 g butter
1 pinch of salt

This mango specialty must seem like a sudden ray of sunshine, given the unpleasant gray, cold, and wet weather that the citizens of Hamburg often suffer through in winter. That was Adolf Andersen's intention, and the eager response to this exotic sponge cake roll with its alluring name shows that he was right on target.

The mango tree is native to India, where it is considered sacred. Nowadays, this delectable fruit, rich in vitamins A, C, and D, is grown in California and Florida, among other places. It is also widely available throughout Europe, but hardly anyone knows that well over a thousand varieties of mangoes exist. For this recipe, use fully ripe fruits that are no longer stringy (the mangoes that grow wild, usually very stringy, are

unsuitable); even so, it will not be easy to remove the large seed from the flesh.

Adolf Andersen prefers mangoes from South Africa, for their texture and flavor. The Julie variety, from the French Antilles, is also an excellent choice. Both varieties go well with the chocolate sponge cake and together create a delicate combination that has found an enthusiastic following.

Avoid baking the sponge cake longer than necessary, as this will dry it out and make it difficult to roll up without breaking. Cover it with plastic wrap after baking if you are not going to use it right away.

1. For the sponge cake, sift the flour and cocoa powder. Melt the chocolate in a double boiler. Whisk the egg whites in another, lukewarm double boiler, remove from heat and gradually add the sugar while beating. Fold in the chocolate, then the flour and cocoa. Spread the mixture on a sheet lined with baking paper and bake for 14–17 minutes at 320 °F / 160 °C. Invert onto a pastry cloth sprinkled with sugar.

2. Moisten the baking paper and remove it. Use the pastry cloth to roll up the sponge and let it cool. To make the buttercream, whisk the eggs with the sugar and salt until foamy in a double boiler. Once they have reached 100 °F / 37 °C, remove from the heat and allow to cool completely while beating. Cream the butter until it is light (about 15 minutes) and combine with the egg mixture.

Roll

3. Peel one mango and cut into very thin segments. Peel the second mango and remove the seed. Mash the flesh and pass through a medium-fine sieve. Combine the fruit puree and buttercream, and then refrigerate.

4. Unroll the sponge cake. Spread it with a generous layer of mango buttercream, then lay the mango segments on top. Carefully roll up the sponge cake again and refrigerate for at least three hours. Serve cut in slices.

Sachertorte

Preparation time: 30 minutes
Cooking time: 1 hour 30 minutes
Difficulty: ☆

Serves 8

Sacher sponge cake: (see basic recipes)

For the chocolate glaze:
1³/₄ oz / 50 g milk chocolate
¹/₂ tbsp / 10 ml liquid honey
2 tbsp / 30 ml condensed milk

Sixteen-year-old Franz Sacher, employed by Prince Metternich, invented Sachertorte in 1832. Without it, where would Viennese baking be now? The fact that it started a quarrel between the two most famous Viennese *konditoreien* (pastry shops), Demel and the Sacher Hotel, attests to the symbolism and importance of this delicacy, valued by a select clientele far beyond the borders of Austria.

Adolf Andersen, who has his own version of Sachertorte, remembers when even the Dresden *konditoreien* once tried to lay claim to the Sachertorte. Andersen's cake is based on what information has leaked about the secret original recipe, apparently strictly guarded, and offers many opportunities for exchanging tips and tricks.

The Sacher mixture will only succeed if certain conditions are met: it must contain plenty of butter and chocolate, and the ingredients should have the same temperature. It should not be stirred too vigorously and must be baked at an even temperature. Since it contains only a little flour, it looks more like a soft chocolate mixture than a sponge cake. Before serving, you might like to garnish the Sachertorte with a cream topping.

The honey glaze, a feature exclusive to German varieties, adds a final touch to the general appearance of the cake. Sachertorte must be prepared well in advance; the glaze must have time to set so that the cake does not collapse when it is cut.

1. Prepare the Sacher sponge cake, following the procedure given in the basic recipes, folding the beaten egg yolk and slightly cooled melted chocolate into the batter as shown below. Bake the sponge mixture in a greased cake pan with a diameter of 12 in / 26 cm for 90 minutes at 275 °F / 140 °C.

2. Allow the sponge to cool in the cake pan. Turn it out onto a cooling rack, cover and allow to rest overnight. To make the chocolate glaze, melt the milk chocolate in a double boiler, allow it to cool a little, add the honey and slightly warmed condensed milk, and stir until smooth.

3. Level out any unevenness in the sponge cake with a serrated knife. Retain the sponge cake that you cut off, and sift it to make sponge cake crumbs. Spread the chocolate glaze over the top and sides of the sponge cake.

4. Finally, press the sifted sponge cake crumbs against the sides of the torte. Before serving, refrigerate for 45 minutes.

Baba

Preparation time: 30 minutes
Cooking time: 40 minutes
Difficulty: ★★★

Serves 12

For the baba dough:
1/2 cup / 125 ml milk
1/2 oz / 15 g bakers' yeast
1 1/2 cups / 200 g flour
5 tsp / 25 g sugar
3 egg yolks
1 pinch of salt
a pinch of vanilla powder
grated peel of 1/2 lemon

6 1/2 tbsp / 100 g butter, melted
6 tbsp / 80 g currants

For the syrup:
1 cup / 250 g superfine sugar
2 cups / 500 ml orange juice
1 cup / 250 ml brown rum
grated peel of 1/2 orange

For the glaze:
9 oz / 250 g fondant

To garnish:
Morello cherries
angelica

In Polish, the word *baba* is a childish variation of *babka* – a fat, old woman, whose appearance this traditional yeast cake is probably supposed to resemble. We probably have the Polish king and later Duke of Lorraine, Stanislaus Leszcynski, to thank for the baba's migration to France; he named it after Ali Baba, his favorite hero from *A Thousand and One Nights*. Then again, people in Austria are firmly convinced that the baba originated in Bohemia. Whatever the case, it is not easy to make an excellent baba, for they require concentrated attention. The same is due the ingredients: finely sifted flour, fresh yeast and only brown rum for soaking.

All the ingredients should be at room temperature, except for the milk, which should be a little warmer (95 °F / 35 °C). The dough should be neither too firm nor too runny; experience will teach you to recognize the right consistency. A pastry bag is used to pipe the dough into greased ramekins or other forms that have been sprinkled with sugar. The forms should only be filled two-thirds full since the babas will rise considerably during baking.

After they are baked the babas are placed upside down; the pressure exerted by the forms produces their bulbous appearance. Do be aware that these seemingly innocent cakes pack quite a punch: the currants are marinated in rum, and the babas themselves are drenched in rum syrup after they have cooled.

1. To make the dough, gently warm a third of the milk and dissolve the yeast in it. Add a quarter of the flour, blend, and leave the mixture to prove in a warm place. Thoroughly mix the remaining flour, sugar, egg yolks, salt, vanilla powder, grated lemon peel, and remaining milk with the dough hook of an electric mixer. Add the yeast mixture, and finally, the lukewarm butter and currants.

2. Place the dough in a large bowl, cover with a cloth and allow to rise at room temperature until it has doubled in size. Grease the ramekins with butter, sprinkle with sugar, and fill two-thirds full with the mixture. Leave to rise again, then bake for 20 minutes at 390 °F / 200 °C.

au Rhum

3. Turn the babas out of the forms. To make the syrup, combine the orange juice, rum, sugar, and grated orange peel into a saucepan and bring to a boil. Allow to cool a little. Prick the babas around the sides with a fork so that they better absorb the liquid. Fill the baba forms half-full with syrup and soak the babas in them.

4. Allow the babas to drain on a cooling rack. Heat the fondant in a saucepan and glaze the babas with it. Arrange on a plate and garnish with morello cherries and angelica.

Cassata

Preparation time: 1 hour
Cooking time: 30–40 minutes
Difficulty: ★★

Serves 8

For the chocolate sponge cake:
6 eggs
1 cup / 240 g sugar
1½ cups / 180 g flour
¼ cup / 30 g cocoa
10 tbsp / 150 g butter, melted

For the light sponge cake:
6 eggs
1 cup / 240 g sugar
2 cups / 250 g flour

4½ tbsp / 70 g butter, melted

For the buttercream:
1½ cups / 350 g butter
¾ cup / 120 g confectioners' sugar
1¾ oz / 50 g chocolate
6 tbsp / 80 g candied fruits, marinated in
    Grand Marnier

For the coating:
apricot jam

To garnish:
9 oz / 250 g marzipan, colored green

Relations between Austria and Italy were not always peaceful, and both countries still have vivid memories of the humiliations they have suffered. An Italian example is the defeat at Caporetto (1917), a name that has become synonymous in Italy with terrible catastrophe. But the art of baking is not a military discipline, and for this delicious bombe filled with candied fruits, Franz Augustin welcomed the inspiration of Sicilian ice cream makers.

For the sake of both the visual effect and the flavor, the finely diced candied fruits should have a variety of colors and be marinated for a long time in order to achieve the optimal consistency, however dry and firm they are to start with. Angelica, cherries, orange peel and – why not? – the amazing pumpkin are all suitable.

The most important item needed to produce the bombe shape is a dome-shaped mold, into which the various elements must be placed with great precision; the candied fruits have to be evenly distributed inside, and the many light and dark chocolate layers of the bombe create a pleasing contrast.

The cassata is easier to cut if it is refrigerated for many hours before serving, overnight at least. This gives it a firmer consistency so that it will not fall apart when cut. Your guests will delight in its colorful slices.

1. For the chocolate sponge cake, stir the eggs and sugar with an electric mixer until foamy, so that the mixture drops off the beaters in smooth ribbons. Sift the flour and cocoa, then fold them into the eggs with a skimmer. Finally, add the lukewarm melted butter. Pour the mixture into a cake pan with a diameter of 9–11 in / 20–24 cm and bake for 20 minutes at 355 °F / 180 °C. Follow the same procedure to make the light sponge cake.

2. To make the buttercream, beat the softened butter and confectioners' sugar for 7–8 minutes with a whisk. Melt the chocolate in a double boiler. Mix a third of the buttercream with the slightly cooled chocolate. Cut both of the sponge cakes horizontally into four layers. Cube one layer of the light sponge cake, and fold the cubes with the finely diced candied fruits into the remaining two-thirds of the buttercream.

3. Line a dome-shaped mold with the chocolate sponge cake, spread it with a thin layer of chocolate buttercream and place a layer of light sponge cake on top. Fill the mold with the mixture of buttercream, candied fruits and sponge cake cubes.

4. Close the top of the mold with a circle of light sponge cake. Refrigerate for 12 hours or overnight. Turn out of the mold and spread apricot jam all over the bombe. Top the cassata with a layer of thinly rolled out green marzipan.

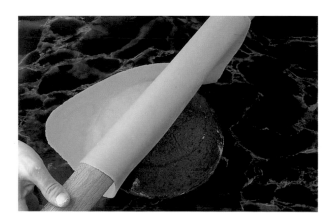

Preparation time: 30 minutes
Cooking time: 30 minutes
Difficulty: ★★

Serves 8

For the sponge cake:
8 eggs, separated
1 cup / 150 g confectioners' sugar
1 cup / 150 g unblanched almonds, very finely
   ground
1 cup, 1 tbsp / 120 g cocoa
6¹/₂ tbsp / 50 g flour

Chocolate buttercream
10 tbsp / 150 g butter
²/₃ cup / 100 g confectioners' sugar
1³/₄ oz / 50 g chocolate coating

For the topping:
1¹/₄ cups / 200 g flaked almonds
confectioners' sugar

To garnish:
confectioners' sugar
chocolate decorations

The Crusades brought nothing but trouble for King Richard the Lionheart of England (1157–1199). After insulting Leopold of Austria at the siege of Acre, he was shipwrecked on his way back to England and fell into the hands of Leopold, who incarcerated him in Dürnstein Castle. Here he was found, if the legends can be believed, by his friend the troubadour Blondel, who by chance was singing an English melody not far from Richard's prison.

This gripping story sheds light on the environment in which the Dürnstein cake was probably created. Today it is made exclusively by the Demel *konditorei*, founded in 1768 and purveyor to the imperial and royal courts in the early 19th century.

Almonds are an important element of the flavor of this torte. In this recipe they are not blanched, as is more common, but are used complete with their skins, giving them a more intense flavor. They also combine better with the flour in the delicate sponge cake mixture. The almonds cannot be replaced by any other ingredients; their flavor, high oil content and mineral salts are integral to this recipe. Roasting the whole almonds and letting them cool off completely before grinding them enhances their flavor greatly.

Bringing all the ingredients for the buttercream to room temperature is important in order to achieve the correct consistency.

1. To make the sponge cake, separate the eggs and beat the egg yolks with half of the sugar in a food processor until the mixture drops off the attachments in smooth ribbons. Blend in the flour, ground almonds, and sifted cocoa by hand. Carefully fold in the egg whites, which have been beaten until stiff with the remaining sugar. Pour the mixture into a greased and floured, round cake pan. Bake for 20 minutes at 355 °F / 180 °C.

2. To make the chocolate buttercream, melt the chocolate coating in the top of a double boiler over lukewarm water. Cream the softened butter and confectioners' sugar for 7–8 minutes with a whisk, then stir in the chocolate coating.

Torte

3. Slice the sponge cake horizontally into three equally thick layers, cover the layers with chocolate cream and place on top of each other. Spread the flaked almonds on a baking tray, dust them with confectioners' sugar, and roast under a grill or in the oven.

4. Spread the remaining cream around the cake and sprinkle the roasted flaked almonds all over. Dust the edge of the top with confectioners' sugar and garnish with chocolate decorations.

Yeast

Preparation time: 30 minutes
Cooking time: 30 minutes
Difficulty: ★★

Serves 8

For the yeast dough:
¹/₂ cup / 125 ml milk
³/₄ oz / 20 g yeast
2 cups / 260 g flour
2¹/₂ tbsp / 35 g superfine sugar

1 tsp vanilla sugar
1 pinch of salt
2 egg yolks
juice and grated peel of ¹/₂ lemon
8 tsp / 40 g butter, melted
¹/₂ cup / 100 g currants
rum

For the coating:
1 egg, slightly beaten

This cleverly plaited yeast loaf looks just like the braid of hair that inconsolable widows were once expected to cut off at their husbands' funerals. But this barbaric custom (originally, women were probably even obliged to follow their husbands into death) barely survived the beginning of the Middle Ages, so the yeast plait awakens only pleasant memories of a leisurely breakfast in a coffee shop near the Kohlmarkt in Vienna, including the excellent and ubiquitous Viennese coffee.

For the yeast braid, be sure to use butter with a very high fat content (96 %), which is important for its flavor and makes the dough easier to knead. The dough must be allowed to rise twice, the first time rolled into a ball and covered immediately

after kneading, and the second time after it has been plaited into a braid.

The ingredients are easier to use at room temperature, though the milk should be heated to 95 °F / 35 °C. The currants, which can be marinated in rum if you wish, should be kneaded into the dough after it has risen the first time. The yeast braid rises by about a third of its size.

In Jewish communities, an almost identical yeast plait called *challah* is served on the Sabbath. The differences between that traditional bread and this recipe are that the *challah* contains no milk, and vegetable oil is used instead of butter.

1. To make the yeast mixture, heat half of the milk in a pan, dissolve the yeast in the warm milk, add about a quarter of the flour and knead. Allow the dough to rise in a warm spot.

2. Combine the remaining flour and milk, the sugar, vanilla sugar, salt, egg yolks, and the lemon juice and zest together with the melted butter in a large bowl. Knead everything to form a smooth dough. Finally, add the rum-marinated currants and the yeast mixture. Place the dough in a clean bowl and allow to rise at room temperature.

Braid

3. Once the dough has risen to twice its original size, divide it into six pieces of equal size, roll them into strips of dough and place them next to each other on a smooth, lightly floured work surface.

4. Use a weight to secure the loose dough strips at one end and form a braid by plaiting the strips of dough. Brush the whisked egg on top and allow the braid to rise at room temperature until it has doubled in size. Brush the braid with egg again and bake for 30 minutes at 375 °F / 190 °C.

Vanilla

Preparation time: 30 minutes
Cooking time: 20 minutes
Difficulty: ✫

Serves 6

Vanilla sugar:
2 vanilla beans
2 tbsp / 20 g confectioners' sugar

For the kipferl dough:
13 tbsp / 200 g butter
¼ cup / 60 g superfine sugar

1½ cups / 180 g flour
⅔ cup / 100 g hazelnuts, very finely ground
3½ tbsp / 50 ml rum

For dusting:
confectioners' sugar

Crème Anglaise:
(see basic recipes)

During the wars between the Turks and the Austrian-German Empire the symbol of the Turkish crescent made its way to Austria. Crescents, or croissants as they are often called today, were allegedly invented by an Austrian baker after the peace treaty at Passarowitz (1718), which led to the final retreat of the Turkish invaders. The influence of Turkey on 18th-century Austria is obvious, as in the famous Turkish March, the Rondo alla turca in Mozart's 11th Sonata (KV 331).

Two different sorts of crescents exist in Austria, where they are called *kipferl* – one firmer and one somewhat softer. The one in this recipe is usually served with tea in the Demel *konditorei*.

For this recipe, the hazelnuts should be freshly roasted and then ground. After kneading the *kipferl* dough, leave it to rest

in the refrigerator and then continue working it with your hands in the traditional manner, just as the bakers of old used to. The crescents can be fairly thick; thinner *kipferl* tend to burn easily when baked. Leave enough space between the crescents on the baking tray so that there will be no problem separating them after baking.

Sugar is used twice in this recipe – first to make the dough sweet, though it is used in moderation, and then to garnish the *kipferl* and round off their flavor. This is the source of the unique *kipferl* taste.

1. To make the vanilla sugar, slit the vanilla beans lengthwise. Scrape out the vanilla pulp using a knife and mix it with the confectioners' sugar.

2. To make the kipferl dough, cream the butter with the vanilla sugar and superfine sugar until light and almost foamy with a mixer. Add the flour, finely ground hazelnuts and rum, and knead everything thoroughly.

Kipferl

3. Form the dough into several rolls, and allow to rest overnight in the refrigerator.

4. Cut each dough roll into pieces 1 in / 2 cm long and shape them into crescents. Place them on a baking sheet and bake for about ten minutes at 410 °F / 210 °C. Allow to cool, then dust them with confectioners' sugar. Serve with Crème Anglaise.

Kipferleier

Preparation time: 30 minutes
Cooking time: 15–20 minutes
Difficulty: ✲

Serves 6

For the kipferleier mixture:
6 eggs
1 cup / 150 g confectioners' sugar
1½ cups / 200 g flour
13 tbsp / 200 g butter

For the marzipan filling:
3½ oz / 100 g marzipan
6½ tbsp / 100 ml brown rum

For the glaze:
9 oz / 250 g chocolate coating

In spite of its curious name, *Kipferleier* (kipferl eggs), this recipe has nothing to do with eggs or oval-shaped things. Ever since the Demel *konditorei* was founded in 1786, its pastry chefs have cracked, beaten, whisked, whipped, cooked or decoratively brushed millions of eggs. They have made a fine art of preparing doughs containing high proportions of egg white, egg yolk or both. These *kipferleier* are made only by the Demel *konditorei*, and the proprietors take great care to preserve the integrity of the original recipe in every way.

Only butter of the best quality should be used for the *kipferleier*. Beat the eggs into the butter mixture one by one, with all the ingredients at room temperature so that the dough achieves the right consistency.

According to Franz Augustin, one should use Lübeck marzipan, the best marzipan in all of Europe. The marzipan is made smoother with a little brown rum, but it is important not to add too much rum as the alcohol bouquet could overpower the almond flavor and impair the composition. The *kipferleier* mixture, which should not be too firm, is piped onto baking paper greased with cooking oil.

As a variation, cocoa powder could be used to make a chocolate glaze to produce a less intense, lighter flavor than chocolate coating, and it does not need to be melted in a double boiler.

1. Cream the butter and confectioners' sugar until foamy in a food processor. Add the eggs one by one, stirring thoroughly after each addition. Then fold in the flour.

2. Line a baking sheet with baking paper. Put the mixture into a pastry bag with a round tip and pipe V-shaped kipferl onto the baking sheet, leaving a small space between them. Bake for ten minutes at 390 °F / 200 °C.

3. In a bowl, stir the marzipan and rum until they form a smooth cream. Place the cream in a pastry bag and use it to garnish half of the kipferl. Place one of the remaining kipferl on top of each.

4. Melt the chocolate coating in a double boiler over warm water and dip one end of each kipferleier sandwich into the chocolate. Place on waxed paper until the chocolate has set.

Amadeus

Preparation time: 30 minutes
Cooking time: 15 minutes
Difficulty: ★★

Makes 25

For the cookie dough:
1¹/₂ cup, 2 tbsp / 400 g butter
2 cups / 300 g confectioners' sugar
3 eggs
5¹/₄ cups / 650 g flour

For the pistachio mixture:
7 oz / 200 g marzipan
rum
³/₄ oz / 20 g pistachio paste
¹/₃ cup / 40 g pistachios, chopped

For the coating:
9 oz / 250 g chocolate coating

The name given to these irresistible cookies might call to mind the composer, Wolfgang Amadeus Mozart, especially since the *Mozartkugeln* chocolates named after him are available throughout Austria (and increasingly in gourmet stores in North America).

Although the two confections share several flavors in common – chocolate, pistachio, and marzipan – Franz Augustin says that he did not invent these cookies in memory of Mozart. He was simply fascinated by the color contrast among the green marzipan, dark brown chocolate, and light cookies.

For the dough to achieve the correct consistency, it is important for all the ingredients, especially the butter and egg yolks, to be used chilled. The recipe was designed to be made with Lübeck marzipan, if possible, and definitely choose a raw marzipan (rather than ready-to-eat) that can absorb more sugar. Instead of chocolate coating, which needs to be melted at a high temperature, one can use liquid chocolate to accent the layered cookies.

One decorative possibility is to use a fluted rolling pin to roll out the dough, giving it a decorative pattern that will be retained during baking if the dough is refrigerated beforehand. The cookies' grooved appearance is sure to please your guests.

1. To make the dough, cream the butter and confectioners' sugar until light, add the eggs and mix everything thoroughly. Add the sifted flour and knead to a smooth dough. Allow the dough to rest in a cool place for about an hour and then roll out to a thickness of ¹/₄ in / 3 mm.

2. Using round, smooth cookie cutters, cut out circles with a diameter of 2 in / 4 cm, place on a baking tray and bake for 15 minutes at 390 °F / 200 °C.

Cookies

3. After baking, allow the cookies to cool on a cooling rack. To make the pistachio mixture, stir the marzipan and rum until smooth with a stiff whisk, then add the pistachio paste and chopped pistachios. Garnish half of the cookies with the pistachio mixture, and then top with the remaining cookies.

4. Melt the chocolate coating in the top of a double boiler. Use a wooden spoon or spatula to cover half of one side of every cookie sandwich with the chocolate coating, being careful not to let any of the glaze run down to the bottom side. Serve 4–5 cookies per person.

Marzipan

Preparation time: 20 minutes
Cooking time: 5 minutes
Difficulty: ★

Serves 6

9 oz / 250 g marzipan
2 cups / 500 ml Calvados
1 egg yolk
red food coloring

To garnish:
cherry stems
angelica (optional)

The production of marzipan fruits has for a long time been the domain of Austrian confectioners, who vie to outdo each other in making these miniature fruits lifelike in shape and color. Along with bananas, cherries, and pears, decorative vegetables are produced in this manner as well, including eggplant, cauliflower and kale.

According to Franz Augustin, color plays a major part in the appeal of these fruits; the venerable traditions of the Demel *konditorei* insist that one pay special attention to distributing the yellow and red colorings evenly so that the marzipan fruits look like real, if miniature, apples.

The marzipan should ideally be that made in Lübeck, for many years the capital of marzipan production, and it must be smooth enough to be shaped into apples. To achieve this texture and to lend the marzipan fruits an intense apple flavor, the marzipan is soaked with French Calvados from the Pays d'Auge, an *appellation d'origine contrôlée* (A.O.C.). After coloring, brush the apples with gum arabic to give them an appealing shine.

One last tip: the cherry stems used as apple stems should be dried in the open air for several days, and need to be carefully trimmed to the correct length before use.

1. Soak the marzipan with Calvados, working the liquid into the marzipan with your hands. Shape the mass into a roll and divide it into small pieces weighing approximately 1/3 oz / 10 g.

2. Roll the pieces between your hands to form apples. Place the apples on a tray lined with baking paper, brush with egg yolk and dry in a warm oven.

Apples

3. Using a pastry brush, brush a little red food coloring, mixed with a drop of water, on to the apples after they have dried. Again, dry them in a warm oven.

4. Place a small real cherry stem on top of each apple.

Strawberry

Preparation time: 45 minutes
Cooking time: 30–40 minutes
Difficulty: ★★

Serves 10 to 12

sponge cake: (see basic recipes)

For the candied strawberries:
10¹/₂ oz / 300 g large strawberries
6¹/₂ tbsp / 100 g sugar
water

For the strawberry puree:
5¹/₄ oz / 150 g strawberries
6¹/₂ tbsp / 100 g sugar

For the buttercream:
1¹/₄ cups / 300 g butter
²/₃ cup / 100 g confectioners' sugar

For the coating:
¹/₂ cup, 1 tbsp / 200 g strawberry jam

To garnish:
10¹/₂ oz / 300 g fondant
candied violets
2 tbsp strawberry puree
red food coloring

Many strawberry lovers regret that the strawberry season is so short. Fortunately, however, Franz Augustin's solution to this problem is sure to satisfy even the most demanding gourmets: the fully ripe berries are carefully selected in summer, preserved with sugar, and stored in canning jars in the cellar or pantry to provide a taste of summer all year round. Their flavor is retained, and even though they have a different texture, it is still possible to make high-quality pastries using candied strawberries.

The majority of strawberry bushes cultivated these days are a result of cross-breeding between a wild Virginian and a cultivated Chilean sort, and have relatively small berries. But for this recipe, Franz Augustin prefers to use larger strawberries, which he considers more flavorful. If you intend to candy your own strawberries, make sure that you choose varieties with a rich flavor.

Prepare the sponge cake a day in advance and allow it to rest overnight; this way, the jam spread on the torte has an opportunity to dry thoroughly, and it will be easier to apply the fondant glaze. The same is true of the cream filling, which thus gains its optimal consistency. Allowing this extra time is essential for the stability of the torte; otherwise, even the slightest pressure exerted when garnishing the cake might be enough to disturb the balance of the various components.

1. Prepare the sponge cake according to the basic recipe and bake for 20 minutes at 390 °F / 200 °C. After it has cooled, cut it horizontally into four layers. Using sugar and water, make a light syrup and candy the strawberries in it over low heat; trying to leave the berries intact. To make the strawberry puree, press the fresh strawberries through a sieve and add sugar to taste.

2. For the buttercream, beat the soft butter and confectioners' sugar for 7–8 minutes with a whisk. Add all but 2 tbsp / 30 ml of the strawberry puree to the cream. Alternate layers of sponge cake, strawberry buttercream, and candied strawberries, finishing with the fourth sponge layer. Spread strawberry jam on the top of the torte, and refrigerate for two hours.

Cream Torte

3. Heat the fondant in a saucepan. Stir in the reserved 2 tbsp / 30 ml of strawberry puree and add a drop of red food coloring to achieve a richer color.

4. Remove the torte from the refrigerator. Glaze the top with the pink fondant, use a pastry bag to pipe a garland along the outer edge of the top, and arrange the candied violets on it.

Brittle Sponge Ring

Preparation time: 1 hour 30 minutes
Cooking time: 40 minutes
Difficulty: ★★

Serves 8

sponge cake, vanilla cream, buttercream,
  Charlotte cream: (see basic recipes)

For the kirsch buttercream:
a little buttercream
$^2/_3$ cup / 150 ml kirsch

For the light vanilla cream:
5$^1/_4$ oz / 150 g Charlotte cream
5$^1/_4$ oz / 150 g vanilla cream
 2$^1/_2$ cups / 600 ml whipping cream
1 vanilla bean

For the brittle:
$^3/_4$ cup, 1 tbsp / 200 g superfine sugar
1$^1/_4$ cups / 150 g chopped almonds
1 tbsp glucose syrup

The vanilla plant was originally native to Mexico (it was the Spanish explorers who introduced it to Europe), but it also thrives in other climactic conditions, as on the island of Réunion, formerly called Bourbon – hence the term "Bourbon vanilla." Part of the orchid family, it is a climbing plant with fleshy, elliptical leaves and narrow green fruits that are 7–9 in / 15–20 cm long and slightly triangular.

After harvesting, the beans are immersed in boiling water, dried in the sun and finally stored in drying chambers, sometimes for several months, as this is the stage during which the beans develop. By the time they reach the stores, they are almost black, soft, and flexible.

For European pastries, sugar is frequently flavored with vanilla by mixing a slit or chopped bean with granulated sugar and storing the mixture in a tightly shut glass jar for a few weeks. The vanilla sugar used in pastry shops is made this way.

The sponge cake ring owes its elegant appearance to its brittle coating. Prepare the brittle in advance and protect it from moisture. It should achieve a strong color when caramelized, but the almond and vanilla flavors must not be impaired in any way. Use only the best quality butter for the light vanilla cream, so that it has the firm consistency necessary when assembling all the layers of the sponge cake ring; if necessary, freeze for a short time.

1. Prepare the sponge cake mixture, vanilla cream, and Charlotte cream according to the basic recipes. Beat the whipping cream until stiff. Grease and flour a savarin form and fill it two-thirds full with sponge mixture. Bake for 40 minutes at 340 °F / 170 °C. Make the buttercream and flavor it with kirsch.

2. To make the light vanilla cream, slowly heat the Charlotte cream until it is soft; remove from the heat, add the vanilla bean which has been slit lengthwise, and infuse for ten minutes. Remove the vanilla bean, scrape out the pulp and mix it into the cream. Add the vanilla cream, combine thoroughly, and then fold in the whipped cream.

with Vanilla Cream

3. Slice the sponge cake horizontally into three layers, and garnish two of them with vanilla cream (about 1 in / 2 cm thick). Assemble the layers and freeze for 30 minutes. Meanwhile, prepare the brittle: caramelize the sugar with the chopped almonds and glucose, without adding water, until it develops a golden yellow color; allow to cool and then crush.

4. Take the sponge cake ring out of the freezer, thinly coat the inside and sides with the kirsch buttercream, and finally press the crushed brittle into the buttercream to coat the entire cake. Refrigerate for four hours before serving.

Preparation time: 45 minutes
Cooking time: 35 minutes
Difficulty: ✶

Makes 16

For the dough casing:
4 cups / 500 g flour
1¹/₃ cups / 325 g butter
²/₃ cup / 165 ml water
1 tbsp / 15 g salt

For the pear weggli filling:
2 lb 9 oz / 1¹/₄ kg basic filling (see basic recipes)
¹/₂ cup / 100 g candied orange peel
³/₄ cup, 2 tbsp / 100 g chopped walnuts

¹/₂ cup / 100 g sultanas
2 tsp / 5 g ground coriander

For the pear weggli spices:
4 tsp / 10 g ground aniseed
4 tsp / 10 g ground cinnamon
2 tsp / 5 g ground cloves
2 tsp / 5 g ground nutmeg
2 tsp / 5 g ground coriander

For the coating:
1 egg yolk

For Eric Baumann, pear *wegglis* (bars) are a special childhood memory. The recipe was handed down by his grandfather, a pastry chef in Lausanne who created these fruit bars toward the end of the last century. It may be that making these cakes simply offers Baumann an occasion to lose himself in his memories of school breaks, when his classmates would proudly display the cakes their mothers and grandmothers had so lovingly packed for them. However, this should not be grounds for us not to take the preparation of pear *wegglis* seriously.

While it is not hard to make the basic filling, it is important to make sure that the correct balance of ingredients is achieved, and that the levels of spices are balanced. The flavor of the few whole pieces of fruit should not be overpowered by the aniseed or cinnamon.

Anyone who likes subtle flavors will love this mixture of various dried and candied fruits – orange peel, sultanas (soak these in water for about an hour before using them), and chopped walnuts. Egg yolk is brushed on to the pear *wegglis*, which are then baked until golden brown. The dough casing should not be too thin, and, according to Eric Baumann, you should "be able to judge both the dough and the filling." Finally, traditional decorations are carved on to the top.

Other hand-held, spiced specialties are also available in Zurich, including the *Leckerle* ("tasty cake") made with honey, almonds, cloves, and cinnamon.

1. Combine the flour and butter thoroughly, add the water and salt, and knead to form a smooth dough. Refrigerate the dough. Mix the ingredients for the basic filling and chop them finely in a blender. To make the pear weggli filling, coarsely chop the orange peel and walnuts, add the remaining ingredients and mix everything with the basic filling.

2. Roll out the dough to a thickness of about ¹/₄ in / 5 mm, and line a wooden weggli form with it (see picture below); the dough should hang over both sides by approximately 1¹/₂ in / 3 cm. Using a pastry bag, pipe the filling into the depression in the center of the form.

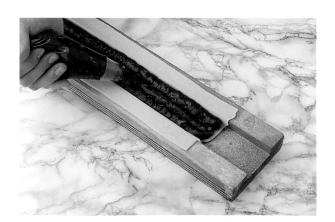

Weggli

3. Brush the edges of the dough with egg yolks, fold over the filling and press down gently so that they stick together; refrigerate for ten minutes. Turn out onto a floured marble slab and cut into pieces 4½ in / 10 cm long.

4. Place the pear wegglis on a baking sheet and brush them with egg yolk. Carve diagonal crosses on the top of each bar and prick three times with a fork. Bake for 35 minutes at 340 °F / 170 °C. Allow to cool for ten minutes before serving.

Mandarin Torte

Preparation time: 40 minutes
Cooking time: 40 minutes
Difficulty: ★

Serves 8

For the Charlotte cream:
1 cup / 250 ml milk
1/3 cup / 90 g sugar
7–8 egg yolks
9 sheets of gelatin

For the orange cream:
7 oz / 200 g Charlotte cream
2 cups / 500 ml whipping cream
7 1/2 tbsp / 110 ml orange juice concentrate

Génoise: (see basic recipes)

For the filling and the topping:
canned mandarin segments

For the syrup for soaking:
6 1/2 tbsp / 100 ml orange juice, freshly squeezed
3 1/2 tbsp / 50 ml sugar syrup

Clear cake glaze:
(see basic recipes)

To garnish:
whipped cream
roasted flaked almonds
brittle

Both oranges and mandarins are used in this recipe. The mandarin is native to China (hence the name "mandarin") and is not very widely available in Switzerland, though it is sold in many markets throughout Europe during November and December. In this tasty recipe, Eric Baumann attempts to familiarize his compatriots with this fruit.

It is best to use Spanish mandarin oranges, or clementines – Spain is one of the leading European producers of mandarins – but be aware that the canned mandarins most widely available are usually grown in Japan. In the modern age of free trade, even fruit is shipped all over the world to make preserves.

The flavor and color of mandarins differ from those of oranges, which in this recipe are used in the form of orange juice concentrate – of the best quality, of course. To retain its full character, it should be incorporated into the orange cream immediately after it is opened. The génoise and Charlotte cream, on the other hand, can easily be made a day in advance.

So that the cake decoration works well, the brittle needs to be prepared very carefully. Spread the flaked almonds on a baking sheet and roast them in the oven at 300 °F / 150 °C, turning every five minutes. Why not treat yourself to a glass of Grand Marnier as you do so?

1. To make the Charlotte cream, bring the milk to a boil with the sugar. Beat the egg yolks with a whisk until foamy, then combine the mixtures and thicken like a custard at 180 °F / 82 °C. Soak the gelatin in cold water and add to the mixture. Refrigerate. For the orange cream, reheat the Charlotte cream, stir in the orange juice concentrate, and then fold in the whipped cream.

2. Prepare the génoise, allow to cool and halve it horizontally. Combine the fresh orange juice and the sugar syrup. Line a cake ring with plastic wrap and place on a cake lid. Place a 1/2 in / 1 cm thick layer of génoise inside, soak with orange syrup, spread the orange cream on top, and cover with drained mandarin segments.

with Orange Cream

3. Cover the mandarin oranges with another layer of cream, place the second layer of sponge cake on them, soak with syrup, and spread the remaining cream on top. Refrigerate for four hours. Meanwhile make the brittle (see Brittle Sponge Ring with Vanilla Cream), allow to cool and crush.

4. Take the torte out of the cake ring, remove the plastic wrap, and spread whipped cream on the top and sides. Arrange mandarin segments around the edge of the top and cover them with the clear cake glaze. Pipe whipped cream rosettes in the center and sprinkle brittle onto them. Decorate the edge of the cake with flaked almonds. Serve well chilled.

Almond

Preparation time: 20 minutes
Cooking time: 40 minutes
Difficulty: ★

Makes 16

2²/₃ cups / 400 g sweet almonds, blanched and ground
1¹/₂ cups, 2 tbsp / 400 g sugar
1 tbsp / 10 g bitter almonds, ground

3 large egg whites
1 tsp grated lemon peel
5 egg yolks
6 eggs
¹/₂ cup / 120 g sugar
1 cup, 2 tbsp / 140 g maizena
9 tbsp / 140 g butter, melted

For sprinkling in the forms:
sponge cake crumbs

According to at least one source, Madeleine Paumier was a chef working for Madame Perrotin de Barmond when she invented the cakes bearing her Christian name, but that is all we know about these two ladies. Madeleines have been around since the Middle Ages, and several French towns have laid claim to being their original home, including Commercy in Lorraine (this version of the story was supported by Stanislaus Leszczynsky in the 18th century), Illiers-Combray near Chartres, and Saint-Yrieix in Limousin.

Several precautions are necessary when making these dry, shell-shaped cakes, particularly with the almonds, which need to be ground twice into a fine almond flour.

Blanched almonds from Spain (Marcona), Italy (Avola) or Provence (Aï) work well. The process of grinding the almonds twice is intended to release the almond oil and produce a dry flour, but overdoing the grinding can have fatal consequences during baking. Find the middle ground and allow the almonds to rest a few minutes after grinding, so that they again become a little softer.

That middle ground is important during baking as well, for the Madeleines must not darken too much. The oven temperature must be low enough for them to develop a lovely golden-yellow color, but high enough for the crust not to become too thick. After baking, they can be stored under a layer of plastic wrap for a few days.

1. Grind the sweet almonds, sugar, and bitter almonds twice in a blender, or finely grind with a handmill.

2. Place the almond flour into a bowl. Stir in the egg whites and grated lemon peel, and combine everything thoroughly.

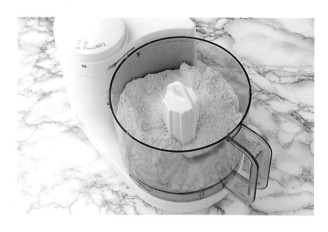

Madeleines

3. Add the egg yolks and whole eggs one at a time, beating to combine after each addition. Stir the mixture to produce a smooth dough. Finally, fold in the sugar, maizena, and the melted butter.

4. Grease the fluted baking forms with butter, and sprinkle sifted sponge cake crumbs into them. Pour the mixture into the forms (approximately 3¹/₂ oz / 100 g per tin). Bake for 40 minutes at 340 °F / 170 °C. Allow to cool before serving.

Lemon-Lime

Preparation time: 2 hours
Cooking time: 10 minutes
Difficulty: ★★

Serves 8

biscuit natur, cigarette pastry:
 (see basic recipes)

For the biscuit spécial:
2 cups / 225 g almonds, very finely ground
1¹/₂ cups / 225 g confectioners' sugar
¹/₂ cup / 60 g flour
4 eggs
3 tbsp / 45 g butter
2 tbsp / 30 g sugar
6 egg whites
yellow food coloring

For the lime mousse:
¹/₂ cup, 1 tbsp / 130 ml lime juice
1 tbsp / 15 ml lime juice concentrate
3 tbsp / 45 g sugar
grated peel of 1 lemon

2 egg yolks
7 sheets of gelatin
1³/₄ cups / 450 ml whipping cream

For the Italian meringue:
4 egg whites
³/₄ cup / 180 g sugar
3 tbsp / 45 ml water

For the syrup for soaking:
3¹/₂ tbsp / 50 ml lemon or lime juice
5 tsp / 25 ml sugar syrup

To garnish:
red currants
cake glaze: green/yellow and clear

Few citrus fruits are more adaptable than lemons and limes. They have a remarkably powerful flavor, lots of vitamin C, and the extraordinary ability to ripen artificially. While lemons originated in southeast Asia and are now grown in tropical regions around the world, limes are indigenous to North and Central America and remain somewhat exotic in European countries. This light, tart, mousse-filled dessert brings out all of its virtues.

Created by Eric Baumann, this torte is rather unusual by Swiss standards, where lemons are well-known, but their green cousin from Mexico, the lime, is quite rare. About the size of a largish walnut, they are decidedly smaller than the lemon. They are a little more difficult to work with – their tough rind is hard to grate – but the strong flavor they lend to the cream makes them the most important element of the torte.

The custard that is the basis for the lime mousse is best prepared a day in advance so that it has time to cool thoroughly before the Italian meringue is folded in, very gently so that it does not collapse. Allow enough time to assemble the torte so you do not have to rush the job.

The same is true of the *biscuit*; much of this can be made in advance and kept under a sheet of plastic wrap. Beginners should start with a smaller sponge cake and not attempt to make larger ones until they feel comfortable with the procedure.

1. Prepare the cigarette pastry, then the biscuit spécial as described in the basic recipes but using the amounts given above; color the biscuit spécial mixture a pleasing yellow. Pipe a thin layer of it onto a sheet of plastic, use a cake comb to draw lines through it, then freeze. After it has set, spread a layer of cigarette pastry on top and bake for 6–7 minutes at 430 °F / 220 °C.

2. Make a lime custard by bringing the lime juice, lime juice concentrate, sugar, and lemon peel to a boil. Beat the egg yolks with a whisk until foamy, combine with the lime mixture and thicken like a custard. Remove from the heat and add the gelatin, which has been soaked in cold water; cool. To make the syrup for soaking, mix the sugar syrup and lemon or lime juice. Prepare the biscuit according to the basic recipe and slice into two layers.

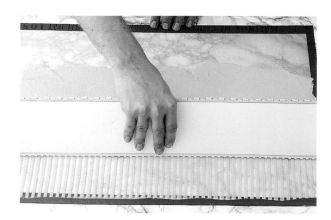

Torte

3. To prepare the meringue, dissolve two-thirds of the sugar in the water and bring to 250 °F / 121 °C. Slowly pour this syrup over the egg whites, which have been beaten until stiff with the remaining sugar. Continue to beat until completely cooled. For the lime mousse, combine the meringue with the lime custard, and finally fold in the whipped cream. Line a cake ring with a strip of baking paper and a strip of the biscuit spécial, leaving about ¹/₂ in / 1 cm free at the top.

4. Place a biscuit natur base in the cake ring, and fill the ring two-thirds full with the lime mousse. Place the second sponge layer on top, soak it with the syrup and fill the ring with the remaining mousse. Freeze for four hours. Coat the top of the torte with the green/yellow cake glaze, then top with a thin layer of clear glaze. Serve well-chilled.

Cherry

Preparation time: 15 minutes
Cooking time: 35 minutes
Difficulty: ★

Serves 8

For the Linz dough:
10 tbsp / 150 g butter
$^1/_3$ cup / 80 g sugar
2 eggs
1 pinch of salt
2 pinches of cinnamon
grated peel of $^1/_2$ lemon
1 cup / 130 g hazelnuts, very finely ground
$1^1/_2$ cups / 200 g flour

For the pudding mixture:
$5^1/_2$ oz / 160 g white bread (without crusts)
$^3/_4$ cup / 200 ml milk
$6^1/_2$ tbsp / 100 g butter
cinnamon
grated lemon peel
$^2/_3$ cup / 100 g blanched almonds, very finely ground
$^1/_2$ cup, 1 tbsp / 140 g sugar
4 egg yolks
4 egg whites
$^1/_4$ cup / 30 g cornstarch
21 oz / 600 g black cherries

The pudding is clearly the preferred domain of English pastry chefs, and Eric Baumann has no intention of trying to compete with them. But this recipe is an excellent opportunity to serve a delicious, economical and relatively simple-to-make dessert, based on ordinary white bread and, of course, enough aromatic black cherries.

Bread is an indispensable component of a balanced diet; in European countries, it is made in a staggering variety of different ways. According to Eric Baumann, the consumption of bread is highest on the European mainland – in Germany, Belgium, and Denmark.

Follow the instructions in this recipe very closely. The milk-soaked bread needs to be thoroughly diced before it is stirred into the pudding mixture. And you should add to the milk only enough cinnamon and grated lemon peel to flavor it without overpowering the taste of the other ingredients.

But you are welcome to vary the original recipe and substitute some of the hazelnuts in the Linz dough with sponge cake crumbs, for example. Instead of the cherries, you can use other seasonal fruits like peaches or apricots. And anything goes as far as the shape of the pudding forms; just take the pudding out of the oven as soon as it is ready.

1. Soak the white bread overnight in the milk. To make the Linz dough, cream the butter, beat in the sugar, and then one after the other add the eggs, salt, cinnamon, lemon peel, and ground nuts. Finally, fold in the flour and knead to form a smooth dough. Refrigerate.

2. To make the pudding mixture, cream the butter with the grated lemon peel and cinnamon. In another bowl, mix the ground almonds, sugar, and egg yolks. Add this and the soaked and thoroughly diced bread to the creamed mixture. Beat the egg whites and sugar until stiff, add the cornstarch, and carefully combine the two mixtures. Finally, fold in two-thirds of the black cherries.

Pudding

3. Roll out the dough thinly and use it to line greased pudding forms. Prick the dough several times with a fork, so that no air pockets form during baking.

4. Fill the forms half-full with the pudding mixture, then sprinkle some cherries on top. Repeat with the remaining pudding mixture and cherries. Bake for 35 minutes at 340 °F / 170 °C. Allow the pudding to cool before serving.

Preparation time: 1 hour 15 minutes
Cooking time: 40 minutes
Difficulty: ★★

Serves 8

hazelnut génoise, biscuit spécial:
  (see basic recipes)

For the milk chocolate mousse:
2 egg yolks
$^1/_4$ cup / 60 ml sugar syrup
4 oz / 110 g milk chocolate coating
$4^1/_2$ tbsp / 35 g chopped hazelnuts
1 cup / 230 ml whipping cream

For the hazelnut mousse:
2 egg yolks
$^1/_4$ cup / 60 ml sugar syrup
$2^1/_2$ sheets of gelatin
sugar syrup
1 cup, 1 tbsp / 120 g roasted hazelnuts, very finely
  ground
$1^1/_2$ cups / 360 ml whipping cream

To garnish:
chopped hazelnuts
confectioners' sugar
chocolate flakes made from chocolate coating

In France, cakes are called either *tourtes* or *tartes* depending on how many layers of sponge cake they contain, and purists consider this difference to be very important. Both the French *tourte* and the German variation *torte* are derived from the Latin word *torta*, meaning a round loaf of bread. The etymology of *tarte* remains unclear.

For this torte, the quality of the chopped and roasted hazelnuts makes the difference between a nice cake and a spectacular one. The round Piedmont hazelnuts in particular are about the right size and need only to be roasted carefully.

To make the mousse, Eric Baumann starts with a foamy egg mixture made using egg yolks and sugar syrup. Use particu-

larly fresh ingredients for this, and use them as quickly as possibly after purchase. It is important that the egg mixture is not overheated (to 175 °F / 80 °C at the most), and that it is allowed to cool thoroughly so that it remains light and fluffy.

The milk chocolate coating must be of good quality, but not too bitter. If you prefer to use a bittersweet chocolate coating, make sure that it contains no more than 60% cocoa. Handle the chocolate just as carefully as the Swiss who, ever since the Josty brothers opened their Berne chocolate factory in 1792, have had a particular predilection for chocolate.

1. Make the hazelnut génoise and the biscuit spécial according to the basic recipes. To make the milk chocolate mousse, whisk the egg yolks with the sugar syrup to a firm foam in a double boiler. Remove from the heat and continue to beat until the mixture has cooled completely. Slowly melt the milk chocolate coating in a double boiler.

2. One after the other, fold the melted milk chocolate coating, chopped hazelnuts and lightly whipped cream into the foamy egg yolks and combine everything thoroughly. For the hazelnut mousse, make an egg yolk and sugar syrup foam as above. Heat the gelatin, soaked in cold water, with a little sugar syrup and add to the foamy egg mixture. Fold in the ground and roasted hazelnuts, and finally the whipped cream.

Chocolate Torte

3. Line a cake ring with a strip of baking paper three-quarters the width of the cake ring; then place a strip of biscuit spécial of the same width as the baking paper in the ring.

4. Place a ½ in / 1 cm thick layer of hazelnut génoise in the cake ring, pipe a ¾ in / 1½ cm layer of milk chocolate mousse onto it, and fill the cake ring with the hazelnut mousse. Decorate the center of the torte with chocolate flakes and dust with a little confectioners' sugar; scatter chopped hazelnuts along the edge of the top. Refrigerate for about four hours before serving.

Caramel Torte

Preparation time: 1 hour 30 minutes
Cooking time: 40 minutes
Difficulty: ★★

Serves 8

génoise, biscuit spécial, clear cake glaze:
  (see basic recipes)

For the chocolate mousse:
3 egg yolks
6¹/₂ tbsp / 100 ml sugar syrup
7 oz / 190 g milk chocolate coating
1¹/₂ cups / 375 ml whipping cream

For the caramel mousse:
3 egg yolks
¹/₄ cup / 55 ml sugar syrup

3¹/₂ sheets of gelatin
1¹/₄ cups / 300 ml whipping cream

For the caramel:
7 tbsp / 115 g sugar
3¹/₂ tbsp / 50 ml glucose
1 tbsp / 15 g butter
³/₄ cup / 165 ml crème fraîche (35% fat)

For the caramel syrup:
a little liquid caramel
a little water

To garnish:
caramel glaze
clear cake glaze
chocolate decorations

So far, there have been three generations of the Baumann family adding to the fame of Swiss pastry chefs in Lausanne, Biel, and Zurich, and they have always adhered to strict quality criteria for their products. This has led to a firmly-rooted family tradition that is founded on extensive expertise, yet has remained open to new ideas all along.

It is in this spirit that Eric Baumann, who continues this family tradition, has been searching for a way to produce a caramel with an intense flavor, in which the sweet and bitter notes balance each other. Experiences have taught him that the best method is to heat the purest English sugar until it has a strong color, but is not too dark, which signals that the caramel has become bitter.

So that the caramel flavor is not overpowered, the milk chocolate used in this recipe must not be too sweet. When using chocolate, keep in mind its characteristic qualities such as flavor, melting properties, and consistency.

There is a certain element of risk when mixing the chocolate coating with the beaten eggs. To reduce this risk, make sure the temperature is not too high and thoroughly combine the chocolate with the cream until the mixture is smooth. Then there should be no problem folding it into the beaten egg mixture. Instead of caramel, hazelnuts, almonds or coffee could also be used to make the torte.

1. To make the chocolate mousse, beat the egg yolks with the sugar syrup in a double boiler until it becomes a firm foamy mixture. Remove from the double boiler and continue to beat until completely cooled. Reduce the hot chocolate coating with a little water until it has a creamy consistency, then fold it into the cold beaten egg mixture. Fold in the whipped cream. Using a pastry bag, pipe 1 in / 2 cm of the mousse into cake rings and freeze.

2. To make the caramel mousse, prepare the egg yolks and sugar syrup as above. Caramelize the sugar until it is fairly brown and dissolve the glucose in it. In another pan, bring the crème fraîche to a boil; add the butter and boiling crème fraîche to the sugars. Heat everything to 215 °F / 103 °C, then allow to cool.

à la Baumann

3. Combine the caramel with the cooled egg yolk mixture. Heat the gelatin (previously soaked in cold water) with a little sugar syrup and add to the caramel. Finally, fold in the whipped cream. Line a cake ring with a strip of baking paper three-quarters the height of the ring, then line the cake ring with a strip of biscuit spécial of the same width.

4. Place a $^1\!/_2$ in / 1 cm thick layer of génoise in the cake ring and soak it with caramel syrup. Fill the ring two-thirds full with caramel mousse. Place the set chocolate mousse on top, then completely fill the ring with caramel mousse. Refrigerate for four hours. Marble the top of the torte with caramel glaze and clear cake glaze, and decorate with chocolate decorations. Serve well chilled.

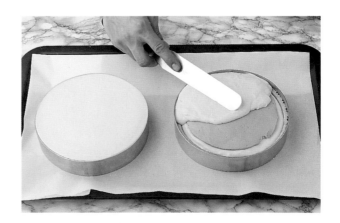

Preparation time: 1 hour 30 minutes
Cooking time: 40 minutes
Difficulty: ★★

Serves 8

génoise, Japonaise sponge cake:
  (see basic recipes)

For the kirsch buttercream:
$^1/_2$ cup / 120 ml milk
$^1/_2$ cup / 120 g sugar
$1^1/_2$ vanilla beans
5 egg yolks
$1^2/_3$ cups / 400 g butter
6 tbsp / 90 ml kirsch, 100% proof
1–2 drops red food coloring

For the Italian meringue:
1 large egg white
6 tbsp / 90 g sugar
2 tbsp / 30 ml water

For the syrup for soaking:
$^2/_3$ cup / 150 ml kirsch, 100% proof
$6^1/_2$ tbsp / 100 ml sugar syrup

To garnish:
flaked almonds, roasted
confectioners' sugar
ground pistachios
Morello cherries marinated in kirsch

The canton of Zug, near Zurich, used to be ruled by the Hapsburg dynasty, and in 1352 it joined the Swiss Confederation, a mutual defense league. Because of the complicated proceedings of the Middle Ages, however, Zug was not incorporated until 1415, when it was finally granted the same rights as the other Swiss cantons. Eric Baumann pays his respects to the culinary traditions of this canton, famous for its *Zuger Pfefferkuchen* (gingerbread), with a kirsch torte.

This versatile fruit schnapps, used to flavor the buttercream in this recipe, can also serve as an excellent complement to chocolate and a variety of fruits. The buttercream is also given a slightly reddish tint to serve as a visual reminder of cherries, though the cherries used to produce kirsch have a very dark juice.

For decorating the cake, Eric Baumann principally uses the type of fruit from which the fruit schnapps used for soaking the sponge cake is made. For this torte, though, he is willing to make an exception and would even accept pineapple as a garnish. He, personally, prefers to decorate the Zug Cherry Torte with Morello cherries, so that it does not pretend to be something it is not. The cherries should have been marinated in kirsch for two months.

Less experienced bakers need to take special care to grease the baking paper thoroughly before spreading the Japonaise sponge mixture on to it. Bake the sponge cake very slowly at a stable temperature so that it bakes evenly, and then keep it in an airtight container.

1. To make the buttercream, bring the milk to a boil with half the sugar and the content of the vanilla beans. Whisk the egg yolks and remaining sugar until foamy. Stir in some hot milk; pour back into the saucepan and thicken at 180 °F / 82 °C like a custard. Let cool. For the meringue, beat the egg whites with 2 tsp / 10 g sugar until stiff. Heat the water and remaining sugar to 250 °F / 121 °C and pour onto the egg whites while beating. Cream the butter, combine with the custard, and fold in the meringue.

2. Finally, tint 1 lb / 450 g of the buttercream red and flavor it with kirsch. Make the Japonaise sponge cake according to the basic recipe. Use a round stencil to spread the mixture on to greased baking paper and bake for 10–12 minutes at 300 °F / 150 °C. Then prepare the génoise, also according to the basic recipe, and turn into a baking paper-lined cake pan of the same diameter as the stencil used for the Japonaise sponge cake. Bake for 20 minutes at 340 °F / 170 °C.

Cherry Torte

3. To make the syrup for soaking, mix the kirsch with the sugar syrup. Spread a thin layer of kirsch buttercream on to one of the Japonaise sponge layers, place the kirsch syrup-drenched génoise on top, spread it generously with kirsch buttercream and cover with the second layer of Japonaise sponge cake.

4. Spread the remaining kirsch buttercream on the top and sides of the cake, and press roasted flaked almonds on to the sides. Dust the top with confectioners' sugar and garnish with chopped pistachios and cherries marinated in kirsch. Refrigerate for about four hours before serving.

Kiwi Torte with

Preparation time: 40 minutes
Cooking time: 40 minutes
Difficulty: ★

Serves 8

génoise, Charlotte cream: (see basic recipes)

For the passion fruit cream:
7 oz / 200 g Charlotte cream
2 cups / 500 ml whipping cream
6$^{1}/_{2}$ tbsp / 100 g passion fruit extract
$^{2}/_{3}$ cup / 100 g confectioners' sugar

For the syrup for soaking:
4 tsp / 20 g passion fruit extract
$^{1}/_{3}$ cup / 80 ml sugar syrup

To garnish:
3 kiwis
1$^{1}/_{2}$ cups / 200 g flaked almonds, roasted
1$^{1}/_{4}$ cups / 300 ml whipping cream

Clear cake glaze: (see basic recipes)

Eric Baumann is quite a fan of some of the exotic fruits increasingly available in our grocery stores. In the following unique and delicious recipe, he uses kiwis and passion fruit, after several experiments convinced him that the flavors of the two fruits complement each other very well.

The best kiwis, also known as Chinese gooseberries, are definitely those grown in New Zealand, where the Hayward variety is cultivated. For some years now this fruit has received the highest praise, for it is full of vitamins and apparently covers our daily requirement of vitamin C, despite being very low in calories. Use ripe kiwis that are still firm and do not give when pressed.

The passion fruit (or granadilla) is not always easy to use. Here it appears in the form of an extract, which preserves the full impact of its flavor without adding enough liquid to the cream to distort its consistency. Using ripe, wrinkled fruits, start by deseeding the flesh, then reduce it with added water and pass it through a sieve. The juice thus produced is reduced a second time. The resulting fruit extract keeps well in the freezer.

The whipped cream should have a fat content of 35% and be very cold. Whip it until stiff, with a twentieth of its weight in sugar. Begin by whipping only 80% of the cream; adding the remaining 20% toward the end of the process. When making the Charlotte cream, it should not be overheated (180 °F / 82 °C at the most) before the gelatin is folded in.

1. Make the génoise and Charlotte cream according to the basic recipes. Slice the génoise horizontally into two layers. For the passion fruit cream, reheat the Charlotte cream slightly and add the confectioners' sugar and passion fruit extract (see text above). Combine everything thoroughly, then carefully fold in the whipped cream.

2. For the syrup to soak, stir the extract into the sugar syrup. Line a cake ring with a strip of baking paper. Place a $^{1}/_{2}$ in / 1 cm thick layer of génoise inside, soak it with passion fruit syrup and fill the ring two-thirds full with passion fruit cream. Place a second layer of génoise on top, soak and cover with the remaining cream. Refrigerate for four hours.

Passion Fruit Cream

3. Remove the cake ring and the baking paper. Spread a thin layer of whipped cream on the top and sides of the cake. Arrange slices of kiwi on the top, leaving a 1 in / 2 cm border free around the outside; cover the kiwi slices with clear cake glaze.

4. Roast the flaked almonds using a salamander and decorate the edge of the cake with them. Pipe a whipped cream garland along the edge of the top. Serve well chilled.

L'Ambassadeur

Preparation time: 30 minutes
Cooking time: 20 minutes
Difficulty: ★

Serves 8

génoise, pastry cream, buttercream:
(see basic recipes)
³/₄ cup / 150 g candied fruits, diced
3¹/₂ tbsp / 50 ml kirsch

For the syrup for soaking: (see basic recipes)
6¹/₂ tbsp / 100 ml water
6¹/₂ tbsp / 100 g superfine sugar
6¹/₂ tbsp / 100 ml kirsch

To garnish:
marzipan

For the egg white icing:
1 egg white
confectioners' sugar
juice of 1 lemon

Because it combines several elements fundamental to pastry-baking, this torte is a classic and was long seen as a way of testing bakers who wanted to prove that they knew their trade. Maybe this is why it is called Ambassadeur. Maurice and Jean-Jacques Bernachon have fastidiously held to the principles by which it is made, and it is still much requested by their customers in Lyon.

To achieve such expertise in baking, the production of the génoise – made with only the best butter and eggs – must be perfectly mastered. The classic pastry cream, made with whole milk, very fresh egg yolks, and particularly aromatic vanilla, and using traditional copper implements, also has to be just so.

Kirsch is distilled from deep black cherries, producing a clear schnapps; a well-known example is that produced by the

Fougerolles community in the Franche Comté region of France. The exquisite aroma of the distilled kirsch gives the pastry cream a delicate touch and gives the "ambassador" a special flavor, sure to be appreciated by diplomats all over the world.

In order to harmonize with this composition, the marzipan needs to be very homogeneous, so knead it carefully with the balls of your hands until it reaches the desired consistency. Before rolling it out, lightly dust the working surface and the rolling pin with confectioners' sugar so that the marzipan does not stick to them.

1. Prepare the simple génoise a day in advance, and slice it horizontally into three equally thick layers. Make both the pastry cream and the syrup for soaking using the basic recipe as a guide with the ingredients listed above. Marinate the diced candied fruits in kirsch. Place a layer of sponge cake on a cake lid and soak it with a third of the kirsch syrup.

2. Pipe a ¹/₂ in / 1 cm thick layer of pastry cream onto the sponge cake base, then sprinkle with half of the (drained) candied fruits. Place the second sponge layer on top, soak with another third of the kirsch syrup, pipe more pastry cream onto the sponge cake and sprinkle with the rest of the candied fruits. Top with the third sponge cake layer and soak with the remaining kirsch syrup.

3. Spread buttercream on the sides and top of the torte and refrigerate for one hour. To make the egg white icing, place the egg white in a bowl and use a wooden spatula to stir in the sifted confectioners' sugar gradually until the mixture has a creamy consistency. Finally add the lemon juice. Cover with a damp cloth.

4. Roll out the marzipan with a rolling pin to a thickness of about ¼ in / 4 mm and cover the torte with it. Trim the excess and finally decorate the torte's surface with the egg white icing, placing a marzipan rose in the center.

Bûche

Preparation time: 1 hour 15 minutes
Cooking time: 15 minutes
Difficulty: ★★

Serves 8

simple génoise, plain ganache, pastry cream:
  (see basic recipes)

For the syrup for soaking:
(see basic recipes)
6¹/₂ tbsp / 100 ml rum
6¹/₂ tbsp / 100 ml water
6¹/₂ tbsp / 100 g superfine sugar

To garnish:
chocolate rolls and flakes

In France, the traditional Christmas dinner is somehow incomplete without this wonderful dessert. Whether made with sweet chestnuts, meringue, chocolate, Grand Marnier or some other creative variation, the chocolate *bûche de noël* (Yule log) is elemental to Christmas. The Bernachons have made it their task to continue this unshakable tradition. A time-consuming procedure, the creation of a *bûche de noël* is best carried out over the three or four days before Christmas.

The génoise should be spread very thinly on to a baking sheet and then baked immediately so that it remains soft. Rolling the sponge cake is easier if you spread some pastry cream or ganache on to it; this produces a slight condensation, making the sponge cake softer. The Bernachon pâtisserie uses an exclusive mixture of twelve varieties of cocoa for the ganache, one of them the much sought-after Chuao, named after a town in the mountains of Venezuela. Touton, a French company, is the sole European importer of this exceptional cocoa.

The effect achieved with a well-chilled *bûche de noël* is a natural result of its combination of fine flavors: génoise, ganache and old rum make this festive dessert unforgettable. Serve it with vanilla ice cream or a delicious crème anglaise.

1. Make the génoise and ganache a day in advance according to the basic recipes. Prepare a classic pastry cream and syrup for soaking, again following those instructions. When you are ready to assemble the cake, heat a third of the ganache in a double boiler, stirring constantly, until it softens and then combine it with the pastry cream. Spread this mixture onto the sponge cake, which has been cut into a rectangular shape.

2. Carefully roll up the sponge cake covered with cream, using a knife or spatula to roll it evenly. Wrap the sponge cake roll firmly in plastic wrap and refrigerate for at least one hour.

de Noël

3. Cut off the ends of the sponge cake roll at an angle with a knife that has been dipped in hot water. Place these pieces on the top of the log to form decorative knotholes.

4. Using a pastry bag with a star-shaped tip, garnish the log all over with the remaining ganache and decorate to taste with chocolate flakes and rolls, meringue mushrooms, or other decorations.

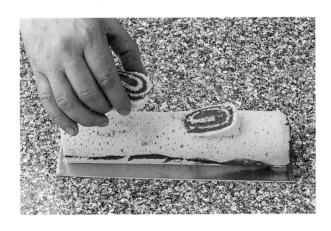

Elysée

Preparation time: 45 minutes
Cooking time: 25 minutes
Difficulty: ★★★

Serves 8

For the génoise:
6 eggs
$^1/_2$ cup, 3 tbsp / 170 g superfine sugar
a little honey
$1^1/_2$ cups / 200 g flour, sifted
$^1/_2$ cup / 120 g best-quality butter

For the ganache:
1 cup / 250 ml crème fraîche with a high fat content
12 oz / 375 g Avellino bar chocolate

$3^1/_2$ oz / 100 g baking chocolate

For the marinated cherries:
10 Montmorency cherries
$^1/_2$ cup / 120 ml cherry brandy

To garnish:
7 oz / 200 g bittersweet chocolate
candied violets
cocoa

This génoise enhanced with refined flavors is a variation of the classic Montmorency Cherry Torte created for the occasion of Maurice Bernachon's old friend Paul Bocuse receiving the Cross of the Legion of Honor, and in honor of Valéry Giscard d'Estaing, the French president at the time. The cake has been known by several names, including Valéry Torte, Anne Aymone Torte and finally, especially for this volume, Elysée Torte. The Elysée ganache consists of cream, chocolate, nut nougat, and very finely chopped brandy-marinated cherries, and the sponge cake is soaked with cherry brandy (like a Montmorency Cherry Torte).

The most distinctive feature of this torte is, however, its decoration, a delicate structure of chocolate flakes that has to be made on a marble slab using a handmill.

Because of the artistic arrangement of chocolate flakes on the top of the cake, it is particularly difficult to cut the cake into many or very thin slices. The record for this is held by the Hermès company with a cake made for a reception of about 500 people in Lyon. Very creative means of transportation had to be arranged for that cake!

When the topic of this torte comes up, Maurice Bernachon never misses the chance to quote one of his customers, who said, "This is a cake you eat twice, the first time with your eyes …" Bernachon was very moved by this at the time and still considers it his nicest compliment.

1. Marinate the cherries in the brandy. For the ganache, bring the crème fraîche to a boil in a saucepan, break the chocolate into small pieces and stir it in. Remove from heat and whisk until smooth. Cover and allow to cool in a refrigerator for at least 12 hours. Then reheat the ganache in a double boiler, stirring constantly, until it softens. Reserve $^1/_4$ of it for covering the cake. Add the drained and finely chopped cherries to the remaining ganache.

2. For the génoise, combine the eggs with the sugar and honey in a double boiler and gently warm. Remove from the heat and continue to beat with a mixer until the mixture hangs down in long ribbons. Fold in the flour and melted butter. Pour into a round cake pan with high sides and bake for 20 minutes at 390 °F / 200 °C. Cut the sponge cake horizontally into three layers. Place one layer on a cake lid, soak with cherry brandy and spread with ganache.

Torte

3. Place the second sponge cake layer on top and again soak with brandy and cover with ganache. Top with the third génoise layer, soak with the remaining cherry brandy, and refrigerate for one hour. Use the reserved ganache to cover the top and sides, smoothing with a spatula.

4. Melt the bittersweet chocolate in a double boiler at 85 °F / 31 °C, spread on to a marble slab and allow to cool. Form rolls, arrange them on top of the cake and dust with cocoa. Serve the torte with crème anglaise or pistachio ice cream, according to taste.

Brittle Baskets

Preparation time: 40 minutes
Cooking time: 30 minutes
Difficulty: ★★★

Serves 8

For the choux pastry:
1/2 cup / 125 ml whole milk
1 tsp / 5 g sugar
1 pinch of salt
1/4 cup / 60 g butter
3/4 cup, 1 tbsp / 100 g flour
3 eggs

For the caramel:
3/4 cup / 200 g sugar
3 tbsp / 50 ml water

For the kirsch pastry cream:
pastry cream (see basic recipes)
kirsch to taste

For the brittle:
3/4 cup / 200 g sugar
1/2 vanilla bean
1 1/4 cups / 150 g chopped almonds, roasted

In many instances, the nearly architectural marvels the French call *pièces montées* (meaning something like "culinary constructions") are merely excuses for extensive feasting. Maurice and Jean-Jacques Bernachon are fully aware of this, and with their original version of a cream puff-filled brittle basket, which is somewhat reminiscent of the traditional French profiterole pyramid called a *croquembouche*, demonstrate just how good they are at preparing exquisite brittle.

Many varieties of almonds, but especially those from Provence, are highly valued for their texture and flavor: the high-fat Matrones, the Béraud almonds, Royales and Tourneforts, and of course the Princess almonds, which have unfortunately become very rare. There are sweet and bitter almonds, which are, of course, used in different ways.

Historians maintain that choux pastry, like macaroon mixture, is one of the oldest types of dough there is. Since it is made of milk and butter, it does not keep very long and should therefore be eaten on the same day it is prepared. It always has to be "burnt off" (hence its German name, *Brandteig*) for a few minutes and kneaded slowly and thoroughly on the stovetop. When baking, be careful not to open the oven door.

Although making the brittle does require some skill, the main things to keep in mind are to make the caramel in a copper saucepan before folding in the almonds and to oil the work surface thoroughly.

1. To make the choux pastry, bring the milk to a boil with the sugar, salt and pieces of butter. As soon as the butter has melted, add the flour and continue to stir vigorously over low heat for as long as it takes for a smooth dough to form. "Burn off" the dough while stirring for one minute, then remove from the heat. Let stand for one minute, then add the eggs one at a time, stirring thoroughly after each.

2. Using a pastry bag with a medium-sized round tip, pipe small puffs onto a baking sheet and bake for 20 minutes at 390 °F / 200 °C. Prepare a pastry cream with the ingredients listed above, using the basic recipes as a guide; flavor with kirsch. Make the caramel, dip the puffs into it and allow them to cool on a cooling rack.

with Cream Puffs

3. For the brittle, caramelize the sugar (without adding any water) with the half vanilla bean in a copper saucepan. Add the roasted almonds and stir to coat thoroughly.

4. Turn the brittle on to an oiled marble slab. While it is still hot, roll it out flat with a rolling pin and cut out a large circle. Line a brioche tin with the brittle. Place the cream puffs in the brittle basket, and garnish with sugar-coated almonds, if desired.

Preparation time: 45 minutes
Cooking time: 15 minutes
Difficulty: ★

Serves 8

For the ganache:
10¹/₂ oz / 300 g baking or bittersweet chocolate
1 cup / 250 ml crème fraîche

For the chestnut puree:
1 cup / 150 g sweet chestnuts, drained
3¹/₂ tbsp / 50 g butter, softened

For the sponge cake:
6 egg whites
³/₄ cup / 180 g sugar
1 cup, 3 tbsp / 180 g blanched almonds

To garnish:
cocoa powder
confectioners' sugar
chocolate decorations
drained chestnuts

Sweet chestnuts do not come from the Indian chestnut tree but are actually the fruits of a related species whose shell contains only a single nut. Though larger and rounder than other chestnuts, they have the same texture. Sweet chestnuts remind Maurice Bernachon of the many autumn morning walks in the Dauphiné on which he used to accompany his father. There are many sweet chestnut trees in neighboring Ardèche, and their fruits are rightly praised.

If you are able to use fresh sweet chestnuts, they must be shelled and blanched in boiling water, wrapped in tulle, and then preserved in the traditional way, in large copper pots. Make sure that they do not fall apart during cooking.

Depending on their size and shape, you can reserve a few chestnuts for garnishing the torte; the rest, even if they have fallen apart, can be used for the cream and should be particularly tender and soft. If you are using canned chestnuts, allow them to drain thoroughly so that the additional liquid does not make the dough too soft. Lightly beat the dough with a wooden spatula, so that it is continually infused with air.

Prepare the ganache a day in advance to ensure that it has the correct consistency. Use only the freshest eggs for the almond sponge cake, and be sure to separate the egg whites and egg yolks carefully.

1. Make the ganache a day in advance: boil the crème fraîche over high heat for one minute while stirring with a whisk, then remove from the heat. Break the chocolate into small pieces, add to the boiled crème fraîche and stir until the mixture is smooth and homogeneous. Cover and allow to cool in the refrigerator for at least 12 hours. Before continuing, reheat the ganache in a double boiler, stirring constantly, until it softens.

2. For the chestnut puree, puree or chop the sweet chestnuts in a blender. Stir in the softened butter until smooth. To make the sponge cake, blend the sugar and almonds with a mixer. Beat the egg whites until very stiff and carefully fold into the sugar and almond mixture. Pipe three rounds of the sponge cake dough (7 in / 16 cm) on to a greased and floured baking sheet and bake for 7–8 minutes at 480 °F / 250 °C.

Chestnut Torte

3. To assemble the torte, pipe a 1 in / 2 cm layer of ganache on to the first sponge base and smooth with a spatula. Place the second layer on top, pipe sweet chestnut cream on to it and cover with the third layer. Spread the remaining ganache on to the top and sides of the torte. Refrigerate for one hour.

4. To garnish, dust the top and sides of the torte with cocoa and sift confectioners' sugar over half of the top. Decorate with chocolate roses or drained canned sweet chestnuts.

Preparation time: 1 hour
Cooking time: 20 minutes
Difficulty: ★★

Serves 8

chocolate génoise: (see basic recipes)

For the Elysée ganache:
1 cup / 250 ml crème fraîche
12 oz / 375 g Avellino chocolate
3¹/₂ oz / 100 g baking chocolate

For the praline buttercream:
¹/₂ vanilla bean
1 pinch of salt
1³/₄ oz / 50 g praline paste

2 egg yolks
5 tbsp / 75 g superfine sugar
3¹/₂ tbsp / 25 g flour
3¹/₂ tbsp / 50 g butter, softened
1¹/₄ cups / 300 ml whole milk

For the syrup for soaking:
(see basic recipes)
6¹/₂ tbsp / 100 ml maraschino liqueur
6¹/₂ tbsp / 100 ml water
6¹/₂ tbsp / 100 g superfine sugar

To garnish:
chocolate flakes or wafers
chopped, roasted almonds

Caracas, the capital city of Venezuela, is a stronghold of high-quality chocolate, so set high standards when selecting the cocoa beans for this torte. The variety preferred by Maurice and Jean-Jacques Bernachon, Caraque cocoa, is ideal. It has a very bitter, sharp flavor and belongs to the Forasteros family, which is harvested from January to April.

Also used in this recipe is Avellino chocolate, from Avellino in the Campania region of Italy, made of bitter chocolate and nut nougat. Chocolate flakes are used for the garnish. Cocoa powder is used in the génoise, which can also be flavored with a little honey if desired. Both the sponge cake and the ganache work best if they are made a day in advance.

In this recipe, the praline paste that flavors the buttercream beautifully complements the maraschino liqueur with which the three sponge layers are soaked. The latter is a delicious liqueur distilled from the marasca cherry, a sour cherry cultivated mainly in northern Italy, and it is used far too infrequently. Generally, it has to mature for several years before it is ready to use.

In order for the top of the torte to be nice and smooth when it is covered with the buttercream, use a knife to smooth out any unevenness in the top layer of génoise.

1. Prepare the génoise a day in advance, baking it in a square cake pan. When it is completely cool, cut it horizontally into three equally thick layers. For the ganache, boil the crème fraîche for one minute over a high heat while stirring with a whisk; remove from the heat. Break the chocolate into small pieces, fold into the hot crème fraîche and stir the mixture until smooth. Cover and refrigerate for 12 hours.

2. To make the praline buttercream, bring 1 cup / 250 ml milk to a boil with the slit vanilla bean and salt; boil for two minutes. Vigorously beat the egg yolks in a bowl with the sugar. Blend in the flour and (to prevent lumps) remaining cold milk, then the hot milk. Pour into a saucepan and return to a boil, and continue to cook for three minutes while stirring constantly with a whisk. Allow to cool.

Torte

3. When the cream has cooled, fold in the softened butter. Fold in the praline paste and stir thoroughly until the mixture is very smooth. Make the syrup for soaking according to the basic recipe. To assemble the torte, place a layer of génoise on a cake lid, soak it with a third of the maraschino syrup and cover with Elysée ganache.

4. Place the second layer on top, soak it and cover with praline buttercream. Place the third layer on top, and soak with the rest of the maraschino syrup. Refrigerate for one hour. Spread ganache on the top and sides of the cake, and smooth with a spatula. Press chopped and roasted almonds halfway up the sides of the cake and use a pastry bag to garnish with the remaining ganache.

Strawberry

Preparation time: 45 minutes
Cooking time: 20 minutes
Difficulty: ★

Serves 8

simple génoise: (see basic recipes)

For the buttercream:
(see basic recipes)
5 tbsp / 75 g butter
$^1/_2$ cup, 2 tbsp / 150 g superfine sugar
4 egg yolks
$6^1/_2$ tbsp / 50 g flour
1 vanilla bean

$2^1/_2$ cups / 600 ml whole milk
2 pinches of salt

For the syrup for soaking:
(see basic recipes)
$6^1/_2$ tbsp / 100 ml kirsch
$6^1/_2$ tbsp / 100 ml water
$6^1/_2$ tbsp / 100 g sugar

For the filling:
2 lb 3 oz / 1 kg strawberries

To garnish:
9 oz / 250 g marzipan
confectioners' sugar

Strawberry cakes are usually available only in spring and early summer, when strawberries are nice and ripe and their flavor has had the chance to develop fully through exposure to sunshine. Gourmets must respect the cycle of the seasons and adjust the pleasures of the palate around the rhythms of nature.

The more aromatic, small, dark red strawberries are best suited for this recipe. Raspberries or wild strawberries could be used instead, as long as they are available in sufficient quantity. Generally, large berries are not suited to this recipe, because you need aromatic berries that are fully ripe but not too soft.

Washing strawberries in a lot of water impairs their flavor, so it is better to wipe them carefully with damp paper towels, especially if there is still some soil on them.

The génoise will be more velvety if it is made with a little honey; the cake will then require a bit less sugar, and also keep longer.

If you decide to make a raspberry cake, replace the kirsch with the best raspberry schnapps you can find. Its delicate bouquet will give the sponge cake a distinctive flavor.

1. Bake the génoise a day ahead. Slice it horizontally into two equal layers. Make the buttercream and syrup for soaking according to the basic recipes, but with the ingredients listed above. Take the stems off the strawberries and wipe them clean. Place a layer of génoise on a cake lid, soak with the kirsch syrup, and spread a $^1/_2$ in / 1 cm layer of buttercream on it. Arrange the strawberries on top, placing a ring of strawberries of equal size around the edge.

2. Cover the strawberries with the remaining buttercream and smooth off the top.

Torte

3. Place the second sponge cake layer on top of the strawberries and buttercream, and soak with the remaining kirsch syrup. Refrigerate for one hour or longer.

4. Roll out the marzipan mixture with a rolling pin to a thickness of 1/8 in / 2 mm, cut a zigzag pattern along the edge, and place it on top of the cake. Dust the torte lightly with confectioners' sugar and use a salamander or hot iron to burn a pattern into the marzipan. Decorate to taste with a marzipan rose or strawberries.

Preparation time: 30 minutes
Cooking time: 20 minutes
Difficulty: ✭

Serves 8

simple génoise:
(see basic recipes)

For the pastry cream:
2¹/₂ cups / 600 ml milk
1 vanilla bean
1 pinch of salt
4 egg yolks
¹/₂ cup, 2 tbsp / 150 g superfine sugar
6¹/₂ tbsp / 50 g flour

For the syrup for soaking:
(see basic recipes)
6¹/₂ tbsp / 100 ml Grand Marnier
6¹/₂ tbsp / 100 g superfine sugar
6¹/₂ tbsp / 100 ml water

For the filling:
9 oz / 250 g buttercream (see basic recipes)
¹/₂ cup / 100 g candied orange peel marinated in
  Grand Marnier
9 oz / 250 g orange-colored marzipan

For the egg white icing:
1 egg white
confectioners' sugar
juice of 1 lemon

For almost fifty years now, Maurice Bernachon has made a Grand Marnier *cordon rouge* (red label) torte with chocolate or ganache, paying tribute to the fine flavor and consistent quality of the well-known liqueur in this and many other creations. Grand Marnier is made by marinating the peels of bitter Antillian oranges in high-quality cognac that has been matured in old oak barrels.

This Grand Marnier torte contains candied orange peel, which our fastidious pastry chefs make themselves from Spanish navel oranges. The peels of the untreated oranges are first blanched, then marinated in large copper pans and flavored with vanilla. But that is not all: as soon as the orange peels are satu-

rated with sugar syrup, they are preserved in stoneware jars and finally marinated again in Grand Marnier for six weeks before use.

The marzipan (ideally made using the Spanish Avola almond) has to withstand quite a bit in this recipe; it needs to be kneaded very thoroughly before it is rolled out and draped over the torte.

The egg white icing can be replaced by other toppings, such as a layer of ganache with some elegantly arranged peach slices. Their color and shine would also enhance the total effect of the Grand Marnier torte beautifully.

1. Make the génoise a day in advance. For the pastry cream, bring 2 cups / 500 ml of milk to a boil with the slit vanilla bean and salt. Whisk the egg yolks and sugar in a bowl until foamy, then fold in the flour. Add the remaining milk, cold (to prevent lumps), then stir in the boiled milk. Pour everything into a saucepan, return to a boil and simmer while stirring with a whisk for three minutes. Allow to cool and refrigerate.

2. Prepare the syrup for soaking according to the basic recipe. Cut the génoise horizontally into three equally thick layers. Place one layer on a cake lid and soak it with a third of the Grand Marnier syrup. Pipe a ¹/₂–1 in / 1–2 cm thick layer of pastry cream on the génoise and sprinkle some marinated orange peel over it. Repeat with the second layer of génoise.

Torte

3. Place the third sponge layer on top, soak it and spread buttercream all over the sides and top of the torte. Refrigerate for one hour. Roll out the marzipan out with a rolling pin to a thickness of ⅛ in / 2 mm, cover the torte with it and trim the excess.

4. To make the egg white icing, put the egg white in a bowl and gradually stir in the sifted confectioners' sugar with a wooden spatula until the mixture has a creamy consistency. Add a dash of lemon juice. Cover with a damp cloth. Decorate the cake with the egg white icing and garnish with a candied orange peel and marzipan leaves.

La Marjolaine

Preparation time: 40 minutes
Cooking time: 15 minutes
Difficulty: ★★

Serves 8

plain ganache: (see basic recipes)

For the almond sponge cake:
(see basic recipes)
6 egg whites
³/₄ cup / 180 g sugar
1 cup, 3 tbsp / 180 g blanched almonds

For the buttercream:
(see basic recipes)
5 tbsp / 75 g butter
¹/₂ cup, 2 tbsp / 150 g superfine sugar

4 egg yolks
6¹/₂ tbsp / 50 g flour
1 vanilla bean
2¹/₂ cups / 600 ml whole milk

For the mocha flavoring:
1 tbsp espresso
2 pinches of salt

For the syrup for soaking:
(see basic recipes)
6¹/₂ tbsp / 100 ml rum
6¹/₂ tbsp / 100 ml water
6¹/₂ tbsp / 100 g superfine sugar

To garnish:
cocoa powder

This mocha buttercream cake may even leave a mark as enduring as Francis Lemarque's song by the same name, a song that has survived the passage of time and remains popular with people of all ages in France. It must have something to do with the clever preparation of the coffee, an espresso that Maurice and Jean-Jacques Bernachon reduce in a double boiler before folding it into the buttercream, and whose flavor is rounded off by a small pinch of salt.

Refrigerate the marjolaine for at least two hours before serving it so that the soaked sponge cake layers, ganache, buttercream, and mocha buttercream reach the same consistency.

Another element is the choice of vanilla, which is actually a type of climbing orchid whose beans contain the aromatic black vanilla pulp. Experts generally prefer what is known as Bourbon vanilla, harvested on the island of Réunion. Fortunately, this is the variety most widely available. But there are also other varieties, including vanilla from Veracruz in Mexico, with which the Aztecs are thought to have flavored their hot chocolate drinks before the Conquistadors' arrival.

In the Bernachons' *pâtisserie*, vanilla is used most generously in the making of chocolate, candies, and ice creams. So to be true to the spirit in which it was created, you should be generous with the vanilla flavor when you make La Marjolaine.

1. Prepare the plain ganache a day in advance. Make the almond sponge cake and buttercream according to the Bernachons' basic recipes but using the ingredients listed above. Flavor half of the buttercream with the espresso. Heat the ganache in a double boiler, stirring constantly, until it is soft. Cut the sponge cake into a square and slice three times horizontally. Place one sponge base on a cake lid and pipe a ¹/₂ in / 1 cm thick layer of ganache on to it.

2. Place the second layer of sponge cake on the ganache, soak with rum syrup, and pipe buttercream on to it. Top with the third sponge cake, soak with rum syrup and garnish with the mocha buttercream.

3. Place the fourth layer of sponge cake on top and soak with rum syrup. Refrigerate for 1–2 hours. Spread the remaining ganache on the top of the torte and dust with cocoa powder.

4. Straighten the edges of the marjolaine with a sharp knife that has been dipped in hot water. Refrigerate before serving.

Preparation time: 45 minutes
Cooking time: 30 minutes
Difficulty: ★★

Serves 8

chocolate génoise, plain ganache:
  (see basic recipes)

For the pistachio buttercream:
buttercream (see basic recipes)
1³/₄ oz / 50 g pistachio paste

For the syrup for soaking:
(see basic recipes)
6¹/₂ tbsp / 100 ml kirsch
6¹/₂ tbsp / 100 ml water
6¹/₂ tbsp / 100 g superfine sugar

For the topping:
pistachios
green marzipan
confectioners' sugar

Since the Bernachon *pâtisserie* obtains its pistachios from Sicily, from the regions of Cefalu or Selinonte for example, they have named this torte after one the island's most popular cities. It is common knowledge among pastry chefs that the fruits of Italian pistachio trees have an incomparable flavor. If ground, they can be used to produce a very fine paste ideal for making an excellent buttercream.

For garnishing, on the other hand, pistachios from Iran are better suited, with their pleasing form and more intense green. The pistachio tree was originally native to Asia Minor. Make sure that both the pistachio cream and the ganache are homogeneous; they must be smooth, appealing and easy to spread.

The génoise, which can be enhanced with ground hazelnuts, is soaked with kirsch – an ideal counterpart to the pistachio flavor. Since the edges of the sponge cake are often uneven and crumbly, spread ganache on the cake before its final trim so that it is nice and smooth all around.

The Palermo torte should be enjoyed fairly soon after it is assembled. It can be served with ice cream or a pistachio coulis. Maybe you will feel transported to Palermo …

1. To make the chocolate génoise, whisk the eggs and sugar in a double boiler until foamy. Allow to cool slightly. Remove from the double boiler and continue to stir with a mixer until the mixture drops off the beaters in long ribbons. Use a wooden spatula to fold in the flour, cocoa powder, and ground hazelnuts.

2. Melt the butter and fold into the génoise mixture while hot. Grease a square baking pan and dust lightly with flour. Bake the sponge cake in a preheated oven for 20 minutes at 390 °F / 200 °C. After baking, immediately turn it out on to a cooling rack. Make the buttercream according to the basic recipe and combine well with the pistachio paste.

Torte

3. Make the syrup for soaking according to the basic recipe. It is best to make the ganache a day in advance. Proceed as described in the basic recipe, adding the pieces of chocolate to the hot crème fraîche as shown below. Cover and allow to cool for at least 12 hours in the refrigerator. Before using, slowly heat in a double boiler until softened.

4. Slice the sponge cake horizontally into three layers. Place one layer on a cake lid, soak it with a third of the kirsch syrup, and cover it with ganache. Soak the second sponge cake layer and coat it with pistachio buttercream. Place the third layer on top, and soak with the remaining syrup. Refrigerate for one hour. Spread ganache on the top and sides of the torte, and cover with a sheet of green marzipan cut to size. Garnish with shelled pistachios.

Sphinx

Preparation time: 30 minutes
Cooking time: 15 minutes
Difficulty: ★

Serves 8

plain ganache: (see basic recipes)

For the almond sponge cake:
6 egg whites
³/₄ cup / 180 g sugar
1 cup, 3 tbsp / 180 g blanched almonds

For dusting:
cocoa powder

Neither an impossible riddle nor a monumental sculpture in the Egyptian desert, this is a classic cake recipe, impressive in its simplicity and its demonstration of the mastery Maurice Bernachon has gained during his fifty years' experience using chocolate. He calls it "black gold," having become acquainted with it during his very first year as an apprentice.

The simplicity of the ganache in this recipe perfectly embodies one of Maurice Bernachon's immutable principles: Use only ingredients of excellent quality, which in this case applies especially to both the chocolate and the crème fraîche.

He enthusiastically recommends the delicious crème fraîche from Isigny in Normandy for the ganache; a top-quality prod-

uct, it was classified a few years ago as an *appellation d'origine contrôlée* (A.O.C.) in France. It is a pasteurized crème fraîche with a high fat content and must be very fresh when used; its fine taste promises a luscious result.

The only difficulty will likely arise in baking the sponge cake bases; do not bake them for too long, so that they retain their velvety texture. If you bake the sponge cake in advance, be sure to wrap it in plastic wrap to protect it from moisture. Use a sieve to sprinkle the cocoa powder garnish very evenly over the cake.

1. Prepare the plain ganache a day in advance, according to the basic recipe, and refrigerate for at least 12 hours. To make the almond sponge cake, grind the sugar and almonds in a blender. Beat the egg whites until they are very stiff. Fold the sugar and almonds into them as carefully as possible so the beaten egg whites do not collapse.

2. Grease and flour a baking sheet. Use a pastry bag with a medium to large round tip (no. 7 or 8) to pipe two sponge cake bases with a diameter of 10 in / 22 cm onto the baking sheet. Bake for 7–8 minutes at 480 °F / 250 °C. After baking, turn the sponge cake bases out on to plates and trim the edges with a knife so that they are evenly round.

Torte

3. Heat the ganache in a double boiler, stirring constantly, until it becomes soft. Place one sponge cake layer onto a cake lid and pipe a 1 in / 2 cm thick layer of ganache on to it with a pastry bag. Place the second sponge cake layer on top, with the smooth side facing up. Refrigerate for one hour.

4. Spread the remaining ganache on the top and sides of the torte and dust with cocoa powder. Using a knife or ruler, create a checkered pattern on the top of the torte.

Le Canotier

Preparation time: 2 hours
Cooking time: 25 minutes
Difficulty: ★★★

Serves 8

génoise, rum syrup for soaking, sweet pastry:
  (see basic recipes)

For the buttercream:
3 eggs
6¹/₂ tbsp / 100 g superfine sugar
5 tsp / 25 ml water
1 cup / 250 g butter
grated peel of 1 lemon

For the marzipan topping:
9 oz / 250 g marzipan
4 egg yolks
1 egg
sugar syrup

For the cigarette pastry:
6¹/₂ tbsp / 100 g butter
²/₃ cup / 100 g confectioners' sugar
3 egg whites
³/₄ cup, 1 tbsp / 100 g sifted flour
cocoa powder

During the France of the Belle Epoque, the *canotier*, a flat, round straw hat, became the symbol of carefree days outdoors; it was a great favorite of the Impressionists. Here, Christian Cottard presents us with a new variation on the torte of the same name.

You need plenty of excellent quality butter for the sweet pastry, and since it must not be kneaded too vigorously, use flour that is not too sticky. Almonds can also be added to the dough, along with a little baking powder to keep it light; almonds absorb excess fat and give the dough a fine flavor. Make sure the oven temperature is not too high.

Cigarette pastry makes an excellent lining, but it has to be used immediately after baking, while it is still hot, because it dries out when cooled. Its texture makes it particularly suited for garnishing, and it is often used for just that purpose.

Recall Maurice Chevalier, who has made the *canotier* known throughout the world, and listen to one of his unforgettable *chansons* while serving Le Canotier with ice cream or chilled fruit on a summer's afternoon. Relive the charm of a past era.

1. Bake the génoise 1–2 days in advance. For the buttercream, whisk the eggs until foamy. Heat the water and sugar to 250 °F / 121 °C and slowly pour the syrup over the eggs; beating continuously until completely cooled. Cream the butter, then fold it into the egg mixture with the grated lemon peel. Make the rum syrup for soaking. Slice the génoise into three layers, soak them with syrup, spread buttercream on two of them, and sandwich them together.

2. Cover the top and sides of the torte with the remaining buttercream and refrigerate. Prepare the sweet pastry according to the basic recipe. After the dough has rested, roll it out evenly and bake; then cut out a round pastry base with the same diameter as the torte. To make the marzipan topping, beat the marzipan until smooth with the egg yolks, then add the whole egg.

3. Using a pastry bag with a flat, ribbed tip, pipe a woven network of marzipan strips onto the torte. Allow to dry overnight in a cool place (but not in the refrigerator). Bake briefly (five minutes or less) at 430 °F / 220 °C. After baking, brush the surface with sugar syrup and place on top of the sweet pastry base.

4. For the cigarette pastry, cream the butter, add the confectioners' sugar, and continue beating with a whisk. Gradually add the egg whites and finally fold in the flour. Pipe the mixture on to a tray lined with baking paper. Use a stencil to make strips of dough and freeze. Spread a thin layer of cigarette pastry mixed with cocoa on to the tray to produce a pattern. Bake at 430 °F / 220 °C. After baking, quickly wrap the pastry around the torte.

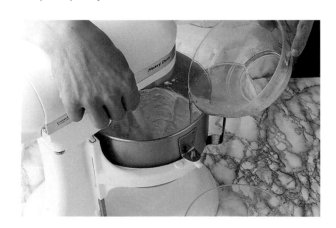

Eclat de Rubis

Preparation time: 1 hour
Cooking time: 30 minutes
Difficulty: ★

Serves 8

For the jelly:
1 lb / 500 g strawberries and raspberries
sugar (according to the acidity of the berries)
grated peel of ¹/₂ orange
1 sprig lemon verbena
12 sheets of gelatin per quart / liter of fruit juice

For the vanilla parfait:
8 egg yolks
¹/₂ cup, 2 tbsp / 150 g sugar

12 sheets of gelatin
2 vanilla beans
2 cups / 500 ml whipping cream

For the financier sponge cake:
3 large egg whites
¹/₂ cup / 125 g superfine sugar
4 tbsp / 40 g very finely ground almonds
¹/₃ cup / 40 g flour
6¹/₂ tbsp / 100 g nut butter (almond butter, hazelnut butter)
1 oz / 30 g raspberries

The Eclat de rubis is a nourishing, delicious sponge cake base topped with vanilla parfait and – for color – the lightly jellied, exquisite juice of red berries. The harmony among these three elements renders this dessert a rare delicacy Christian Cottard reserves for his most demanding customers.

The source of the delicate flavor of this tarte is the juice of the red berries, made in a double boiler and flavored with vanilla and, for a final touch, lemon verbena. Make the juice a day in advance, but do not squeeze the berries; use only the juice released while they are steamed.

Christian Cottard prefers to use raspberries for the sponge cake, because their acidic flavor balances the sweetness of the cake. Fully ripened, untreated fruits are best, though you can also substitute deep-frozen berries.

Less practiced bakers might worry about how to get the jelly out of the mold, and this is a legitimate concern. Usually, it is enough to expose the jelly to a slight increase in heat; if you heat the mold slightly as soon as the jelly has set, it can then be turned out with no trouble. Christian Cottard remembers his family in Normandy doing it just this way.

1. Combine the berries, sugar, orange peel, and verbena in the top of a double boiler, cover tightly, and simmer for one hour over low heat. Allow to cool. Place in a sieve, but do not squeeze the berries, simply retain the juice that flows from them. Stir in the soaked gelatin. Pour into a round mold with a diameter of 8 in / 18 cm. Refrigerate for 12 hours.

2. To make the vanilla parfait, beat the egg yolks until foamy. Heat the sugar to 250 °F / 121 °C and slowly pour it on to the egg yolks. Continue to stir until completely cooled. Soak the gelatin in hot sugar syrup, then add it to the egg yolk mixture with the vanilla. Whip the cream until stiff and carefully fold it into the parfait.

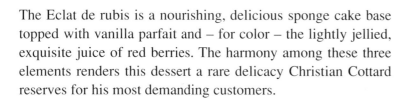

3. Fill the parfait into a pastry bag and pipe it into the mold on top of the red berry jelly. Refrigerate for at least five hours.

4. For the financier sponge cake, whisk the egg whites slightly. Fold in the sugar, ground almonds, flour, and nut butter; allow the mixture to rest. Pour into a springform pan two sizes larger than the one used for the parfait. Spread the raspberries on top of it and bake for 10–15 minutes at 390 °F / 200 °C. Remove from the pan and allow to cool. Invert the parfait onto the sponge cake base, and garnish the edge of the sponge cake with raspberries.

La Marjolaine aux

Preparation time: 2 hours
Cooking time: 15 minutes
Difficulty: ★★

Serves 8

Italian meringue: (see basic recipes)

For the marjolaine sponge cake:
4 egg whites
6^1/$_2$ tbsp / 100 g superfine sugar
3 tbsp / 20 g flour
^{3}/$_4$ cup / 110 g almonds, unblanched
^{3}/$_4$ cup, 2 tbsp / 125 g hazelnuts, blanched

For the almond and pistachio mousse:
4^1/$_2$ oz / 125 g marzipan
^{1}/$_2$ oz / 12 g pistachio paste
2 egg yolks
6^1/$_2$ tbsp / 100 g butter

For the orange ganache:
^{3}/$_4$ cup / 200 ml cream
grated peel of 1 orange
14 oz / 400 g orange colored or white chocolate
    coating
2^1/$_2$ tbsp / 40 ml glucose
4 tsp / 20 ml Grand Marnier

To garnish:
dried fruits

In the Mediterranean area, the expansion of the Roman Empire also served to spread the eating habits of the conquerors to the conquered, particularly the use of dried fruits such as almonds, hazelnuts, pine nuts, and dates (plums do not seem to have appeared in the West before the Crusades).

This marjolaine, with a high content of almonds (preferably of the Aï, Ferraduel or Ferragne varieties), is part and parcel of Provençal tradition (Provence became part of the Roman Empire during the first phase of conquest). As for the hazelnuts, choose Piedmont hazelnuts, which are well-known for their flavor, or Spanish Avelinos.

The pistachios for the almond and pistachio mousse should be of excellent quality. Originally introduced by the Arabs, these nuts are cultivated all around the Mediterranean (the Roman *mare nostrum*) and have become integral to the traditional baking of most Mediterranean cultures. This member of the *Anacardiaceae* family should be small – small nuts are more aromatic – and preferably from Spain.

Allow the cake to cool a little before serving. By the way, marjolaine is also the French word for marjoram, which suggests delicate and enticing flavors.

1. For the marjolaine sponge cake, grease a baking sheet thoroughly with butter and place in the freezer. Roast the almonds and hazelnuts and grind them finely with two-thirds of the sugar. Stir in the flour. Beat the egg whites and remaining sugar until stiff, then carefully fold into the nuts and flour. Spread the sponge cake mixture on to the cold baking sheet. Bake·at 390 °F / 200 °C. Remove from the tray immediately after baking and allow to rest for a few hours.

2. To make the almond and pistachio mousse, combine the marzipan and pistachio paste with the egg yolks. Cream the butter, add it to the marzipan mixture and stir until smooth. Continue beating the mixture until it has the consistency of a foamy cream.

Saveurs de Provence

3. To make the orange ganache, heat the cream with the grated orange peel. Add the chocolate coating, broken into pieces, along with the glucose and stir until melted. Remove from heat. Before the mixture has cooled completely, stir in the Grand Marnier. Prepare an Italian meringue according to the basic recipe.

4. Assemble the Marjolaine aus Saveurs de Provence as a rectangle: spread orange ganache on to a layer of sponge cake, place another sponge layer on top, and coat it with almond and pistachio mousse. Top with the final layer of sponge cake, and cover it with the Italian meringue. Brown the meringue with a salamander and garnish with dried fruits and a slice of orange.

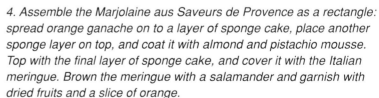

Puff Pastry Cake

Preparation time: 2 hours
Cooking time: 30 minutes
Difficulty: ★★★

Serves 8

For the puff pastry:
(see basic recipes)
8¹/₃ cups / 1 kg flour
2 tbsp / 30 g salt
2 cups / 500 ml water
4 cups / 1 kg butter
superfine sugar

For the pastry cream:
(see basic recipes)
1 cup / 250 ml milk
2 egg yolks
3¹/₂ tbsp / 50 g sugar
3¹/₂ tbsp / 50 ml whipping cream
5 tbsp / 50 g confectioners' sugar

For the light cream:
2 oz / 350 g pastry cream
2³/₄ cups / 700 ml whipping cream
6 sheets of gelatin
¹/₂ cup / 70 g confectioners' sugar

To garnish:
confectioners' sugar

To say that this mille-feuille consists of precisely 1,000 layers, as the French word for puff pastry suggests, is the same as saying a millipede actually has 1,000 feet. The term dates back to the Renaissance, when the first experiments were performed on the composition of puff pastry, which had been brought by the Crusaders back from the Middle East. It is still used widely today – in croissants, for example, since the 18th-century retreat of the Turks after their defeat at Vienna, and in puff pastry turnovers.

A genuine mille-feuille pastry, such as the one required for the palmiers that ring the side of this spectacular torte, needs to be folded and turned six times; first four normal turns, for which one must allow approximately two hours, and then another two turns in which superfine sugar is generously added to the pastry.

Christian Cottard insists that the butter used for the puff pastry be very fresh and of the best quality; it is wrapped in a simple flour and water dough and it is the butter alone that makes the pastry exquisite. If you are curious about the precise number of layers, a brief calculation certifies that puff pastry that has been folded and turned six times contains 729 layers of butter and 730 layers of flour and water dough; hence the melting, pure taste of butter!

The fruit of all these efforts is a great puff pastry classic, frequently used to gauge young bakers' abilities and one of the most famous gifts of this vocation in which patience and creativity work in concert with a love of flavors.

1. *Make a classic puff pastry (without sugar), roll it out ¹/₈ in / 2 mm thick and allow to rest for two hours. Cut into strips 9 in / 20 cm long and ¹/₂ in / 1 cm wide. Use them to weave the lid, and rest for one hour. Bake for 20 minutes in a hot oven, turning it over and dusting it with confectioners' sugar after ten minutes. The lid must be baked thoroughly and have a caramelized sheen. Make two puff pastry bases with the same diameter as the cake ring being used.*

2. *For the palmiers, prepare a normal puff pastry and make four normal turns; during the two final turns generously incorporate superfine sugar into the pastry. Roll it out to a thickness of ¹/₂–1 in / 1–2 cm and cut into strips 2¹/₂ in / 5 cm wide. Refrigerate until firm, but no longer. Cut the strips into pieces ¹/₂ in / 1 cm wide, place on a baking sheet next to each other and bake. Line a cake ring with the palmiers while they are still hot.*

with a Woven Lid

3. To make the light cream, start by preparing a pastry cream (see basic recipes for method). Allow to cool. Whip the cream with the confectioners' sugar until stiff; soak the gelatin in cold water. Heat a little pastry cream and fold in the gelatin. Add the remaining pastry cream, beat until smooth with a whisk, and carefully fold in the whipped cream.

4. Assemble the mille-feuille by alternating the puff pastry bases with a layer of light cream piped from a pastry bag with a round, $^1/_2$ in / 10 mm-wide tip. Finally, place the woven puff pastry lid on top. Refrigerate for about three hours before serving.

Coffee Mill

Preparation time: 2 hours
Cooking time: 25 minutes
Difficulty: ★★★

Serves 6 to 8

génoise: (see basic recipes)

For the bavaroise au café:
1³/₄ oz / 50 g ground coffee beans
1¹/₃ cups / 330 ml milk
5 egg yolks
6¹/₂ tbsp / 100 g sugar
4 sheets of gelatin
1¹/₃ cups / 330 ml whipping cream

For the rum parfait:
5 egg yolks
6¹/₂ tbsp / 100 g sugar
4 sheets of gelatin
5 tsp / 35 ml rum
1¹/₃ cups / 330 ml whipping cream

For the syrup for soaking:
6¹/₂ tbsp / 100 g sugar
6¹/₂ tbsp / 100 ml water
soluble chicory coffee

For the glaze and garnish:
7 oz / 200 g clear cake glaze
3¹/₂ oz / 100 g bittersweet chocolate coating

There are all sorts of mills – windmills, watermills and, of course, wooden coffee mills – the ones with a small drawer, most often found in antique stores nowadays, which were used for generations when coffee beans still had to be ground by hand. Christian Cottard created his Coffee Mill as an homage to this simple household appliance, for the 1986 Best Craftsman of France competition.

To ensure the success of this assembled parfait, the individual stages of work, as well as the baking utensils and ingredients, need to work well together. It is also vital to keep to the given times, as when preparing the coffee. A strong coffee, such as the Robusta from Ecuador, is recommended.

First, the coffee beans must be properly roasted: sandwich them between two sheets of waxed paper (or a towel) and crush them with a rolling pin. Then roast them on a baking tray at 390 °F / 200 °C until the edges blacken. Immediately stir them into the hot milk, just before it begins to boil.

Bake the thin génoise sponge cake at a temperature 30–50 °F / 20–30 °C higher than that used normally. It is best to bake the génoise a day (or several) in advance, because it becomes easier to work with. Either way, make the génoise sponge cake base first, and then the bavaroise au café.

1. To make the bavaroise, crush and roast the coffee beans, then stir them into the boiling hot milk. Cover and let steep until cooled. Strain through a sieve. If necessary, add milk to make 1¹/₃ cups / 330 ml. Beat the egg yolks with the sugar until the mixture runs down in smooth ribbons, add the infused milk, and reduce like a custard. Pass through a sieve and add the gelatin, which has been soaked in cold water. Allow to cool, then fold in the whipped cream.

2. Place a hemispherical mold into a bowl so that it does not tip over, and coat it with bavaroise au café. To make the rum parfait, beat the egg yolks until foamy. Heat the sugar to 250 °F / 121 °C, pour onto the egg yolks and continue beating until the mixture has completely cooled. Add the gelatin (soaked in cold water) and the rum, then carefully fold in the whipped cream.

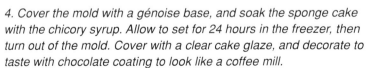

3. Pour the rum parfait into the bavaroise-coated mold. To make the syrup for soaking, boil the sugar and water, remove from the heat and whisk in the soluble chicory coffee. Allow to cool. Prepare the génoise according to the basic recipe but using the ingredients given above, spread the mixture on a tray lined with baking paper, and bake for ten minutes at 430 °F / 220 °C. Cut out a round base the same size as the bavaroise mold.

4. Cover the mold with a génoise base, and soak the sponge cake with the chicory syrup. Allow to set for 24 hours in the freezer, then turn out of the mold. Cover with a clear cake glaze, and decorate to taste with chocolate coating to look like a coffee mill.

La Paillote

Preparation time: 1 hour 30 minutes
Cooking time: 20 minutes
Difficulty: ★★

Serves 8

For the Italian meringue:
(see basic recipes)
2 large egg whites
$^1/_2$ cup / 125 g superfine sugar
$^1/_4$ cup / 60 ml water

For the coconut mousse:
$^1/_2$ cup / 125 ml cream
9 oz / 250 g coconut meat, grated
4 sheets of gelatin
2$^1/_2$ tbsp / 35 ml sugar cane rum

For the succès sponge cake:
2 large egg whites
$^1/_2$ cup, 2 tbsp / 150 g superfine sugar
1 tbsp / 10 g cornstarch
$^1/_3$ cup / 50 g almonds, very finely ground
7$^1/_2$ tbsp / 50 g pecan nuts, chopped

For the caramelized bananas:
2 tbsp / 30 g superfine sugar
2 tbsp / 30 g butter
2 bananas, sliced

To garnish:
bittersweet chocolate coating

Prized by pastry chefs, coconut is used to make pastries like coconut macaroons as well as this coconut mousse paillote, which has the shape of a straw hat. The coconut meat available in stores is of a good quality, but you can also puree copra, the dried coconut meat containing milk.

The liquid ingredients have to be added to the meringue mixture very slowly so that the mousse becomes light but not runny. Fold the whipped cream in at the end.

As soon as these first steps have been completed, you can devote all your attention to the paillote. Use bittersweet choco-late coating of about 70% cocoa; its slightly bitter taste will contrast with the sweet flavor of the coconut mousse and the succès sponge cake, which provide the base for the mousse. The "chocolate roof" may look rather complicated, but you will get the hang of it quickly and undoubtedly take pride in your architectural abilities.

One final word about pecans, which originated in North America: An easily digested dried fruit that does not spoil, they are very difficult to shell. They can replaced with ordinary walnuts, but these will be a little less exotic.

1. To make the coconut mousse, first prepare an Italian meringue according to the basic recipe, but using the amounts given above. Beat the cream until stiff and warm the coconut meat slightly. Soak the gelatin in cold water and dissolve it in the heated rum. Fold it into the meringue with the coconut meat, then gently blend in the whipped cream.

2. For the succès sponge cake, whisk the egg whites and beat with some of the sugar until stiff, then add the cornstarch. Combine the remaining sugar with the ground almonds and chopped pecans, and fold into the beaten egg whites. Using a pastry bag with a round hole ($^1/_2$–$^3/_4$ in / 12–14 mm), pipe the mixture on to baking paper and bake at 430 °F / 220 °C. Caramelize the sugar and butter in a saucepan. Brown the banana slices in it and then set aside.

Coco-Créole

3. Make a Chinese hat using a sheet of plastic and invert it on a cake ring to keep it level. Place an equally large but lower ring inside the hat to form the base for the paillote.

4. Fill the hat with coconut mousse, arrange the banana slices on top and cover with the sponge cake base. Freeze for at least 12 hours. Remove the plastic hat and cake ring, and use a pastry bag to garnish the mousse with melted chocolate in the shape of a straw hat.

Preparation time: 1 hour 30 minutes
Cooking time: 15 minutes
Difficulty: ★★

Serves 8

génoise: (see basic recipes)

For the biscuit mixture:
3 egg yolks
6¹/₂ tbsp / 100 g superfine sugar
3 egg whites
¹/₂ cup, 2 tbsp / 75 g flour
a pinch of baking powder
confectioners' sugar

For the Grand Marnier parfait:
6 egg yolks
¹/₂ cup / 125 g superfine sugar

7 sheets of gelatin
¹/₂ cup / 125 ml Grand Marnier
2 cups / 500 ml whipping cream

For the syrup for soaking:
(see basic recipes)
6¹/₂ tbsp / 100 ml grapefruit juice
2 tbsp / 30 ml Grand Marnier
³/₄ cup / 200 ml sugar syrup
6¹/₂ tbsp / 100 g sugar
6¹/₂ tbsp / 100 ml water

Fruit (according to season):
apricots, peaches, strawberries, currants,
    raspberries, blackberries, blueberries

Where to find a mold in the shape of a painter's palette? Christian Cottard once saw a form for a headcheese being made at a manufacturer's, and this inspired him to convert a cake ring, bending it to reproduce the curve of the hand-hold on a palette. All that remained was to cut out the opening for the thumb, and the palette mold was ready. Of course, after being manipulated and re-formed, the cake ring can only be used for painter's palettes …

In obeisance to the wise teachings of our ancestors, one should use only seasonal fruits. In this instance, Christian Cottard has had to do without the star fruit, papayas and other exotic fruits that he otherwise prizes.

Here, the biscuit mixture functions just as it does in a charlotte: It binds the fat of the parfait and absorbs the liquid without let-ting it seep through. With no taste of its own, it cannot impair the delicate flavor of the parfait. The sponge cake ingredients should be mixed very carefully so that it stays airy and light, and the flour must be folded in last. If you are using double-acting baking powder, as is common in the United States, reduce the amount by one-third.

While Grand Marnier is listed as an ingredient here, it can be replaced by any of the various white fruit schnapps, depending on the choice of fruit. Rum should be reserved for exotic fruits, if you insist on using those. Grapefruit juice is ideal for drenching the génoise, as it contains little sugar and gives the finished torte a very fresh flavor.

1. To make the biscuit mixture, beat the egg yolks with 2¹/₂ tbsp / 40 g sugar until they are foamy and the mixture falls from the beaters in smooth ribbons. Beat the egg whites until stiff with the remaining sugar. Combine both mixtures, then fold in the sifted flour and baking powder.

2. Pipe the mixture on to baking paper using a pastry bag with a round ³/₄ in / 14 mm tip, dust with confectioners' sugar and bake for 12 minutes at 390 °F / 200 °C. For the parfait, beat the egg yolks with a whisk until foamy. Heat the sugar to 250 °F / 121 °C and slowly pour it onto the egg yolks. Continue to beat until completely cool. Add the gelatin soaked in cold water and the Grand Marnier, then fold in the whipped cream. Combine the ingredients for the syrup for soaking.

Palette

3. Prepare the génoise, spread the mixture on to a tray lined with baking paper and bake for 20 minutes at 430 °F / 220 °C. When cooled, slice it horizontally. Place one layer of génoise into a palette-shaped cake ring, soak it with syrup, cover it with half the Grand Marnier parfait, and arrange fresh pieces of fruit on top. Place the second sponge layer in the ring, soak it, and spoon the remaining parfait on top. Freeze.

4. Take the palette out of the cake ring and cut out a "thumb hole" to one side. Arrange the piped biscuit all the way around it, and garnish the top attractively with seasonal fruits.

Preparation time: 3 hours
Cooking time: 20 minutes
Difficulty: ★★

Serves 8

clear cake glaze: (see basic recipes)

For the apricot puree:
7 oz / 200 g apricots
8 tsp / 40 g sugar
1/2 vanilla bean
water

For the dacquoise:
2 egg whites
1/2 cup, 2 tbsp / 150 g sugar

1/2 cup, 1 tbsp / 100 g unblanched almonds, very
finely ground
4 tsp / 10 g cornstarch

For the apricot mousse:
3 1/2 oz / 100 g Italian meringue: (see basic recipes)
3/4 cup / 200 g apricot puree
2 tsp / 10 ml Amaretto
6 1/2 tbsp / 100 ml whipping cream
2 sheets of gelatin

For the Bavarian cream:
2 1/2 tbsp / 30 g very finely ground almonds, roasted
3/4 cup / 200 ml milk
3 egg yolks
3 1/2 tbsp / 50 g sugar
3 sheets of gelatin
3/4 cup / 200 ml whipping cream

For the Roussillon Torte, Christian Cottard prefers fully ripe-ned apricots from the Roussillon region of France; they have a nice velvety red color, "a color that excuses nothing," as the famous French author Victor Hugo once said. The name of this fruit is derived from the Arabic *al-barqúq*, or its Catalan deriv-ative *abercoc*.

Choose apricots that have small spots, but no bruises. The very simple apricot puree consists only of superfine sugar, apri-cots,and a vanilla bean. Steam the apricots for about twenty minutes to allow the puree to reach the right consistency and preserve its tartness. It would be unfair to Christian Cottard to use a ready-made product here.

If the cake is to be a success, its surface must be completely smooth. To ensure this, assemble it upside down and remember that it will shrink a little in the refrigerator. Bavarian creams, and parfaits in general, tend to do so.

Christian Cottard advises making the roasted almond Bavarian cream a day in advance. Use almonds with a very high fat con-tent that are aromatic and develop their full flavor when eaten. The dash of Amaretto (an Italian liqueur made with almonds and apricots) accentuates the harmony of almonds with apricots. One final tip: place the various mixtures in the cake ring without delay, and refrigerate the finished cake as soon as possible.

1. For the puree, place the halved apricots in a saucepan with the sugar, vanilla, and a little water and steam for 20 minutes. Allow to cool. To make the dacquoise, beat the egg whites with 3 1/2 tbsp / 50 g sugar until stiff. Combine the ground almonds, cornstarch, and remaining sugar and carefully fold into the egg whites. Use a pastry bag with a round 1/2–3/4 in / 12–14 mm tip to pipe circles of the sponge mixture on to baking paper and bake at 430 °F / 220 °C.

2. To make the apricot mousse, prepare an Italian meringue according to the basic recipe, and whip the cream until stiff. Soak the gelatin in cold water, dissolve it in Amaretto and warm. Carefully combine the meringue, apricot puree, Amaretto and whipped cream.

Torte

3. Roast the ground almonds for the Bavarian cream in the oven, add them to the boiling milk, then remove from heat. Cover with plastic wrap and leave to infuse; do not strain. Beat the egg yolks and sugar until the mixture is foamy and falls from the whisk in smooth ribbons. Add the almond milk; thicken like a custard, and then add the soaked gelatin. Allow to cool and then fold in the whipped cream.

4. Assemble the torte upside down. Cover a cake round with plastic wrap and place a 8 x 2 in / 18 x 4 cm cake ring on it. Pour in the apricot mousse and top with a layer of dacquoise. Spoon in the Bavarian cream and cover with a second layer of sponge cake. Refrigerate. Turn out of the ring, cover with clear cake glaze and garnish with almond halves.

Saint-Honoré

Preparation time: 2 hours 30 minutes
Cooking time: 30 minutes
Difficulty: ★★★

Serves 8

pastry cream, Italian meringue, choux pastry, puff
pastry: (see basic recipes)

For the Chiboust cream:
1 cup / 250 ml milk
1–2 egg yolks
3¹/₂ tbsp / 50 g sugar
3¹/₂ tbsp / 25 g flour

3–4 egg whites
³/₄ cup / 200 ml sugar syrup
5¹/₂ sheets of gelatin

For the caramel glaze for the cream puffs:
³/₄ cup, 1 tbsp / 200 g sugar
¹/₄ cup / 60 ml glucose
4¹/₂ tbsp / 70 ml water

Both the famous Saint-Honoré and the Chiboust cream, which is its signature, were created in the previous century in a *pâtisserie* in Paris. The cake was named after St. Honoré, the patron saint of bakers, and the cream bears the name of the pastry chef who invented it, Chiboust. His name is frequently misspelled, which is not exactly an homage to the artist. To this day the cake is an excellent exercise in stylistic composition for all pastry chefs, as it contains two "pillars" of the art of baking, puff pastry and choux pastry.

Given the size of the cake, Christian Cottard is happy to make use of leftover puff pastry. It may not be balled together or shaped, and must contain butter. One could even use deep-frozen puff pastry as long as it contains no stabilizers.

The oblong cream puffs that garnish the cake are an elegant variation of classic choux pastry. Make sure they dry thoroughly during baking, giving off plenty of steam.

While some pastry chefs might fill the Saint-Honoré with whipped cream for the sake of simplicity, doing so diminishes its character; the Chiboust cream filling, also known as Saint-Honoré cream, is its hallmark.

1. For the Chiboust cream, make a pastry cream using the milk, egg yolks, sugar, and flour, and make an Italian meringue with the egg whites and sugar syrup (see basic recipes for procedure). Soak the gelatin in water, then fold it into the warm pastry cream. Carefully combine the pastry cream and meringue while both are still warm. Prepare the puff pastry, roll it out, and cut out a round base with a diameter of 8 in/18 cm. Refrigerate and leave to rest for two hours.

2. Follow the basic recipe to make the choux pastry. Fill it into a pastry bag with a medium round tip (no. 6) and pipe a ring of choux pastry around the puff pastry base, then bake it for 20 minutes at 430 °F / 220 °C. Pipe oblong cream puffs (of choux pastry) onto a baking sheet and bake for 20 minutes at 430 °F / 220 °C. Make the caramel and glaze them with it.

Torte

3. Place the puff pastry base on a cake round and, using a pastry bag with a triangular tip, pipe the Chiboust cream onto it. Lightly brown the surface with a salamander, or in the oven.

4. Halve the cream puffs. Use the remaining caramel to affix the lower halves of the cream puffs to the choux pastry ring of the Saint-Honoré. Use a pastry bag with a wave-shaped tip to garnish them with Chiboust cream and place the glazed upper halves on top. Serve immediately.

Pain de Gênes with

Preparation time: 40 minutes
Cooking time: 1 hour
Difficulty: ★★

Serves 8

For the poached pears:
3 cups / 750 ml red wine with well developed tannins
4 tsp / 30 g honey
5 tbsp / 70 g sugar
1 cinnamon stick
grated lemon and orange peel
5 Williams pears

For the red wine jelly:
2 cups / 500 ml pear liquid
1 oz / 25 g pectin
3½ tbsp / 50 g sugar

For the pain de Gênes:
9 oz / 250 g marzipan
3 eggs
⅓ cup / 80 g butter, melted
2½ tsp / 12 ml rum
⅓ cup / 40 g flour
2 tsp / 10 g baking powder

For dusting:
confectioners' sugar

Christian Cottard fondly remembers the small Seckel pears he enjoyed as a child, which are less widely available nowadays. The children at his school actually fought over them on the playground. But among cooks, they were best known for their firmness even after steaming, their compatibility with wine, and their tendency to quickly become wrinkled and as sweet as sugar.

Since Seckel pears are not easy to come by, Christian Cottard makes do with juicy, aromatic Williams pears. Bred in Britain from the yellow Christ pear variety, its flesh is evocative of nutmeg. These pears also remain firm when they are steamed and go very well with good wines that are full of character.

When making the red wine jelly, choose a wine with well-developed tannins and a balanced bouquet, such as a wine from the Hérault region – not because this wine is particularly fruity, but because it can take on the complementary flavors well: the pears, of course, as well as cinnamon, lemons, oranges, and honey.

The *pain de Gênes* (French for Genoese bread) is a cake that is well-suited to being served with jelly. The batter, consisting mostly of marzipan flavored with rum, needs to be stirred until smooth before the creamed butter is added, so that no lumps form. If you are using double-acting baking powder, reduce the amount by one-third. Because it contains little sugar, this cake must be baked slowly.

1. In a saucepan, combine the wine, honey, sugar, cinnamon stick, and zests, and bring to a boil. Peel the pears, but do not cut them. Remove the remains of the flowers, but leave the stems intact.

2. Place the pears in the boiling syrup and simmer over low heat, uncovered, until they shrink slightly. Allow them to cool in the cooking liquid. Drain the pears, but retain the liquid. To make the red wine jelly, bring the pear liquid to a boil again, and add the pectin mixed with sugar. Boil for two minutes, then allow to cool.

Williams Pears

3. To make the pain de Gênes, beat the marzipan with a mixer until smooth. Add the eggs one by one and stir the mixture until foamy. Melt the butter, cool it slightly and pour it onto the marzipan with the rum; finally fold in the flour sifted with the baking powder. Pour the mixture into a greased and floured fluted cake pan and bake for 20 minutes at 375 °F / 190 °C. After baking, turn out of the pan immediately.

4. Slice the cake horizontally into two layers. Place one layer on a cake round, liberally coat it with red wine jelly, and place the second layer on top. Spread jelly in the center of this layer and arrange the sliced poached pears on it in the form of a rosette. Cover with the remaining red wine jelly. Dust the edge of the Pain de Gênes with a little confectioners' sugar.

Preparation time: 1 hour 30 minutes
Cooking time: 20 minutes
Difficulty: ★★★

Makes 12

Joconde sponge cake, pastry cream:
(see basic recipes)

For the filling:
6 bananas
6¹/₂ tbsp / 100 g butter
6¹/₂ tbsp / 100 g sugar
6¹/₂ tbsp / 100 ml rum

For the almond cream:
14 oz / 400 g pastry cream

14 oz / 400 g marzipan
1²/₃ cups / 400 g butter
5 tbsp / 75 ml rum

For the chocolate sauce:
1 cup, 2 tbsp / 280 ml water
1¹/₂ cups / 360 g sugar
1 cup, 1 tbsp / 120 g cocoa powder
1 cup / 240 ml cream
4 sheets of gelatin

For the chocolate glaze:
3¹/₂ oz / 100 g bittersweet chocolate
6¹/₂ tbsp / 100 g cocoa butter

To garnish:
3¹/₂ oz / 100 g milk chocolate
1 banana

In French, the word banane means not just banana, but also describes a kiss-curl or the rubber that covers bumpers. French privates in the trenches of the First World War even used it as a nickname for a certain military decoration. Lucas Devriese would likely have earned a medal for this rich, exotic dessert made with real bananas. Despite the distance between Knokke-Le-Zoute in Belgium and the Caribbean, where they grow, several varieties of this delicious fruit are very popular there.

Lucas Devriese prefers to use ripe bananas that are still firm. If necessary, they can be wrapped in newspaper and further ripened. For the preparation of the fruits to be an all round success, brown them first over moderate heat (210 °C / 100 °C) for 20 minutes, then over high heat (390 °C / 200 °C). The resulting caramel crust keeps the bananas from drying out when flambéed with the rum. Take particular care with this stage of the work, and do it all on the same day. The almond cream, on the other hand, does not suffer if it is made a day, or even several days, in advance; it can even be frozen.

For the almond cream, Lucas Devriese recommends using Portuguese almonds, which are relatively small and noticeably different in taste from the almonds with which we are more familiar. They are fragrant and give the dessert a distinctive flavor that offers a definite contrast to the sweetness of the bananas.

1. Halve the six bananas for the filling lengthwise and brown them with the butter and sugar in a saucepan for 20 minutes over low heat, and then a few minutes longer over high heat. Slice the bananas into bite-size pieces and flambé them with the rum. Prepare the Joconde sponge cake and pastry cream according to the basic recipes.

2. To make the almond cream, thoroughly mix the butter and marzipan until they form a smooth mixture, then carefully combine with the pastry cream and rum.

Dessert

3. Spread a layer of almond cream into hemispherical molds. To make the chocolate sauce, bring the water, sugar, cocoa powder, and cream to a boil in a saucepan. Remove from the heat and add the gelatin, which has been soaked in cold water. For the chocolate glaze, melt the bittersweet chocolate with the cocoa butter and set aside.

4. Fill the molds with flambéed banana slices, top with a spoonful of almond cream, and cover with a round layer of sponge cake. Refrigerate for one hour. Turn the dessert out of the molds and cover with chocolate glaze. Allow to set in the refrigerator and decorate with melted milk chocolate, using a tiny pastry bag. Arrange on a plate with slices of banana and serve with the chocolate sauce.

Bavarois with Tea

Preparation time: 1 hour 30 minutes
Cooking time: 30 minutes
Difficulty: ★★

Serves 8

For the chocolate sponge cake:
6 eggs
³/₄ cup / 180 g sugar
³/₄ cup, 1 tbsp / 110 g flour
¹/₄ cup / 35 g cornstarch
¹/₄ cup / 30 g cocoa powder

striped Joconde sponge cake, clear cake glaze
(see basic recipes)

For the chocolate mousse:
5 egg yolks
²/₃ cup / 150 ml sugar syrup
11¹/₂ oz / 330 g baking chocolate, melted
2 cups, 3 tbsp / 540 ml whipping cream

For the bavarois:
1 cup / 250 ml milk
¹/₄ oz / 8 g tea (Earl Grey)
4 egg yolks
3¹/₂ tbsp / 50 g sugar
5 sheets of gelatin
1 cup / 250 ml whipping cream

In a Zeebrugge inn where he was asked to sample several refined teas, Lucas Devriese decided to create a dessert that would show off tea to its full advantage, once and for all. Tea is said to be the oldest drink in the world. The tea bush, probably native to China originally, is cultivated in many places around the world with varying success according to altitude and climate, and many countries actively trade in tea. The inhabitants of the English colonies brought tea to Europe in about the 17th century, where myriad varieties remain popular to this day.

Among these is Earl Grey tea, which derives its particular flavor from essence of bergamot, a substance won from the peel of small bergamot oranges. Its name is attributed to the resourcefulness of the fourth Earl Grey (1812–1898), governor of Australia and later of New Zealand.

The preparation of the bavarois (Bavarian cream) needs to move rapidly, because tea stays fresh for little longer than 24 hours, particularly when it is infused in milk (the best way to develop its full aroma). This means that the tea can be made at most a day in advance, shortly before you begin making the mousse.

One last note: unsweetened cocoa works better for making the chocolate sponge cake than does sweetened cocoa.

1. To make the chocolate sponge cake, beat the eggs with the sugar until the mixture drops off the beaters in smooth ribbons. Sift the flour with the cornstarch and cocoa powder, and carefully fold into the eggs with a wooden spatula. Use a pastry bag to pipe the sponge mixture onto a baking sheet lined with baking paper and bake for 25 minutes at 355 °F / 180 °C. Prepare the striped Joconde sponge cake according to the basic recipe and bake.

2. To make the chocolate mousse, whisk the egg yolks and pour the lukewarm sugar syrup over them while continuing to beat. Heat the mixture to 195 °F / 90 °C in a double boiler. Once it starts to thicken, pour into a mixer and continue to beat at high speed until completely cooled. Stir in the melted chocolate and then gently fold in the whipped cream.

and Chocolate

3. For the bavarois, bring the milk to a boil with the tea, cover, and allow to infuse for up to 24 hours. Pour through a sieve. Beat the egg yolks and sugar thoroughly, then add the milk. Pour the mixture into a saucepan and thicken at 185 °F / 85 °C. When the desired consistency has been reached, remove from heat. When just lukewarm, add the soaked gelatin and, finally, fold in the whipped cream.

4. To assemble the torte, line the sides of the mold with a narrow strip of striped Joconde sponge cake. Slice the chocolate sponge into two layers, place one in the mold, and fill halfway with chocolate mousse. Top with the second sponge layer and pipe the bavarois onto it. Refrigerate for three hours. Garnish the top with cocoa and cover with a clear cake glaze.

Puff Pastry Torte with Chiboust

Preparation time: 2 hours
Cooking time: 30 minutes
Difficulty: ★★★

Serves 8

puff pastry, Italian meringue: (see basic recipes)

For the Chiboust cream:
1¹/₂ cups / 375 ml milk
6 egg yolks
5 tbsp / 75 g sugar
6 tbsp / 40 g powdered cream
1 vanilla bean
5 sheets of gelatin

For the crème anglaise:
1 cup / 250 ml milk
2 cups / 500 ml crème fraîche

13 tbsp / 190 g butter
6 eggs
2 tbsp / 30 ml Calvados

For the caramelized apples:
8 apples (Jonagold)
2 cups / 500 g sugar
1 cup / 250 g butter

For the filling and garnish:
1 cup / 200 g sultanas, marinated in Calvados
shelled walnuts
superfine sugar

The Jonagold apple, a cross of the Jonathan and Golden Delicious varieties, is widely available in Belgium and neighboring countries. Its skin is bright yellow with blushes of elegant orange-red, and its crunchy flesh has a pleasant tartness that is retained even when the apple is cooked. It works well for this dessert, because the individual slices become tender and almost transparent when caramelized, but do not collapse into puree. In Belgium, the Jonagold is highly valued as a national product. It comes as no surprise, then, that Lucas Devriese also recommends it.

For this version of Chiboust cream, which immortalizes the name of the famous pastry chef who invented the classic Saint-Honoré cake, powdered cream is used. One could also use dried milk or cornstarch, as long as they are sifted to ensure a homogeneous cream that is easy to work with.

Lucas Devriese recommends making the base out of puff pastry that has been folded and turned five times and allowed to rest for one and a half hours in the refrigerator between each turn. This extra time and effort is definitely worthwhile, because it makes the finished pastry extremely light and yet well able to carry the other parts of the dessert.

1. For the Chiboust cream, prepare the Italian meringue according to the basic recipe. Bring the milk to a boil with the vanilla and half the sugar. Whisk the egg yolks, remaining sugar, and powdered cream until pale yellow. Pour a little hot milk into the egg yolks, blend, then return everything to the pan and continue stirring until thickened. When the mixture has cooled to 140 °F / 60 °C blend in the soaked gelatin, then fold into the Italian meringue.

2. For the crème anglaise, bring the milk and crème fraîche to a boil. Beat the butter with the eggs. Pour a little hot milk onto the butter mixture, stir and return to the saucepan. Heat, stirring continuously, until the crème anglaise thickens. Add the Calvados and set the crème anglaise aside. Peel, core and slice the apples. Caramelize the sugar without adding water until it is light brown, then carefully add the butter. Place the apple slices in the caramel and steam over low heat for 30 minutes, then drain.

Cream and Apples

3. Make the puff pastry and use it to line a springform pan to a height of 1 in / 2 cm. Fill the shell with dried lentils or baking beans so it does not dry out, and bake blind. Allow to cool. Place a 2 in / 4 cm wide strip of doubled waxed paper or baking paper around the puff pastry base to form a collar. Pour in the crème anglaise, then top it with the caramelized apples, marinated sultanas, and a handful of shelled walnuts.

4. Finally, spoon in a layer of Chiboust cream to fill the collar. Dust the top with superfine sugar and caramelize with a salamander. Garnish with shelled walnuts.

White Wine

Preparation time: 1 hour
Cooking time: 30 minutes
Difficulty: ★★

Serves 8

Duchess sponge cake: (see basic recipes)

For the crème anglaise with white wine:
1¹/₂ cups / 375 ml white wine
1²/₃ cups / 400 g sugar
14 egg yolks
juice of 1 lemon

For the white wine mousse:
15 oz / 420 g crème anglaise with white wine

3²/₃ cups / 820 ml whipping cream
9 sheets of gelatin

For the syrup for soaking:
15 oz / 420 g crème anglaise with white wine
5 tbsp / 75 ml sugar syrup

To garnish:
fresh fruits of the season, e.g. blueberries, red
currants, blackberries, raspberries, strawberries,
apples, star fruit, limes

Clear cake glaze: (see basic recipes)

These days there are fewer genuine duchesses, but the number of inanimate objects holding this title have grown. In Belgium, duchesse describes a type of daybed and a pear (Duchess d'Angoulême), and in France it names a fabric. And then there are a few famous dishes like duchess potatoes (creamed with egg and butter, piped into shapes and baked) and duchess sponge cake, used in this recipe, that attest to this phenomenon.

As long as one follows these instructions, preparing and baking this pastry should be fairly straightforward. Actually, the end result depends mainly on the quality of the white wine used to flavor the crème anglaise, which is used both in the mousse and the syrup for soaking the sponge cake.

The mousse with which Lucas Devriese covers the sponge cake is composed mainly of crème anglaise. Choose one of the lovely golden yellow wines made only with light grapes. Lucas Devriese, a great fan of wines from the Champagne region, prefers Chardonnay for the custard because he feels its bouquet offers the best complement. Whichever wine you select, be sure to prepare the crème anglaise rapidly and then use it right away.

In this case, a great deal of experimentation is to be discouraged. If you had thought to flavor the crème anglaise with cinnamon, you need not go to the trouble. Lucas Devriese himself tried this and bitterly regretted it.

1. To make the crème anglaise, bring a little white wine, the lemon juice, and half the sugar to a boil in a saucepan. Beat the egg yolks with the remaining sugar until foamy in a bowl. Add the remaining white wine to the eggs, pour them into the saucepan with the hot wine syrup, and thicken at 185 °F / 85 °C. Allow to cool. To make the white wine mousse, mix 15 oz / 420 g of the white wine custard with the dissolved gelatin and whipped cream.

2. Prepare the duchess sponge cake according to the basic recipe. Use a pastry bag to pipe it on to a baking sheet lined with baking paper and bake. To make the syrup for soaking, combine the white wine crème anglaise and sugar syrup. Slice the duchess sponge cake horizontally into two layers. Place one layer in a cake ring and soak with syrup.

Duchess

3. Pipe a generous layer of the white wine mousse on top of the sponge base. Arrange the raspberries on the mousse and top with the second sponge layer. Fill the cake ring with mousse. Refrigerate for two hours.

4. Take the torte out of the cake ring, and spread the remaining mousse on the sides of the cake. Cover with clear cake glaze and garnish with fresh fruits of the season.

Preparation time: 45 minutes
Cooking time: 25 minutes
Difficulty: ✳

Serves 8

7 oz / 200 g Morello cherries

For the chocolate sponge cake:
  (see basic recipes)
7 eggs
³/₄ cup, 1 tbsp / 200 g sugar
1 cup / 130 g flour
¹/₃ cup / 45 g cornstarch
¹/₄ cup / 30 g cocoa powder

For the chocolate mousse:
5 egg yolks
²/₃ cup / 150 ml sugar syrup
12 oz / 330 g chocolate, melted
2¹/₄ cups / 540 ml cream, whipped

For the whipped cream:
3 cups / 750 ml whipping cream
³/₄ cup / 120 g confectioners' sugar

For the chocolate leaves:
9 oz / 250 g milk chocolate coating

Because the Black Forest in southwestern Germany is renowned for the cherries that grow in its orchards, which are used to distill a very pure fruit schnapps, its name graces this classic of the baker's trade. The Black Forest Torte is easy to make and shows off the exquisite flavor of Morello cherries to full advantage.

The various types of cherries fall into two categories: sweet and sour. Sweet cherries range in color from reddish-yellow (Bigarreau cherries, used to distill kirsch) to the dark red, almost purple Black Tartarian and Bing varieties. More acidic, sour cherries are generally smaller and include Belle de Choisy, Montmorency, and Morello. Accordingly, cherry trees are divided into sweet cherry and sour cherry trees.

The Black Forest Torte is one of Lucas Devriese's favorites, and he takes particular care in preparing it. Morello cherries, best marinated in kirsch beforehand, are an excellent complement to bittersweet chocolate, whose intense flavor is pleasantly tempered by whipped cream.

Some skill and experience are required to turn a plain block of chocolate into the garnish for the cake. When the chocolate coating has been tempered and spread thinly on a slab, use one hand to warm it slightly so that it softens, and guide the spatula with the other hand. To produce large chocolate leaves, you will have to work rapidly.

1. Make the chocolate sponge cake according to the basic recipe, but using the ingredients listed above. Pipe the mixture on to a baking sheet and bake. When completely cooled, slice the sponge through twice. For the chocolate mousse, beat the egg yolks with the syrup, then stir in the melted chocolate. When this has cooled, fold in the whipped cream. Place one sponge base in a cake ring and garnish with Morello cherries.

2. Whip the cream with the confectioners' sugar, and pipe a layer of whipped cream to cover the cherries. Place the second sponge layer in the cake ring and cover with chocolate mousse. Again garnish with Morello cherries, top with the third sponge cake layer, and pipe whipped cream onto it. Refrigerate for two hours.

Torte

3. Melt the milk chocolate coating in a double boiler and spread thinly on to a slightly warmed slab. Refrigerate for 30 minutes and then bring back to room temperature. Using a metal spatula, draw up large flakes. Take the cake out of the cake ring.

4. Completely cover the cake with the individually shaped chocolate flakes. Dust with cocoa and confectioners' sugar.

Leaf Torte with

Preparation time: 2 hours 30 minutes
Cooking time: 1 hour
Difficulty: ★★★

Serves 8

For the dacquoise sponge cake:
9 egg whites
1 cup / 250 g superfine sugar
1³/₄ cups / 200 g lightly roasted almonds, very finely ground
5 tsp / 25 ml milk

crème anglaise: (see basic recipes)

For the chocolate leaves
1 lb / 500 g milk chocolate coating
5 tbsp / 75 ml nut nougat, liquid

For the pistachio Bavarian cream:
5¹/₄ oz / 150 g crème anglaise
2¹/₂ oz / 75 g pistachio paste
3 sheets of gelatin
1¹/₂ cups / 375 ml sweetened whipped cream

For the praline cream:
3 egg whites
³/₄ cup / 180 g sugar
13 tbsp / 200 g butter
3 egg yolks
¹/₂ cup / 125 ml nut nougat, liquid

To garnish:
chocolate wafers

Combining the crème anglaise and its Bavarian counterpart may seem daring, even with Lucas Devriese's dacquoise sponge cake to serve as a platform for the meeting. The astonishing result is fresh and delicious, and the chocolate decorations add an elegant touch.

To produce a truly impressive confection, it is advisable to improve the pistachio paste that flavors the Bavarian cream. While pistachio paste is available in stores, its taste is often inadequate and can be improved by roasting. The procedure for the crème anglaise basis of the Bavarian cream is essentially the same as a basic custard recipe; take the usual care performing this step so that the egg yolks do not curdle.

The dacquoise sponge cake should also be uncomplicated, as long as you use only high-quality ingredients. The almonds should be finely ground; roast them briefly before doing so to intensify their flavor. For the praline paste, be sure to cream the butter thoroughly before adding the egg yolks

The "leaves" that adorn the top of this torte are made of milk chocolate and, if desired, nut nougat can be added to lend it a special coloring effect. Add just enough oil to make the chocolate supple, and spread it onto a warm slab so that it does not set too quickly. Afterwards, put it in a cool place (a little below room temperature), and its consistency will be ideal for scraping the decorations.

1. To make the dacquoise sponge cake, beat 8 egg whites and ¹/₂ cup plus 2 tbsp / 150 g sugar until stiff. Mix the ground almonds, remaining sugar and egg white, and the milk. Carefully combine both mixtures. Using a pastry bag, pipe the sponge cake mixture on to a tray lined with baking paper, then bake for 15 minutes at 340 °F / 170 °C. Reduce the temperature to 300 °F / 150 °C and bake an additional 45 minutes.

2. For the chocolate leaf garnish, melt the chocolate with a little oil in a double boiler. Spread a thin layer of chocolate on to a warm slab and put in a cool place for one hour. Using a metal spatula, make the leaves and two circles of the diameter of the cake ring to be used. To make the pistachio Bavarian cream, prepare a crème anglaise, combine it with the pistachio paste, add the soaked gelatin and carefully fold in the whipped cream.

Pistachio-Praline Cream

3. For the praline cream, beat the egg whites until stiff. Heat the sugar to 250 °F / 121 °C and then pour it on to the egg whites, beating continuously until completely cooled. Whisk the butter and egg yolks together, add the nut nougat, stir thoroughly, and fold into the egg white mixture.

4. To assemble the torte, place the dacquoise base inside a cake ring on a cake round, and pipe a generous amount of praline cream on to it. Place a circle of milk chocolate on the cream and spread it with pistachio Bavarian cream. Top with the second chocolate circle, then fill the cake ring completely with praline cream. Refrigerate for one hour. Decorate the sides of the torte with chocolate wafers, and garnish the top with decoratively arranged chocolate leaves.

Montblanc

Preparation time: 1 hour
Cooking time: 8 minutes
Difficulty: ★★★

Serves 8

Duchess sponge cake: (see basic recipes)

For the Italian meringue:
8 egg whites
2 cups / 500 g superfine sugar

For the quark cream:
5 egg yolks
3¹/₂ tbsp / 50 ml water

³/₄ cup, 1 tbsp / 200 g sugar
1 lb 5 oz / 600 g quark
2²/₃ cups / 640 ml whipping cream
6 sheets of gelatin

For the syrup for soaking:
6¹/₂ tbsp / 100 g sugar
³/₄ cup / 200 ml water
¹/₃ cup / 80 ml kirsch

To garnish:
2 pint baskets of raspberries

Lucas Devriese did not mean to be provocative in naming this dessert after Europe's highest mountain. Despite the fact that they live in Belgium, which Jacques Brel described in song as *le plat pays* (the flat country), when Devriese's wife Hilde first tasted it, she was reminded of a mountain. In any case, this exquisite creation's elegance and flavor certainly more than live up to the name.

The various elements of this dessert should be prepared in one day, and since the dessert must be frozen for a while after the first layer of cream is applied, one must be careful to allow sufficient time to assemble it. For that reason, choose quark with a

firm consistency and a medium fat content (20% to a maximum of 30%) so that it does not collapse later.

If you start by beating the egg yolks alone and then add the sugar, the cream will be lighter. If necessary, replace the quark with crème fraîche, but make sure that its distinctive taste is retained. All ingredients must be at room temperature when they are mixed for the dessert to succeed.

The cream will not keep for longer than three days and calls for high quality ingredients. If you like, you can flavor it; raspberry puree would be one obvious choice.

1. Prepare the duchess sponge cake and spread it on to a baking sheet lined with baking paper (allow 1 lb 5 oz / 600 g sponge mixture for a 18 x 27 in / 40 x 60 cm baking tray). Bake for six minutes at 480 °F / 250 °C. Let cool on a cooling rack. To make the meringue, beat the egg whites and sugar in a mixing bowl over a source of heat until they have a firm consistency, then continue to beat with an electric mixer until completely cooled.

2. For the quark cream, beat the egg yolk until foamy. Heat the sugar and water, slowly pour the syrup over the egg yolks while beating at the highest speed. Allow to cool a little and add the dissolved gelatin. Once the mixture has completely cooled, rapidly fold in the quark and whipped cream. Follow the basic recipe for the kirsch syrup for soaking.

3. To assemble the dessert, slice the duchess sponge cake horizontally to make two layers. Place one layer on a cake round, soak with kirsch syrup and spread it with quark cream. Soak the second layer and place it on the cream. Freeze for one hour. Once the dessert is cold, cut out tartlets using a round cookie cutter (2³/₄ in / 6 cm diameter).

4. Place each tartlet on to a somewhat larger base to make it easier to apply the meringue with a pastry bag. Put the tartlets in the oven until the meringue is golden grown, then place on dessert plates and fill the center with fresh raspberries.

Banana

Preparation time: 45 minutes
Cooking time: 30 minutes
Difficulty: ✶

Serves 8

striped Joconde sponge cake, chocolate sponge
  cake: (see basic recipes)

For the banana mousse:
1 lb / 500 g bananas
1 tsp / 5 ml lemon juice
3¹/₂ tbsp / 50 ml banana liqueur
5 sheets of gelatin
3 cups / 750 ml whipping cream

For the syrup for soaking:
³/₄ cup / 200 ml sugar syrup
5 tbsp / 75 ml banana liqueur

Bananas, a wonderful source of both roughage and vitamins, grows on a lovely tree that grows up to thirty feet / ten meters tall, which is a member of the Musaceae family. Originally cultivated mainly in Guinea, it has been systematically commercialized since the 1920s. In Europe, the emergence of banana steamboats led to their wide availability.

Here, Lucas Devriese, who enjoys using this soft fruit, introduces us to a dessert that is easy to make and gentle on the digestion, in which bananas are prepared as a mousse with liqueur. Do not allow the fact that they are being pureed lead you to compromise on quality or use overripe bananas. They must be firm and fragrant and, ideally, come from the Antilles.

Lemon juice gives the banana puree a light color and keeps the mousse from becoming dark. The addition of banana liqueur emphasizes the individual flavor of the fruit, offering a chance to savor and appreciate the unique, full flavor of banana in this dessert. An old-fashioned kitchen utensil like a potato masher is actually a more appropriate tool for mashing the bananas than the efficient blender. Beat the cream, which should be well-chilled, at low speed.

To garnish the mousse, make the chocolate decorations according to your personal taste, or your abilities. There are no limits on what you can make, other than your own skill.

1. Follow the basic recipe for the striped Joconde sponge cake. Mix the cocoa powder into half of the sponge mixture and spread it onto a tray lined with baking paper. Use a cake comb to draw stripes into it and freeze. When it has set, spread a thin layer of the light sponge mixture over the cocoa sponge cake. Bake for five minutes at 390 °C / 200 °C, then turn out immediately onto a cooling rack.

2. To make the banana mousse, puree the bananas with the lemon juice and banana liqueur, add the dissolved gelatin, and fold into the whipped cream. Prepare a chocolate sponge cake according to the basic recipe, allow the cool thoroughly, and slice it horizontally twice to form three layers.

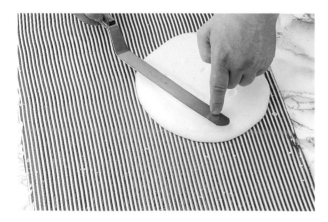

Mousse

3. Line the perimeter of a 2¹/₂ in / 5 cm high cake ring with a 1¹/₂ in / 3 cm wide strip of the striped Joconde sponge cake.

4. Place a chocolate sponge base in the cake ring, soak it with banana syrup, and coat it with banana mousse. Top with a second sponge layer, another layer of banana mousse, and cover with the third sponge cake layer. Finally, spread more banana mousse on top and smooth over carefully. Refrigerate for two hours. Cover with a clear cake glaze, then remove from the cake ring. Garnish with bittersweet and milk chocolate decorations.

Raspberry Mousse

Preparation time: 45 minutes
Cooking time: 25 minutes
Difficulty: ★

Serves 8

Duchess sponge cake, striped Joconde sponge
cake: (see basic recipes)

For the raspberry mousse:
3 egg whites
$^1/_2$ cup, 2 tbsp / 150 g sugar
$3^1/_2$ tbsp / 50 ml water
$1^1/_4$ cups / 300 ml whipping cream
$^3/_4$ cup / 165 g raspberry puree
4 sheets of gelatin

For the raspberry jelly:
2 cups / 500 ml raspberry juice
1 pinch of pectin
2 cups / 500 g superfine sugar
$^1/_2$ cup / 120 ml glucose syrup

For the raspberry coulis for soaking:
$^1/_4$ cup / 100 g raspberry puree
5 tsp / 25 ml raspberry liqueur
$6^1/_2$ tbsp / 100 ml sugar syrup

For this dessert, use raspberries that are both firm and juicy. The raspberry bush, a member of the rose family, is very popular but also sensitive and demanding to cultivate. When selecting the berries, look for drupelets (the botanical term for the little juicy spheres making up the raspberry) that are nice and round, and clearly distinct from each other.

Raspberries have a distinctly acidic flavor that pleasantly tickles the tastebuds; there is no other fruit like it. Use the same variety of raspberry for the mousse, coulis, and jelly in order to avoid clashes in flavor.

The raspberry jelly for glazing the dessert should be fairly light. If time allows, it is best to make it yourself using good

berries, boiling the mixture until a candy thermometer shows a temperature of 150 °F / 64 °C. This ensures that the jelly has the right concentration of sugar, will keep well and, most importantly, will have a very smooth surface.

As soon as it has reached this temperature, pour the jelly directly onto a slab measuring 27 x 18 in / 60 x 40 cm, and allow it to cool to 100 °F / 30 °C. Finish by removing any air bubbles that might form on the surface. If you prefer a more exotic dessert, passion fruit could be substituted for the raspberries.

1. Follow the basic recipes for the duchess sponge cake and striped Joconde sponge cake. To make the raspberry mousse, prepare an Italian meringue: beat the egg whites until stiff, heat the sugar and water to 250 °F / 121 °C and pour the syrup onto the egg whites, beating continuously until completely cooled. Add the dissolved gelatin, and finally the raspberry puree and whipped cream.

2. For the raspberry jelly, bring the raspberry juice to a boil with the pectin and half of the sugar in a copper saucepan. Allow to boil for one minute, then add the remaining sugar and glucose syrup. Continue to heat the mixture until a candy thermometer shows a temperature of 150 °F / 64 °C. Allow to cool and whisk until the jelly is perfectly smooth. For the raspberry coulis for soaking, mix the raspberry puree with the syrup and raspberry liqueur.

à la Lucas

3. Set a cake ring onto a cake round and line it with striped Joconde sponge cake. Slice the duchess sponge cake horizontally and place one layer in the cake ring. Soak it with raspberry coulis and cover with a layer of raspberry mousse. Place another sponge base on top and repeat the process, finishing with a thick layer of mousse. Refrigerate for two hours.

4. Cover the entire surface of the dessert with raspberry jelly. Allow to set in the refrigerator for an additional two hours, then remove the cake ring. Garnish with raspberries and a sprig of mint.

La Feuillantine

Preparation time: 1 hour
Cooking time: 1 hour 30 minutes
Difficulty: ★★

Serves 8

makes 2 cakes measuring 7 in / 16 cm

For the Japonaise sponge cake:
1²/₃ cups / 400 g sugar
8 egg whites
6¹/₂ tbsp / 100 ml water
1 cup / 130 g hazelnuts, very finely ground

For the chocolate wafers:
14 oz / 400 g bittersweet chocolate coating

For the honey mixture:
2¹/₂ oz / 75 g white chocolate coating
²/₃ cup / 150 ml crème fraîche
3 tbsp / 60 g honey
1 sheet of gelatin
vanilla sugar
1¹/₂ cups / 350 ml whipping cream

To garnish:
1 honey praline
confectioners' sugar

Anyone familiar with Victor Hugo's works may well wonder why the Florentine, a puff pastry cake popular in the 17th century, is now called a Feuillantine. There is a cloister by the same name, the Feuillantines in the Fauburg Saint-Victor region, which long served as a prison for ladies of the oldest profession, but any surmised connection between the two would be purely speculative.

At first, this composition contained only bittersweet chocolate. Then a young pastry chef named Laurent Buet added a honey mixture, for which high-quality honey is used – that found in the Swiss Jura, for example, and preferably pine honey. It is a good idea to prepare the honey mixture a day in advance so that it develops a uniform consistency.

Philippe Guignard also recommends making the vanilla sugar yourself, using the finest superfine sugar and first-class vanilla beans that have been ripened over a long period of time in drying chambers.

The crème fraîche should be beaten neither too long nor too briefly. At one extreme it tastes too much like milk, and at the other it becomes too firm and loses its characteristic flavor. The hazelnuts give the Japonaise sponge cake a firmer consistency and will absorb some of the sugar, so they are preferable to almonds. This base is actually a meringue base similar to the French succès sponge cake. Philippe Guignard normally uses a pastry bag to pipe it directly onto a baking sheet, which makes it lighter when baked.

1. For the Japonaise sponge cake, whisk the egg whites until stiff with one-quarter of the sugar. Heat the water and remaining sugar to 250 °F / 121 °C, then slowly pour onto the beaten egg whites, beating continuously until cooled. Fold in ¹/₂ cup / 50 g finely ground hazelnuts. Pipe the mixture in a spiral onto a tray lined with baking paper, sprinkle the rest of the hazelnuts onto the sponge mixture, and bake for 60–90 minutes at 320 °F / 160 °C.

2. To make the chocolate wafers, melt the bittersweet chocolate coating, spread it thinly onto a tray lined with waxed paper, and allow it to cool for at least one hour. Before the mixture is completely hard, cut out two round wafers the same size as the Japonaise sponge base. Cut each wafer into eight triangles.

au Miel

3. Prepare the honey mixture a day in advance: melt the white chocolate coating in a double boiler. Heat the crème fraîche and stir into the chocolate coating. Add the honey, dissolved gelatin and vanilla sugar. Allow the mixture to cool and set aside until needed. The following day, whip the cream until stiff and fold into the honey mixture.

4. Melt a little bittersweet chocolate coating, spread it on the Japonaise sponge base, and use a pastry bag to pipe the honey mixture onto it. Place one of the chocolate wafers (divided into triangles) on top, pipe more of the honey mixture onto it and cover with another chocolate wafer. Dust with confectioners' sugar and garnish with the honey praline.

Pithiviers

Preparation time: 1 hour
Cooking time: 35–40 minutes
Difficulty: ★★

Serves 8

vanilla cream, puff pastry: (see basic recipes)

¹/₂ fresh pineapple
2 tbsp / 30 g butter
sugar
cinnamon
1 tbsp rum

For the almond cream:
¹/₂ cup / 125 g butter
³/₄ cup, 1 tbsp / 125 g blanched almonds, ground
²/₃ cup / 100 g confectioners' sugar
¹/₃ cup / 40 g cornstarch
3 small eggs
5 tsp / 25 ml rum
12 oz / 350 g vanilla cream

To garnish:
2 egg yolks
1 pinch of salt
sugar

Though it may be surprising to find a specialty that made the French town of Pithiviers famous in Switzerland, fans of Three Kings' Cake, or *Dreikönigskuchen* in German, should only be pleased. This torte is so-called because it is traditionally enjoyed on Epiphany, the day when the arrival of the three wise men in Bethlehem after Jesus's birth is celebrated. Consisting of almond cream and puff pastry and enhanced by the fresh flavor of pineapple, it is delicious all year around and is not particularly difficult to make.

The choice of almonds is an important consideration. Most suitable are medium-sized blanched almonds like the Spanish Marcona or Californian Thomson. Mix the ingredients for the almond cream very gently and carefully – they should be neither beaten nor stirred until foamy. Round off the cream's flavor with brown Jamaican rum, a vital ingredient of the Pithiviers Torte.

Start by making a light puff pastry that contains only pure butter (82% fat). The Swiss have a great deal of experience making puff pastry, and one pastry they make with it is *Waadter Cremehörnchen* (Waadt cream horns). They know how important it is to bake puff pastry at precisely the right temperature and use only the freshest ingredients. In this case, the pastry should be made three days in advance and folded and turned twice each day, leaving it to rest for 24 hours each time.

A Pithiviers has to be baked slowly so that it bakes all the way through and has a tender consistency. The top is slightly caramelized, which not only enhances its appearance but also further accentuates the flavor of the puff pastry.

1. Prepare the puff pastry and 12 oz / 350 g of vanilla cream according to the basic recipes. To make the almond cream, beat the butter with the ground almonds, confectioners' sugar, and cornstarch, then add the eggs one at a time and stir until smooth. Add the rum and finally blend in the vanilla cream.

2. Peel a fresh pineapple, dice the flesh finely and brown half of it in butter. After one minute dust lightly with sugar and cinnamon. After another two minutes, add 1 tbsp / 15 ml rum, reduce and then allow to cool. Whisk the egg yolks for the egg wash with the salt and sugar.

Torte

3. Roll out the puff pastry and cut out two circles, one slightly larger than the other. Place the smaller layer onto a cake plate. Brush a $^1/_2$ in / 1 cm wide path around the edge with the whisked egg yolk, and spread almond cream in the middle. Arrange the diced pineapple on top of the cream. Cover with the larger circle of puff pastry, pressing the edges together.

4. Brush the top of the Pithiviers with egg yolk and make rosette-shaped marking with a knife (be careful not to cut all the way through the pastry). Slit the edge at even intervals and push in the dough to make a border of half moon shapes. Allow to rest for 20 minutes, then bake for 35–40 minutes at 430 °F / 220 °C. Dust the cake with confectioners' sugar before the last five minutes, and put back in the oven to caramelize. Serve lukewarm.

Preparation time: 30 minutes
Cooking time: 20 minutes
Difficulty: ★★

Serves 12

For the dough:
1³/₄ oz / 50 g yeast
3¹/₂ tbsp / 50 ml milk
4¹/₂ cups / 550 g flour
3¹/₂ tbsp / 50 g sugar
5 eggs
2 tsp / 10 g salt
grated peel of 1 lemon
13 tbsp / 200 g butter

For the filling:
2 cups / 500 ml cream
³/₄ cup / 100 g flour
³/₄ cup, 1 tbsp / 200 g sugar
1 pinch salt
pulp of 1 vanilla bean

To glaze:
1 egg yolk, lightly beaten

Philippe Guignard shows his true colors as a champion of the Swiss canton of Waadt by presenting us with one of the oldest recipes from this region: a dessert that tastes sweet, though it may not appear to be at first.

Guignard is a master of this yeast dough delicacy, which can be prepared in myriad variations, as long as it contains a delicious cream with a 33% fat content. Heavy cream can also be used, if you prefer the taste. In Switzerland, the cream tastes strongly of the alpine pastures where the dairy cows graze, and this takes some getting used to. Be careful not to beat the cream for too long or too vigorously. Otherwise, it may turn into butter when baked.

Preparing the dough demands concentrated attention. It is kneaded for quite a while, like a brioche dough, so that the gluten in the flour makes it soft and elastic. If you have time to make it a day in advance and refrigerate it overnight, the butter will nearly retain its original consistency, and the dough will be firmer and easier to work with. Brushing the edges with egg yolk twice gives the dough color and added suppleness.

When this pastry is baked, two contrasting effects result: the melting and liquefaction of the filling, and the rising of the dough, which keeps the filling from seeping out.

1. To make the dough, dissolve the yeast in the milk. Using the dough hook of an electric mixer, knead the flour with the sugar and dissolved yeast. Add the eggs, salt, and grated lemon peel. Knead for 7–8 minutes, then add the butter to the dough in small pieces. It is best to make the dough a day in advance and allow it to rest in the refrigerator overnight.

2. Grease a flat pie pan with butter. Roll out the dough and line the pan with it. Allow it to rise in a warm place for one hour. Brush the edges with egg yolk twice, and prick the base with a fork. Using a pastry wheel, cut off the surplus dough.

Cream Flan

3. For the filling, beat the cream until stiff. In another bowl, mix the flour with the sugar, a pinch of salt, and a little vanilla pulp.

4. Cover the dough with this mixture of dry ingredients. Use a pastry bag to pipe the whipping cream on too of it and dust the surface with superfine sugar. Bake for 15–20 minutes at 445 °F / 230 °C. Allow to cool before serving.

Preparation time: 45 minutes
Cooking time: 5 minutes
Difficulty: ★

Serves 6

For the vanilla sauce:
2 cups / 500 ml milk
1$^1\!/_2$ vanilla beans
7 egg yolks
6$^1\!/_2$ tbsp / 100 g sugar
3$^1\!/_2$ tbsp / 50 ml heavy cream
1 tsp rum

For the apples:
3 large cooking apples (Pippin, Granny Smith)
3$^1\!/_2$ tbsp / 50 g butter
3$^1\!/_2$ tbsp / 50 g superfine sugar
1 pinch of cinnamon
juice of $^1\!/_2$ lemon

To garnish:
halved pistachios

Everything started with Jamin and the renowned pastry chef Joel Robuchon, of whose extraordinary expertise Philippe Guignard is honored to have partaken no fewer than nineteen times. This is how he discovered Fried Apples with a Pistachio and Chocolate Coulis, which inspired him to create this dessert.

The *vanilla planifolia*, actually an orchid, has greenish pods about as thick as a finger, which are painstakingly dried over a period of months before being sold as the familiar dark vanilla beans. Each contains about 25,000 black seeds, with a very subtle taste, containing the flavoring vanillin. In this recipe, Philippe Guignard prefers vanilla from the formerly French colonial island of Réunion, still known as Bourbon vanilla.

Bourbon vanilla goes well with other flavors, especially rich spirits such as rum and kirsch, as in this version of custard, a crème anglaise or English cream, which is esteemed for its creaminess and versatility.

For the dessert, slightly tart apples should be used to contrast with the subtle vanilla. Reinette are one kind of apple that works well, or use more widely available Cox's Orange Pippin, since they also stay firm when they are cooked. Philippe Guignard is open-minded about other flavor variations, though; instead of apples, you could use pineapple, fried banana slices or prunes fried in clarified butter.

1. To make the vanilla sauce, cut open the vanilla beans, scrape out the pulp and add to the milk. Bring to a boil. Beat the egg yolks with the sugar until they are white and foamy. Pour the boiling milk over them while stirring constantly. Pour everything back into the pan and heat, still stirring, until the mixture thickens. Pass through a sieve and add the rum and heavy cream. Allow to cool, stirring occasionally.

2. Peel the apples, and cut balls out of the flesh using a melon baller. Mix the lemon juice with 2 tbsp / 30 ml water and cover the balls in the liquid so that they stay nice and white.

Vanilla Sauce

3. Melt the butter in a pan, add the apple balls, and brown them slightly over low heat, turning often so that they brown evenly on all sides. Reduce the heat.

4. After one minute, sprinkle superfine sugar and a little cinnamon onto the apples. If necessary, add more butter. The apples are sufficiently tender once you can easily push the tip of a knife into them. Arrange the apple balls in a circle in soup plates, garnish with halved pistachios and then pour the vanilla sauce in the middle.

Orange and Almond

Preparation time: 45 minutes
Cooking time: 45-50 minutes
Difficulty: ★★

Serves 8

puff pastry, vanilla cream: (see basic recipes)

1 lb / 500 g puff pastry
6 oranges

For the almond cream:
$^1/_2$ cup / 125 g butter
1 cup, 3 tbsp / 125 g almonds, very finely ground
$^2/_3$ cup / 100 g confectioners' sugar

2 tbsp / 15 g cornstarch
1 pinch of salt
2 small eggs
1 tbsp / 15 ml Grand Marnier (or rum)
$4^1/_2$ oz / 125 g vanilla cream

For the coating:
oranges
apricot jelly

To garnish:
half-candied orange peel
grenadine

You can never be too careful with fruit that has a very thick peel. Once, because Philippe Guignard failed to take this into consideration, he was very disappointed in an orange cake he made, and resolved to create a dessert that satisfied him. The result is this delicious tart incorporating a thoroughly baked puff pastry shell, almond cream, and a coating of thinly sliced oranges.

Take care when baking the puff pastry. Put the pastry into a hot, pre-heated oven, and then reduce the temperature quickly to allow the inner layers to rise nicely as well as the outer ones. If the pastry is not baked through properly, the edges will be a nice, golden yellow, but the tart's flavor will not be optimal.

In this recipe, the choice of oranges plays an important role. Guignard recommends Minneola oranges from Israel, a medium sized variety with a relatively thin skin. Marinate the peel in grenadine overnight or longer, so that it takes on a delicate purple-red color. This half-candied orange peel is both soft and crunchy. Though it does taste delicious, its main purpose is to lend a decorative effect.

For the almond cream, use Marcona almonds. Grind them yourself, adding a dash of Grand Marnier to intensify their flavor. A very fruity Chardonnay or a good Riesling goes well with this pastry.

1. Make the puff pastry and vanilla cream according to the basic recipes. Line a cake ring with puff pastry, and allow to rest in the refrigerator for one hour. For the almond cream, cream the butter, then stir in the ground almonds, confectioners' sugar, cornstarch, and salt. Add the eggs one at a time and beat the mixture with a whisk until it is smooth and light. Blend in the Grand Marnier and, finally, the vanilla cream.

2. Pipe a thin layer of almond cream onto the puff pastry base. Cut the orange peel into thin strips. Blanch the strips, lightly candy them in grenadine syrup for 7–8 minutes, and leave in the syrup to cool overnight.

Cream Tart

3. Using a pastry jagger, trim the excess paste at the height of the almond cream. Halve the oranges and cut them into very thin slices.

4. Cover the surface evenly with orange slices, sprinkle a little superfine sugar on top and bake for 45–50 minutes at 355 °F / 180 °C. Coat with the apricot jelly flavored with oranges. Before serving, garnish the center of the tart with the candied orange peel.

Preparation time: 40 minutes
Cooking time: 10 minutes
Difficulty: ★

Serves 8

For the sweet short pastry:
10 tbsp / 150 g butter
5 tbsp / 75 g sugar
1 egg
1 egg yolk
2 cups / 250 g flour
1 pinch of salt
vanilla pulp, ground

For the chocolate mixture:
14 oz / 400 g chocolate coating
1¼ cups / 300 ml cream
1¼ cups / 300 ml unsweetened whipping cream

To garnish:
cocoa powder
confectioners' sugar

When one talks about Switzerland, the subject of its marvelous chocolate is sure to come up, a national specialty of almost mythical fame in each of the country's 26 cantons. In this mountainous country, where cattle farming has been elevated to a noble art, chocolate has the status ordinarily accorded to select wines, caviar or goose liver pâtés. Large Swiss chocolate companies like Suchard, Lindt, and Nestlé, to name only the best known, have closely monitored the quality of their products for more than a century in a continual effort to improve them. For this rich and satisfying tart, use a chocolate coating with a relatively high cocoa content (around 70%).

The preparation of the short pastry is integral to the success of this pastry. Prepare it in a very cool place and allow it to rest for at least six to eight hours before rolling it out and lining the pan. Carry out this last stage of the work with great care; the paste needs to fit the pan precisely. Be sure there are no air pockets whatsoever in the paste before pouring in the chocolate mixture.

This pastry is enjoyed cold, so once it has been baked and cooled, and shortly before serving, refrigerate it for 20 minutes and then dust it with cocoa powder and confectioners' sugar. Serve the tart with a glass of Banyuls, a delicious wine with a deep earth color.

1. To make the pastry, knead the butter thoroughly with the sugar, egg and egg yolk, then sift the flour, pinch of salt, and ground vanilla pulp over the butter mixture and combine. Form the pastry into a ball and allow it to rest in a cool place for 6–8 hours.

2. Divide the pastry into two portions and roll them out evenly. Grease two springform pans (or cake rings) with butter and line them with pastry. Bake for eight minutes in a moderate oven.

Tart

3. For the chocolate mixture, heat the cream in a saucepan. Break or chop the chocolate coating into small pieces and pour the hot cream over it. Stir with a whisk until the mixture is smooth. Allow to cool.

4. Beat the unsweetened cream until stiff and carefully fold into the chocolate mixture. Pour onto the pastry shell and bake for two minutes at 390 °C / 200 °C. Allow to cool, dust with chocolate powder and confectioners' sugar, and refrigerate briefly before serving.

Preparation time: 30 minutes
Cooking time: 60–70 minutes
Difficulty: ☆

Serves 8

For the sweet short pastry:
10 tbsp / 150 g butter
5 tbsp / 75 g sugar
1 egg
1 egg yolk
2 cups / 250 g flour
1 pinch of salt
vanilla pulp, ground

For the filling:

1³/₄ oz / 50 g nillon (pressed walnut mixture), ground
6¹/₂ tbsp / 100 ml milk
6¹/₂ tbsp / 100 ml cream
6 tbsp / 90 g sugar
1 egg
2 egg yolks
1 tbsp walnut oil

Nowadays, few gourmets outside Switzerland are likely to have heard of *nillon*. For the Swiss, this word conjures up childhood memories, almost as vividly as does the traditional *nillon* cake eaten by schoolchildren as a mid-morning snack during walnut season. *Nillon* is the tasty remains of walnuts after all the oil has been pressed out of them; it can either be packed into a solid mass for children to nibble, or turned into the powder that, among other things, is used to create this truly Swiss dessert.

Hazelnut *nillon* is also available and is made exactly the same way as walnut *nillon*. Both keep well stored in airtight metal tins.

When making the pastry shell, be sure that the pastry contains not even the smallest of holes or air pockets before covering it with the *nillon* filling. As with every pudding mixture, this tart must be baked at a very low temperature.

It is easier to find *nillon* than you might think: wherever walnut oil is made, there has to be a way to make use of the solid material left over from pressing, though the name of this substance will vary from region to region. Walnut oil also emphasizes the flavor of the *nillon* tart filling, which the famous pastry chef Fredy Girardet regularly features on his dessert menu.

1. In a glass bowl, mix the nillon with the milk and allow it to infuse for 15 minutes. To make the pastry, thoroughly knead the butter with the sugar, egg and egg yolk. Sift the flour, salt, and ground vanilla pulp over the butter mixture and combine. Form the pastry into a ball and allow it to rest in a cool place for one hour.

2. Roll out the pastry evenly and use it to line a cake ring or small springform pan with a diameter of 8 in / 18 cm. Bake at a moderate temperature. Allow to cool and then turn out of the cake ring.

Tart

3. Add the cream, sugar, egg, egg yolks, and walnut oil to the nillon mixture. Beat thoroughly with a whisk.

4. Pour this mixture into the pastry shell, put in the oven and bake for 40–50 minutes at 265–275 °F / 130–140 °C. Allow to cool and then serve.

Preparation time: 40 minutes
Cooking time: 25 minutes
Difficulty: ✶

Serves 8

For the sweet short pastry:
10 tbsp / 150 g butter
5 tbsp / 75 g sugar
1 egg
1 egg yolk

2 cups / 250 g flour
1 pinch of salt
vanilla pulp, ground

For the pudding mixture:
1¹/₂ cups / 350 ml pear wine (Raisinée)
1 cup / 250 ml cream
4 eggs
2 egg yolks

The wine in this recipe is a particular cooked wine, similar to that which used to be served in the Provence region of France with the famous "thirteen desserts" associated with the Christmas season. This cooked wine, known as Raisinée, is made in the canton of Waadt using whole, ripe pears. They are cooked over very low heat for several days in a copper pan, with a little sugar, to produce a black, syrupy mixture that looks like Turkish coffee or balsamic vinegar.

The traditional nature of the recipe does not mean that variations are not allowed; sometimes apples are used along with pears, though they need to be equally ripe and flavorful.

The cooked wine is filtered to remove any traces of fruit flesh before it is sold, most often directly from farms in the cantons of Waadt and Fribourg, and anything cooked or baked with it tastes marvelous. Any type of pear can be used, and the production of Raisinée is a genuine folk custom; every village, even every producer, has its own festivities to celebrate the wine-making season.

It is not difficult to make Raisinée yourself, as long as you use only whole fruit and not pear juice, which at first glance might not seem as sour.

1. To make the pastry, knead the butter thoroughly with the sugar, egg and egg yolk. Sift the flour, pinch of salt, and ground vanilla pulp over the butter mixture and combine. Form the pastry into a ball and allow it to rest in a cool place for 1–2 hours. Combine all the ingredients for the pudding, except for 6¹/₂ tbsp / 100 ml of the cream, which should be set aside. Allow to rest for two hours.

2. Roll out the pastry and use it to line a cake ring or springform pan with a diameter of 8 in / 18 cm. Refrigerate for 20 minutes and then bake at a low temperature. Take the pastry shell out of the cake ring and allow to cool.

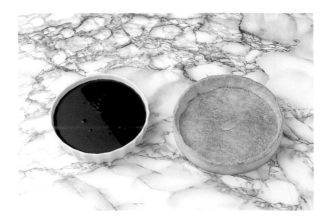

Tart

3. Place the pudding mixture in a pan and heat it to 105 °F / 40 °C. Whip the reserved 6¹/₂ tbsp / 100 ml cream until stiff, and fold it into the pudding.

4. Pour the mixture into the pastry shell. Bake for 15 minutes at 390 °C / 200 °C. Allow to cool and then serve.

Royal Pineapple

Preparation time: 1 hour
Cooking time: 8–10 minutes
Difficulty: ★★★

Serves 8

For the biscuit roulade:
15 egg yolks
1/2 cup / 120 g sugar
2/3 cup / 80 g flour
grated peel of 1 lemon
6 egg whites
1 pinch of salt

For the pineapple mousse:
Vanilla custard:
1 cup / 250 ml milk

3 1/2 tbsp / 50 g sugar
1/2 vanilla bean
1 egg yolk
1/4 cup / 25 g powdered cream, heated

3 sheets of gelatin
2 tsp / 10 ml kirsch
2 tsp / 10 ml rum
1 lb / 500 g diced pineapple
1 2/3 cups / 400 ml whipping cream

For the coating:
4 1/2 tbsp / 100 g apricot jam

To garnish:
pistachios
1 pineapple slice

Tourte is the Swiss term for desserts consisting of a sponge cake base topped with a flavored cream. Philippe Guignard named this classic recipe Tourte royale (Royal Cake), and he feels that it is unforgettably good. In this recipe, he strives to bring out the character of pineapple, particularly pineapples grown on the island of Réunion, which are highly valued for their consistency and flavor.

We can thank the Swedish botanist Olaf Bromel for discovering bromeline, an enzyme in pineapple and other bromeliads that gives the ripe fruit its singular flavor and also stimulates the digestive system.

The Tourte royale hinges on the clever combination of pineapple and custard; because it contains whipped cream, the resulting cream is very light, but also nutritious and rich in flavor. Blend the two mixtures carefully. The cream can also be flavored with rum and kirsch.

Take some pains when making the biscuit roulade, a popular sponge cake frequently used as a base for tortes. It is manageable and, thanks to the jam spread on it, delicious; bake it rapidly at a very high temperature so that it does not dry out. After it is baked and cooled, roll it up immediately. Spread the jam thinly so that it does not seep out.

1. To make the biscuit roulade, beat the egg yolks with 1/4 cup / 65 g sugar until the mixture falls from the whisk in long ribbons, then fold in the sifted flour and grated lemon peel. Whisk the egg whites, salt and the remaining sugar until foamy. Carefully combine the two mixtures. Spread the sponge cake mixture onto a tray lined with baking paper.

2. Bake the biscuit roulade at 480 °F / 250 °C, making sure that it stays soft; after baking carefully sprinkle it with sugar. As soon as it has cooled, spread the biscuit with a thin layer of apricot jam. Wrap it up very tightly in plastic wrap and refrigerate for three hours.

Cake

3. To make the vanilla custard, heat the milk with the sugar and slit vanilla bean. Whisk the powdered cream with the egg yolk and add a little hot milk. Return everything to the saucepan with the hot milk, bring to a boil and allow to cool. Add the gelatin dissolved in cold water, kirsch, rum, and diced pineapple, then carefully fold in the whipped cream.

4. Place a cake ring on baking paper. Line the base and sides with thin, uniformly sliced rounds of biscuit roulade. Fill with the pineapple mousse, cover with more slices of biscuit roulade and allow to set in the refrigerator. Turn out onto a serving dish and cover with apricot jam. Garnish the center of the cake with a rosette of whipped cream, a pineapple slice and halved pistachios. Refrigerate for one hour before serving.

Rum

Preparation time: 1 hour 15 minutes
Cooking time: 20 minutes
Difficulty: ★★

Serves 10

For the génoise:
5 eggs
$^1/_2$ cup, 2 tbsp / 150 g sugar
$^3/_4$ cup, 1 tbsp / 110 g flour
6 tbsp / 40 g unsweetened cocoa powder
1 tbsp / 10 g almonds, very finely ground

For the chocolate cream:
7 oz / 200 g bittersweet chocolate
1$^1/_4$ cups / 300 ml whipping cream, unsweetened

For the syrup for soaking: (see basic recipes)
$^3/_4$ cup / 180 g sugar
$^3/_4$ cup / 200 ml water
1$^1/_4$ cups / 300 ml rum

To garnish:
chocolate powder
chocolate sprinkles
pistachios

In Switzerland, chocolate is almost an object of worship, but Philippe Guignard feels that the truffé (chocolate truffles) made there tend to be somewhat dry and too dense for his palette. His solution for improving the texture was to add rum, a classic combination with chocolate, to this recipe.

Guignard always uses chocolate with at least a 60 to 70% cocoa content, whether he is making a truffle torte, a light chocolate puff pastry or a rich cake with ganache. Chocolate gourmets go weak at the knees at the sight of his truffé, with its garnishes of ground chocolate and chocolate sprinkles.

The old Jamaican rum for soaking the génoise should have been aged for at least three years in oak casks. This turns it a lovely golden color, with a bouquet so exquisite that it should never be blended. While there is no universal recipe for soaking, it works well to brush the sponge base with the rum, going over it several times until it is fully drenched. Ideally, assemble the rum truffle torte an entire day before serving it.

When the International Athletic Meeting takes place in Lausanne, the Guignard *pâtisserie* employs the help of 23 other bakers to make as many as an almost unimaginable 24,000 Rum Truffles. "Everything is possible" say the staff, as they mobilize for this truly "sporting" effort.

1. To make the génoise, beat the eggs with the sugar until the mixture falls from the beaters in long ribbons, then sift the flour, cocoa powder, and ground almonds over it and gently blend. Grease and flour a springform pan, pour the mixture into and bake for 20 minutes at 355 °F / 180 °C. Immediately turn out onto a cooling rack.

2. Melt the bittersweet chocolate in a double boiler and allow to cool. Whip the cream until stiff, and carefully fold the melted chocolate into it. Make the syrup for soaking, following the basic recipe but using the amounts listed above.

Truffle

3. Slice the génoise horizontally in such a way that the bottom layer is thicker than the top one. Soak the bottom layer with rum syrup and spread two-thirds of the chocolate cream on it. Place the second layer on top and soak it, as well.

4. Spread chocolate cream around the torte. Press chocolate sprinkles into the cream around the edge and decorate the top with chocolate cream rosettes. Dust with ground chocolate and garnish with pistachios. Serve well-chilled.

Amandine

Preparation time: 3 hours
Cooking time: 30 minutes
Difficulty: ★★★

Serves 6

biscuit, pastry cream, Italian meringue, génoise,
   cream for decorating: (see basic recipes)

For the almond cream:
6¹/₂ tbsp / 100 g butter
¹/₂ cup, 1 tbsp / 85 g almonds, very finely ground
1 tbsp / 15 ml apricot schnapps
4¹/₂ oz / 125 g pastry cream
3 oz / 90 g Italian meringue

For the apricot jelly:
³/₄ cup / 170 g coarse apricot puree
5 tsp / 25 g superfine sugar
2¹/₂ sheets of gelatin
1¹/₂ tsp / 8 ml apricot schnapps

For the syrup for soaking:
2 tbsp / 30 ml sugar syrup
¹/₂ cup / 125 ml water
2 drops of bergamot oil

To garnish:
14 oz / 400 g apricot glaze
3 apricot halves
1 blanched almond

Amandine may owe its place in French literature to the famous line in the second act of Edmond Rostand's *Cyrano de Bergerac*, "Quickly glaze the sides with apricot …" Here is another work of art, this one created by Pierre Hermé, who for a decade headed the team of pastry chefs in the famed Fauchon food emporium, and is now responsible for *pâtisserie* at the pastry shop, tea salon, and café Ladurée in Paris. Each element of his composition deserves special attention.

Making the diagonal stripes in the biscuit requires a steady hand. Rather than trying to pull the cake comb diagonally, it is easier to turn the baking paper at an angle so the comb can be pulled in a straight line toward you. Then the sponge mixture is baked without steam (see glossary) at 390–445 °F / 200–230 °C.

Use only top-quality, fleshy, perfect fruit for the apricot jelly and glaze; wash the apricots before removing their stems and stones. The reddish apricots from Roussillon or the more orangeish apricots from Provence are ideal; their textures can be checked by pressing them slightly. Be precise when weighing the puree, and remember that the jelly mixture is dependent on the puree's consistency.

Choose high-quality apricot schnapps as well – knowing its place of origin is helpful in making this selection. Pierre Hermé, for example, prefers using Valais de Morand, or possibly a good peach liqueur, which usually has a stronger flavor.

1. Prepare and bake the génoise, then slice it into two layers. Make the biscuit mixture and spread it ¹/₂ in / 1 cm thick on a rectangular piece of baking paper. Use a cake comb to draw diagonal stripes through the mixture, then bake. For the almond cream, cream the butter with a whisk until foamy, add the ground almonds and apricot schnapps while stirring, then fold in the pastry cream and Italian meringue.

2. To make the apricot jelly, combine the coarsely pureed apricots with sugar. Soak the gelatin and dissolve it in the apricot schnapps with a quarter of the apricot puree. Heat to 105 °F / 40 °C and add to the remaining puree while stirring vigorously. Pour into a cake ring with a diameter of 7 in / 15 cm and refrigerate until set. Line a cake ring with a diameter of 8 in / 18 cm and height of 2 in / 4 cm with a strip of baking paper and a 1¹/₂ in / 3 cm wide strip of the biscuit.

3. Place a ¹/₂ in / 1 cm layer of génoise inside the cake ring and soak it with bergamot syrup. Fill the ring two-thirds full with almond cream, and place the set apricot jelly on it. Top it with more cream and the second génoise layer, soak the sponge cake, and fill the ring with the remaining almond cream. Smooth the top and freeze for 30 minutes. Mark a circle 5 to 5¹/₂ in / 11 to 12 cm in diameter on the surface. Use a pastry bag with a medium tip to pipe the cream for decorating onto it in the shape of lamellas.

4. Freeze the torte for one hour, then use a ladle to cover it with apricot glaze. Refrigerate for two hours and allow to set. Remove the cake ring, and garnish the cake with apricot halves and blanched almonds.

Cannelés

Preparation time: 1 hour 20 minutes
Cooking time: 1 hour
Difficulty: ☆

Serves 6

2 cups / 500 ml milk
1 vanilla bean (Tahiti vanilla)
1²/₃ cups / 250 g confectioners' sugar, sifted

2 eggs
2 egg yolks
1 tbsp / 15 ml brown rum made with sugar cane
3¹/₂ tbsp / 50 g melted butter, cooled
³/₄ cup / 100 g flour, sifted

The name of this crunchy yet tender little cake – a specialty of Bordeaux – is derived from the fluted tin in which it is baked (the French *cannelure* means groove, or flute).

Brown rum and Tahiti vanilla make for a delicious combination. Pierre Hermé maintains that the only truly suitable spirit is brown rum made with sugar cane and aged for at least three years in oak casks, which gives the rum a marvelous amber color and an intense flavor. Hermé also likes the Tahiti vanilla's "rounded" flavor and prefers it to Bourbon vanilla.

When making cannelés, all the ingredients should be used cold, and, for optimal results, chill the tins before pouring in the batter. While the completed, unbaked mixture will keep for a few days if need be, the baked cannelés should not be kept overnight. Allow them to cool a little before serving

"When they turn black, they are ready" is a rule of thumb for recognizing when the cannelés have finished baking; they should be very dark, which is when, gourmets say, these delicious little cakes are at their best.

1. To make the batter, bring the milk to a boil with the cut open and scraped out vanilla bean a day in advance. Refrigerate. On the next day, remove the vanilla bean. Combine the confectioners' sugar with the eggs, egg yolks, rum, cooled melted butter, flour, and cold milk. Refrigerate the mixture for at least 24 hours before baking.

2. Brush butter into each of the fluted baking forms or ramekins and then refrigerate them – they should be very cold when the batter is poured into them.

3. Take the batter out of the refrigerator and stir for two minutes with a whisk, then fill the baking forms leaving ¹/₂ in / 1 cm space at the top (stir the mixture again before filling each form).

4. Bake the cannelés for one hour at 390–430 °F / 200–220 °C (355–375 °F / 180–190 °C in a convection oven) if the forms have a diameter of 2¹/₂ in / 4¹/₂ cm, or 50 minutes if the forms have a diameter of 1³/₄ in / 3¹/₂ cm. Turn out of the forms immediately, cool for one hour and enjoy the same day.

Banana Fans with

Preparation time: 1 hour
Cooking time: 20 minutes
Difficulty: ★★

Serves 6

6 bananas
1 pinch of coarsely ground pepper
3 passion fruits
3 sheets of phyllo pastry

For the honey butter with citrus fruits:
3¹/₂ tbsp / 50 g butter, melted
8 tsp / 40 g superfine sugar
1 tsp honey

5 tsp / 25 ml lemon juice
5 tsp / 25 ml orange juice

For the allspice ice cream:
1¹/₂ cups / 340 ml fresh whole milk
1 pinch of ground allspice
4¹/₂ tbsp / 70 ml cream
1 tbsp / 15 g invert sugar
6¹/₂ tbsp / 100 g superfine sugar
1 pinch of stabilizer
5 egg yolks

The shape of this delicate, exotically flavored banana fan brings to mind the famous Madagascariensis, or "traveller's tree," native to Madagascar; its fruits look like wooden bananas. The hallmark of this dessert is the unusual peppered ice cream, flavored with allspice, a versatile spice also known as Jamaica pepper, which was probably first used by the Arawak Indians of Guyana.

To retain the fullest flavor, buy only whole seeds of allspice and grind them shortly before use. Prepare the ice cream at least two hours before serving to ensure that the flavor has a chance to develop.

In this composition, the sweetness of bananas makes for a vivid contrast with the familiar tartness of passion fruit; to emphasize it, choose very ripe, small, wrinkled passion fruits, and scrape out as much of the flesh as possible. Cut the bananas into thin, even slices, and drizzle a little lemon juice onto them so that they do not turn brown.

It can be difficult to brown the phyllo pastry in convection ovens, for it is so light that it tends to blow away before it is crunchy enough. In this case, it is better not to bake it in advance. A most fitting drink to accompany this fan would be a good white sugar cane rum.

1. To make the honey butter, melt the butter and then gently stir in, one after the other, the sugar, honey, lemon juice, and orange juice. Without delay, spread out the phyllo pastry on a work surface and spread the honey butter on to it. Cut in half lengthwise and then two times across to make six rectangles. Pleat each piece into a fan shape.

2. Hold the pleated phyllo pastry at one end and open up the fan. Place the fans on a tray and brown for a few minutes in the oven at 430 °F/220 °C. Select ripe passion fruits, open them and scrape out the flesh. Refrigerate the passion fruit flesh.

Passion Fruit Coulis

3. For the ice cream, bring 5 tbsp/70 ml milk to a boil, infuse the allspice in it for two hours and then strain through a sieve. Put a third of the allspice back into the milk. Bring the remaining milk to a boil with the cream and invert sugar, and stir in 5 tbsp/70 g sugar and the stabilizer. Stir in the allspice milk. Beat the egg yolks with 2 tbsp/30 g sugar, pour the milk mixture over them, and thicken like a custard. Cut a banana into slices ¹/₈ in / 2 mm thick and arrange as a fan.

4. Sprinkle a little coarsely ground pepper onto the bananas, and spread the passion fruit flesh on top. Place a crunchy phyllo pastry fan in the center and place a ball of ice cream between the banana and fan. Serve immediately.

Torte with Wild Strawberries

Preparation time: | 1 hour
Cooking time: | 1 hour
Difficulty: | ★★★

Serves 6

Joconde sponge cake, Italian meringue, biscuit, strawberry juice and cigarette pastry: (see basic recipes)

For the beaten egg mixture:
2 eggs
$^1/_4$ cup / 60 g sugar
4 tsp / 20 ml water

For the mascarpone mousse:
10 oz / 135 g mascarpone cheese
1 tbsp / 15 ml milk
$6^1/_2$ tbsp / 100 ml cream
5 sheets of gelatin
$1^1/_4$ oz / 35 g Italian meringue
$^1/_2$ cup / 120 ml cream, whipped until stiff

To garnish:
wild strawberries, red currants

This original French recipe briefly unites Casanova and Leonardo da Vinci's *Mona Lisa*: Casanova, apparently, had a great love of mascarpone cheese, and in France, the *Mona Lisa* is known as La Joconde, a name she shares with the French almond sponge cake. This great leap into history may require a bit of imagination, but this recipe has no shortage of that.

Pierre Hermé considers the biscuit the third part of the alliance, for it absorbs the strawberry juice well and is softened by it. Use only very red, fully ripened, fleshy berries to make the juice for soaking.

The garnish, also of red berries, harmoniously combines wild strawberries with red currants. While the little wild strawberries spoil quickly, they do have an incomparably delicate flavor. They also freeze well, which serves to soften the slightly bitter taste some people find unpleasant. Filter out the hard seeds on the berries' surface by using a pointed sieve when preparing the coulis.

Mascarpone, still a favorite of Casanova's countrymen, comes from Lombardy and is made using the cream from cows' milk.

1. Prepare all the elements according to the basic recipes; bake the Joconde sponge cake and biscuit. Prepare the beaten egg mixture like a zabaglione and spread a little on to the Joconde sponge cake, dust with confectioners' sugar, and caramelize with a salamander. Repeat, then burn regular thin lines into its surface. For the mascarpone mousse, combine the mascarpone and milk. Bring the cream to a boil, add the soaked gelatin and mix with the mascarpone.

2. Carefully fold in the Italian meringue and stiffly whipped cream. Line a $1^1/_2$ in / 3 cm high cake ring with a strip of baking paper and a strip of Joconde sponge cake of the same width. Slice the biscuit horizontally, place one layer in the cake ring and soak it with strawberry juice. Fill the ring halfway with mascarpone mousse and arrange the wild strawberries and red currants on top.

and Red Currants

3. Cover with mascarpone mousse and a second layer of biscuit thoroughly soaked with strawberry juice. Freeze the torte for two hours.

4. Remove the cake ring and place the torte on a cake round about $^1/_2$ in / 1 cm larger than the torte. Spread a little sweetened Italian meringue on top and lightly brown it with a salamander. Garnish with wild strawberries and lightly glazed red currants. Place two leaves made of cigarette pastry on top of the berries.

Macaroons with Aniseed

Preparation time: 45 minutes
Cooking time: 35 minutes
Difficulty: ★★

Serves 6

For the vanilla macaroon mixture:
1 cup / 140 g almonds, very finely ground
4 egg whites
1²/₃ cups / 240 g confectioners' sugar
ground vanilla

pastry cream: (see basic recipes)

For the aniseed cream:
7 oz / 200 g pastry cream
¹/₄ cup / 60 ml whipping cream
1 tsp / 6 ml aniseed liqueur
2 tsp / 10 ml Ricard

To garnish:
3 pints of raspberries
star anise

In France, the macaroon has given rise to many legends and traditions whose myriad variations, throughout all the French provinces, are always based on a marzipan mixture.

For Pierre Hermé, the appeal of this dessert lies in the contrast of the creamy filling with the firmer shell, crunchy in the center but a little softer at the edge. Achieving this effect hinges on the very process of making the macaroon mixture, so devote your full attention to it.

Adhere strictly to the baking instructions as well, particularly if you have a convection oven. If so, reduce the temperature to 275 °F / 140 °C, and increase the baking time, if necessary, because there may be temperature differences of up to ten degrees depending on the model. A certain degree of caution is advisable here.

The aniseed cream harmonizes well with the slightly caramel-like flavor of the Ricard, and with the flavor of the aniseed liqueur from Spain that Pierre Hermé uses. Carefully select the raspberries for the garnish and use only ripe, aromatic, perfect berries. Raspberries are low in calories and contain a lot of vitamin C.

1. For the macaroons, beat the egg whites without sugar, then fold in the almonds, confectioners' sugar, and vanilla powder with a wooden spatula. The mixture should collapse a little when stirred. Pipe spirals on to baking paper, place on to two baking trays (one on top of the other) and bake for 15 minutes, starting at 480 °F / 250 °C, then reduce the temperature to 355–390 °F / 180–200 °C. To remove the macaroon, pour a little water between the tray and baking paper.

2. Prepare the pastry cream as described in the basic recipe, pouring the boiling milk into the beaten egg yolks as shown below. Pour everything back into the saucepan and boil for two minutes, stirring continually so that the mixture does not stick. Add the butter to the cream once it has cooled to 120–130 °F / 50–55 °C.

Cream and Raspberries

3. Weigh 7 oz / 200 g pastry cream, stir in the aniseed liqueur and Ricard with a whisk, and finally fold in the stiffly whipped cream using a wooden spatula. Place a macaroon upside down on a cake round. Using a pastry bag with a small to medium-sized tip, pipe a layer of aniseed cream on to it that is slightly smaller than the macaroon base.

4. Arrange raspberries around the edge of the cream, using the largest berries for the outermost circle, and place the remaining raspberries in the center. Cover with another layer of cream and top with the second macaroon layer. Garnish with raspberries and star anise. Refrigerate for 30 minutes before serving.

Puff Pastry with Spiced

Preparation time: 1 hour 30 minutes
Cooking time: 20 minutes
Difficulty: ✲✲

Serves 6

spiced puff pastry: (see basic recipes)

spiced cake e.g. *lebkuchen*

For the ice cream with Dijon spiced cake:
2¹/₂ cups / 600 ml milk
2 oz / 55 g spiced cake, crumbled
6¹/₂ tbsp / 100 ml cream
1 tsp lebkuchen spices
7¹/₂ tbsp / 110 g superfine sugar
7 egg yolks

generous pinch / 3 g stabilizer
1 tbsp / 25 g pine honey
1 tsp / 5 ml Ricard

For the candied orange slices:
7 oz / 200 g oranges
1 cup / 250 ml water
¹/₂ cup / 125 g sugar

For the orange butter:
3¹/₂ oz / 100 g candied oranges
6¹/₂ tbsp / 100 ml orange juice
4 tsp / 20 ml lemon juice
generous pinch of ground cardamom
generous pinch of Sarawak ginger, freshly ground
1 pinch of black pepper
¹/₄ cup / 60 g butter

To garnish:
2 oranges and 2 lemons

Pierre Hermé was undoubtedly inspired to create this fascinating dessert in his Alsatian homeland, where the feast day of St. Nicholas is still celebrated on December 6. In addition to oranges and nuts, children enjoy long pieces of *lebkuchen* on that day. This recipe draws on that tradition.

Lebkuchen are perhaps most strongly associated with Germany, but similar spiced cakes are beloved in many European countries. The spice mixture that makes them so alluring varies from region to region, but invariably contains cinnamon, nutmeg, ginger, and cloves. While the German blend is dominated by cinnamon, the French mixture of spices is more balanced, often containing a note of aniseed, and corresponds more to French taste. It gives the spiced cake ice cream a somewhat sweet and rounded flavor and contrasts with the mild tartness of the orange butter, which is cleverly highlighted

by cardamom, pepper, and ginger. The spiced cake should be soft, with a well-browned, crunchy top.

Making the puff pastry is the most difficult aspect of this recipe. It will turn out perfectly only if you are able to turn the pastry over without breaking it after three-quarters of the baking time. This is easier if you place a second piece of baking paper on the puff pastry before putting it in the oven.

Assembling the dessert, also an important part of the process, requires significant concentration, for it is integral to the success of the final presentation. The orange and lemon segments added at this stage are not merely decorative but offer yet another delicious contrast, as well as highlighting the perfect balance of the various flavors. To reduce the acidity of the lemon segments, dip them briefly in simmering sugar syrup of 16 °Beaumé.

1. For the spiced cake ice cream, bring the milk to a boil, add the crumbled spiced cake, allow to infuse for one hour, then blend in a blender. Bring the cream to a boil with the lebkuchen spices. Combine all the remaining ingredients, except the Ricard, in a bowl and whisk thoroughly. Add the milk and cream and thicken the mixture like a custard. Allow to cool, stir in the Ricard and pour into an ice cream maker.

2. To candy the oranges, slice them very thinly and spread them on a tray. Make a syrup with the water and sugar and pour the boiling syrup over the oranges. Refrigerate and marinate for 24 hours. To make the orange butter, drain the orange slices and puree them as finely as possible with the orange and lemon juice, and freshly ground cardamom, ginger, and black pepper. Refrigerate this spice mixture for 30 minutes.

Cake, Oranges and Lemons

3. Shortly before arranging the dessert, heat 7 oz / 200 g of the spice mixture and stir it into the butter, which has been whisked until foamy. Cut the spiced cake into very thin slices measuring 4¹/₂ x 2¹/₂ in / 10 x 5¹/₂ cm. Spread butter on both sides of the cake slices and toast with a salamander. Melt the remaining butter. Using a silver spoon, form balls of spiced cake ice cream.

4. On dessert plates, layer a slice of toasted spiced cake, a ball of ice cream, a second slice of spiced cake and ball of ice cream, and finish off with a rectangle of caramelized spiced puff pastry. Place this in the center of the plate, pour hot orange butter to one side and garnish with skinned orange and lemon segments.

Chocolate Eggs

Preparation time: 1 hour
Cooking time: 8 minutes
Difficulty: ★★

Serves 6

6 sheets of phyllo pastry
1 egg carton

For the coffee cream:
1¼ cups / 300 ml cream
¾ oz / 20 g coffee beans, ground

For the rum zabaglione:
3 egg yolks
6 tbsp / 90 g sugar

3 tbsp / 45 ml old brown rum made with sugar cane
2 tbsp / 30 ml water

For the egg ganache:
1 egg
2 egg yolks
8 tsp / 40 g superfine sugar
5¼ oz / 150 g Guanaja chocolate coating, melted
6½ tbsp / 100 g melted butter

While there are in existence surely a thousand recipes that use eggs, for many people the egg's strongest connotation is still the Easter holiday. In inventing this dessert for Easter Sunday, Pierre Hermé has created the one thousand and first.

In this recipe, only the ganache can be prepared in advance. Its consistency should be almost sponge-like – crispy at the edge, firm on top, but creamy and almost liquid inside. The rest, especially the phyllo pastry, should not be prepared until the last minute.

To prepare the egg shells, use a knife with a very sharp point to make the initial cut into the shell and a pair of sharp scissors to

cut around it, and work with great precision and all the patience you can muster. Afterward, the main concern is the temperature of the various components, for the surprise of this dessert lies in the astonishing combination of lukewarm zabaglione with colder coffee cream.

Serve the eggs with an old rum made with sugar cane, or simply a very strong, hot coffee. If you think using the phyllo pastry will be too difficult, or if you are short on time, serve the lukewarm eggs in egg cups.

1. Use an egg carton to shape the phyllo pastry so that it can support the eggs, sprinkle it with sugar and bake in a hot oven until golden brown. For the coffee cream, bring the cream to a boil, remove from the heat, infuse the coffee in it and then strain through a pointed sieve lined with cheesecloth. Refrigerate at 4 °C for six hours. Beat until the cream is as stiff as whipped cream. Refrigerate again until serving.

2. Cut open the top of the eggs, first with a pointed knife and then with scissors. Empty the eggs, rinse out the shells with cold water, and allow them to dry upside down. Whisk together all the ingredients for the zabaglione in a saucepan over a low heat until the mixture thickens. Keep warm.

with Coffee Cream

3. To make the ganache, beat the egg, egg yolks, and sugar until foamy. Fold in the melted chocolate and stir with a whisk until smooth, then add the melted butter and stir again until smooth.

4. Place the eggshells in the indentations in the baked phyllo pastry and fill each halfway with ganache. Bake for eight minutes at 390 °F / 200 °C. Fill the eggshells completely with cold coffee cream and serve immediately. Serve the rum zabaglione separately.

Riviera

Preparation time: 1 hour 30 minutes
Cooking time: 1 hour 30 minutes
Difficulty: ★★★

Serves 6

Candied lemon, Joconde sponge cake, flourless chocolate sponge cake, chocolate mousse: (see basic recipes)

For the lemon cream:
grated peel of 2 lemons
2 small eggs
6 tbsp / 90 g superfine sugar
4½ tbsp / 65 ml lemon juice
½ cup / 120 g butter

For the lemon cream with candied lemon:
6½ oz / 180 g lemon cream
⅓ cup / 60 g diced candied lemon
Sarawak pepper

To garnish:
9 oz / 250 g bittersweet chocolate coating
½ cup / 125 g cocoa butter
1 lemon

The elegant look of the Riviera Torte perfectly mirrors the delicacy of the various flavors it contains. First, though, we should thank the great Italian and Spanish explorers Christopher Columbus and Hernán Cortés for their brilliance in bringing cocoa beans to Europe from America, where natives used them as a unit of currency. If not for these gentlemen, we would not now be able to make sponge mixtures, without using flour, as soft and light as this one.

Pierre Hermé displays his genius in filling this particular sponge cake with a lemon cream, its tartness further emphasized by candied lemons, which you should prepare yourself.

Sarawak pepper, the berry of a pepper plant that grows in Indonesia, also deserves mention; though rarely found in European stores, its sharpness is vital in rounding off the flavor of the torte.

Combining chocolate and lemon is a tightrope walk that means balancing the bitterness of chocolate with the acidic flavor of lemons, a dicey business. Weigh the lemon cream precisely before using it in the torte, to ensure that the carefully considered proportions remain intact.

1. Candy the lemon overnight. For the cream, combine the finely grated zest of the lemons with the sugar. Whisk vigorously with the eggs and lemon juice. Poach in a double boiler to 180 °F / 84 °C, stirring regularly. Pass the cream through a sieve, let it cool to 115 °F / 45 °C, then stir in the butter. Whip for five minutes in a blender, then add the candied lemon peel. Spoon the cream into a ring 1 in / 2 cm high and 8 in / 18 cm around and smooth. Freeze for four hours.

2. Prepare the Joconde and flourless chocolate sponge cakes and chocolate mousse. Slice the chocolate sponge into two layers. Line a 2 in / 4 cm high cake ring with baking paper and a 1¾ in / 3.5 cm wide strip of Joconde sponge cake. Place a chocolate sponge base inside and fill the ring one third full with chocolate mousse. Top with the frozen layer of lemon cream. Cover with chocolate mousse, a second layer of sponge cake, and fill the ring with chocolate mousse. Smooth the surface and freeze for one hour.

Torte

3. Using a pastry bag with a special Chiboust tip, decorate three-quarters of the top with long, adjacent chocolate mousse lamellas. Freeze again.

4. Melt the bittersweet chocolate coating and cocoa butter at a maximum temperature of 90–105 °F / 35–40 °C. Pass through a pointed sieve lined with cheesecloth. Take the cake out of the cake ring and, using a spray-gun, dust all around with the mixture of chocolate coating and cocoa butter. Garnish with a chocolate lemon leaf and a lemon third.

Impératrice

Preparation time: 1 hour 30 minutes
Cooking time: 1 hour
Difficulty: ★

Serves 6

8 apples (Granny Smiths)
butter
cane sugar
5¼ oz / 150 g apricot glaze

For the pastry shell:
13 tbsp / 190 g butter
1 pinch of very fine salt
1 pinch of superfine sugar
1 egg yolk

3½ tbsp / 50 ml milk
2 cups / 250 g flour

For the creamy rice pudding:
½ cup / 90 g rice (Arborio or Vialone Nano)
4 cups / 1 l whole milk
¼ cup / 65 g superfine sugar
½ cup, 2 tbsp / 125 g sultanas
3 egg yolks
8 tsp / 40 g butter
1 small egg

Apples have been eaten for as long as anyone can remember, and with so many varieties one can always conjure up a new surprise. Various apples may be used in this recipe, depending on whether you prefer crunchy, tart apples or fragrant ones. Pierre Hermé likes several types, including Boskoop (firm and tart), Cox's Orange Pippin (despite their small size), Reinnette (their firm, aromatic flesh is a great favorite in France), Calville blanche (somewhat rare, but highly regarded by gourmets) and Granny Smith (green, juicy, and very tart).

The choice of rice is equally important. Pierre Hermé is particularly fond of Italian short grain rice, which releases starch when cooked while remaining pleasantly firm to the bite. For the rice pudding to have the right consistency, soak the sultanas in water a day in advance until plump but drain them thoroughly before adding them to the pudding.

Some final tips: the dough should not be kneaded longer than necessary or it will become too elastic and lose its crunchiness when baked. Keep the tart in the refrigerator, but take it out two hours before serving so it can come to room temperature. The ideal beverage to serve with this is an excellent *cidre* (fresh hard cider), though this may not be readily available in the US.

1. To make the pastry shell, knead the butter until soft with the dough hook of an electric mixer, then add the salt, sugar, egg yolk, milk, and finally the flour. Do not knead the dough longer than necessary. Form it into a ball and refrigerate wrapped in plastic wrap. It is best to make the dough a day in advance. Line a 8 in / 18 cm pie pan or flan ring with a height of 1½ in / 3 cm with the pastry. Cover with baking paper and dried peas, and bake blind for 15 minutes at 355 °F / 180 °C.

2. For the rice pudding, bring the rice, milk, and sugar to a boil in a saucepan and then bake in a 355 °F / 180 °C oven until the rice has absorbed the liquid (30 minutes). Add the egg and egg yolks and briefly bring to a boil again. Stir in the butter and the marinated and drained sultanas. Using a pastry bag, pipe the rice pudding into the tart shell to three-quarters the height of the pan.

Apple Tart

3. Bake until the rice forms a crust. Allow to cool. Peel the apples, cut them into eight segments and remove the core. Steam at 445 °F / 230 °C on a baking sheet with small amounts of butter and cane sugar until soft. Then allow to cool.

4. Arrange the apples in a circle on the rice pudding and cover the entire top of the cake with apricot glaze. Refrigerate until shortly before serving.

Preparation time: 1 hour
Cooking time: 20 minutes
Difficulty: ✳

Makes 30

For the choux pastry:
¹/₂ cup / 125 ml water
¹/₂ cup / 125 g butter
2 tbsp sugar
vanilla sugar
1 pinch of salt
1 cup / 125 g flour
2 eggs
6 egg yolks

For the pastry cream:
1 cup / 250 ml cream
2 egg yolks
8 tsp / 40 g sugar
1 tbsp / 15 g vanilla sugar
2 tbsp / 15 g cornstarch

For the vanilla cream:
2¹/₂ cups / 600 ml cream
10¹/₂ oz / 300 g pastry cream

For dusting:
confectioners' sugar

Throughout Europe there are a fabulous variety of *beignet* specialties, delightful hand-size pastries, and they have different names depending on the language spoken where they are made. In France they are called *bugnes*, *frivoles*, *oreillettes* or *guenilles*; in Spain, *churros*; in Italy, *cannoli*; and in Greece, *loukoumade*. Diverse ingredients are used for these pastries, and there are all manner of traditions and occasions for which they are made, from birthdays and public holidays throughout the year to religious feasts in honor of patron saints, and more.

These cream puffs are made using choux pastry, cooked on the stove top and then cooled before the eggs are added (hence its German name, *Brandteig*, which means burnt). But this recipe is for a regional Austrian specialty and, of course, there are other ways to make it.

Homemade vanilla sugar gives a more satisfying flavor and, in the long run, is the most economical use of vanilla beans. To make it, store sugar with dried vanilla beans in an airtight container, occasionally adding new beans to strengthen the flavor. Sugar flavored in this way is used for both the choux pastry and the vanilla cream.

When making the cream puff pastry, you will first make a sort of syrup that softens the dough and causes it to give off steam while baking, which is essential because that is what makes the dough rise. The puffs must be baked in an oven that closes properly and can reach a very high temperature. During baking, do not open the oven door for any reason.

1. To make the choux pastry, combine the water, butter, sugar, vanilla sugar, and salt in a saucepan and bring to a boil. Add the flour and stir the pastry vigorously with a wooden spatula until it is smooth and comes away from the sides of the pan. Remove from the heat and cool slightly. Add the eggs one by one and beat thoroughly after each one.

2. For the pastry cream, heat the cream in a saucepan. Beat the egg yolks with the sugar and vanilla sugar in a bowl until they are creamy and almost white. Add the cornstarch, and slowly pour the boiled cream over the mixture. Pour everything back into the saucepan, bring to a boil, then pour into another pan and allow to cool.

Cream Puffs

3. Using a pastry bag with a star-shaped tip, pipe cream puffs the size of small cream rosettes onto a tray and bake until golden brown. Start by baking for ten minutes at 390 °F / 200 °C, then continue at 355 °F / 180 °C so that they dry thoroughly. To make the vanilla cream, stiffly whip the cream and fold it into 10½ oz / 300 g of the pastry cream.

4. Carefully halve the cream puffs horizontally. Use a pastry bag with a star-shaped tip to fill them with vanilla cream, then replace the pastry "lids" and dust with confectioners' sugar. Arrange three on each plate.

Viennese Carnival

Preparation time: 2 hours
Cooking time: 10 minutes
Difficulty: ★★

Serves 8

For the doughnut dough:
1¹/₂ oz / 40 g yeast
³/₄ cup / 200 ml milk
5³/₄ cups / 600 g flour
1 pinch of salt
2 tsp / 10 g vanilla sugar

¹/₃ cup / 80 g butter, melted
4 tsp / 20 ml rum
2 eggs
¹/₃ cup / 80 g sugar

For the filling:
³/₄ cup, 1¹/₂ tbsp / 300 g apricot jam

For dusting:
confectioners' sugar

Vienna's Carnival period, famous for its brilliant festivities, starts at New Year's and continues right into February, with the opera ball as its festive conclusion. During Carnival, a season of parties and fun leading up to Lent celebrated with varying intensity in different European cities, all sorts of excesses are permitted – Vienna is no exception in this – and there are of course plenty of culinary delights on offer, including baked specialties.

The Carnival doughnuts may look like ordinary jelly doughnuts to American eyes, but they have their own distinctive shape and delicate flavor. In Vienna, they are available only at the climax of the Carnival season, in the four days leading up to the opera ball. They are filled with jam using a pastry bag

(apricot or mirabelle plum jam or, according to taste, different types of jelly).

To be faithful to the traditional recipe, the doughnut dough must be light enough that the doughnuts swim while they fry in the boiling lard (or oil). When both sides have been fried, a light, almost raw dough circle will appear around in the middle. The color contrast, a welcome sight during the Carnival period, does not escape notice by doughnut connoisseurs.

These doughnuts are based on a very old country recipe traced by Helmut Lengauer back to the beginning of the 18th century. The Austrian term for doughnuts, *Krapfen*, likely derives from *Ranftl*, which means "ring" or "border."

1. To make the doughnut dough, prepare the yeast mixture by combining the yeast with a third of the lukewarm milk, and a quarter of the flour. Beat the eggs and sugar until foamy in a double boiler. Mix the remaining flour, milk, salt, and vanilla sugar and knead thoroughly. Add the yeast mixture, the melted butter, rum and finally the beaten egg mixture. Allow the dough to rest for ten minutes.

2. Form the dough into a roll, cut off pieces of about 1¹/₂ oz / 40 g each, and shape them into balls.

(Doughnuts

3. Heat a deep-fat fryer to 355 °F / 180 °C, then fry the doughnuts in the hot fat for 4–5 minutes on both sides, leaving an unbrowned ring in the middle. Allow to drain on paper towels.

4. Use a pastry bag to fill the doughnuts with apricot jam or another filling of your choice. Dust them lightly with confectioners' sugar and arrange on a plate. Serve with coffee.

Preparation time: 1 hour
Cooking time: 20 minutes
Difficulty: ★★

Makes 20

For the dough:
¹/₃ cup / 80 ml milk
6¹/₂ tbsp / 100 g butter
1 pinch of salt
5 tsp / 25 g sugar
¹/₂ oz / 15 g yeast
2 tsp / 10 g vanilla sugar
2 cups / 250 g flour
juice of ¹/₂ lemon

For the nut filling:
1 cup / 150 g walnuts, shelled and halved
³/₄ cup / 180 ml milk
3¹/₂ tbsp / 50 g sugar
2 tsp / 10 g vanilla sugar
1 cinnamon stick
4 tsp / 20 ml rum
2 eggs
3¹/₂ oz / 100 g nougat
4¹/₂ oz / 130 g sponge cake crumbs
mint leaves

For the egg wash:
1 egg

In 1683, a vast army of 200,000 Turks besieged Vienna in the largest Turkish attack in the country's history. It finally took an enormous mobilization of the Christian world, with the active assistance of the Polish king and the duke of Lorraine, to force the retreat of the Grand Vizier Kara Mustapha's troops. This historic threat is remembered in this pastry shaped like the Turkish crescent; it became an icon of Vienna's skill in baking and is known the world over as a typically Viennese pastry.

Many variations of this *Nußßbeugel* (Austrian for nut crescent) are available in Vienna, all having in common that they are invariably served with coffee in the Sacher Hotel, whether *Schwarzer Kaffee* (espresso), *Kapuziner* (with whipped cream) or *Franziskaner* (with grated chocolate).

The walnut tree is the best-known member of the *Juglandaceae* family (a term that really melts in the mouth). Use only fresh walnuts for the filling, and shell them yourself to make sure that the texture and flavor are perfect. Walnuts, even those of high quality, quickly become rancid, and the flavor of the shelled nuts frequently sold in plastic bags leaves much to be desired.

Italian and Greek walnuts can be recommended, as are French walnuts from the Périgord and Dauphiné regions. If no first-class walnuts are available, another delicious alternative would be a poppy seed filling.

1. Knead together all the ingredients for the dough thoroughly with the kneading attachment of an electric mixer. Shape the dough into a long roll and allow to rest in the refrigerator for one hour.

2. Cut the dough roll into slices of about 1 oz / 25 g each. Shape these into balls and use a rolling pin to roll them out to a slightly oval shape. Refrigerate the rolled-out ovals.

Crescents

3. To make the nut filling, chop the nuts finely. Bring the milk to a boil with the sugar, vanilla sugar, cinnamon, and rum. In another pan, combine the slightly beaten eggs, nougat, sponge cake crumbs and mint leaves, pour the hot milk over them, add the chopped walnuts and heat for 2–3 minutes. Pour the mixture into another bowl and allow to cool.

4. Using a pastry bag, pipe a little walnut paste onto each oval piece of dough, roll them up and bend slightly into a crescent shape. Place the crescents on a baking sheet, brush with whisked egg, and bake for 20 minutes at 355 °F / 180 °C. Serve warm.

Plum Pancakes

Preparation time: 30 minutes
Cooking time: 10 minutes
Difficulty: ✶

Serves 4

For the dough:
¹⁄₃ oz / 10 g yeast
1 cup / 250 ml milk, warm
2 cups / 250 g flour
2 tbsp / 30 g sugar
1 tsp vanilla sugar
3 egg yolks
1 pinch of salt
grated peel of ¹⁄₂ lemon
2 tbsp / 30 g butter, melted

For the sour cream sauce:
1 cup / 250 ml sour cream
¹⁄₃ cup / 50 g confectioners' sugar

For the Slivovitz ice cream:
1 cup / 250 ml milk
1 cup / 250 ml cream
4 egg yolks
6¹⁄₂ tbsp / 100 g sugar
4 tsp / 20 ml slivovitz

To garnish:
plum jam or plum
butter
rum
candied lemon or
lime peel

Many anecdotes are told in connection with this recipe that goes back to the Middle Ages; its existence in what used to be known as Czechoslovakia has been documented as early as the 14th century. In one story, a cook forgets that she has plum jam cooking on the stove, and it turns very dark, as dark as prunes, which were probably also first produced in much the same manner.

This somewhat "diabolic" method of making prunes (during cooking, the skin of the plums must withstand the pressure of the boiling juice) conjures the Knights Templar, whom we can thank for the secret of this process. They brought it with them from the Crusades to the Middle East, along with a few other

bits of witchcraft at which they excelled. Then again, there comes a point at which the distinction between fact and fiction becomes blurry …

An imaginative component of this recipe is the sauce made of sour cream and slivovitz, a plum brandy. Sour cream is beloved in both central and eastern Europe and in Great Britain.

Slivovitz (from the Serbian *sliva*, plum) is distilled from a special plum native to Bosnia-Herzegovina, the Pocegace. Its area of origin was once one of the border regions of the Austro-Hungarian empire. Slivovitz is distilled there to this day.

1. To make the yeast mixture, mix the yeast with a third of the lukewarm milk in a bowl, then add a third of the flour. Combine the remaining flour and milk, sugar, vanilla sugar, egg yolks, salt, and grated lemon peel in a mixing bowl. Knead thoroughly with the dough hook of an electric mixer. Add the yeast mixture, which should have doubled in size, and finally, the melted butter.

2. Using a blini pan, cook pancakes that are approximately ¹⁄₂ in / 1 cm thick. Prepare the sauce by whipping the sour cream, and blending in the confectioners' sugar. Refrigerate.

with Sour Cream

3. Spread plum jam on a pancake and drizzle a little rum on it. Place another little cake on top, spread it with plum jam and garnish with very fine strips of candied lemon or lime peel.

4. To make the slivovitz ice cream, bring the milk and cream to a boil. Beat the egg yolks with the sugar until the mixture falls from a spoon in long ribbons. Stir a little hot milk into the eggs, pour everything into a saucepan, and return to the heat until thickened. Allow the custard to cool, pass it through a sieve, add the slivovitz and pour into an ice cream maker. Serve the pancakes drizzled with sour cream sauce, accompanied by a scoop of ice cream.

Almond Brittle Mousse

Preparation time: 20 minutes
Cooking time: 10 minutes
Difficulty: ★

Serves 4

3¹/₂ oz / 100 g white almond brittle chocolate
2 tbsp / 30 ml milk
1 cup / 250 ml whipping cream
1¹/₂ sheets of gelatin

For the zabaglione:
1 egg
1 egg yolk

2 tbsp / 30 g sugar
4 tsp / 20 ml white port

For the strawberry salad:
1 lb / 500 g strawberries
¹/₃ cup / 50 g confectioners' sugar
6¹/₂ tbsp / 100 ml Grand Marnier

To garnish:
mint leaves
flaked almonds, roasted

This dessert, a clever combination of almond mousse with zabaglione, is derived from an old Austrian recipe, and is served in the variation described here in Vienna's famous Sacher Hotel. If you wish, you can alter the recipe somewhat and use milk chocolate instead of white almond brittle chocolate for the mousse; if you do so, however, flavor the zabaglione more strongly by adding a little instant coffee to it.

When almonds are coupled with chocolate, they develop many complementary flavors that produce subtle contrasts when eaten. In order to preserve the balance among them, stick precisely to the given quantities and use only ingredients of the highest quality.

Strawberries are always an excellent complement to chocolate, and there are myriad ways to combine the two. Other red fruits can be used for the salad in this dessert, including forest fruits or Morello cherries. The salad goes wonderfully well with the mousse; its essential flavors are emphasized especially by the Grand Marnier, the world-famous liqueur distilled from bitter orange peel marinated in cognac.

1. To make the zabaglione, beat the egg and egg yolk, sugar, and white port in a pan in a double boiler until foamy. Set aside until needed. Melt the white chocolate in a second double boiler with the milk. Whip the cream until stiff.

2. Add the melted chocolate to the zabaglione, then add the gelatin, which has been soaked in cold water. Finally, carefully fold in the whipped cream. Pour into molds and refrigerate for six hours.

on a Strawberry Salad

3. Slice the strawberries lengthwise, put them in a container that is large enough that they are not crowded, and marinate them in a mixture of the Grand Marnier and confectioners' sugar.

4. Arrange the strawberries on dessert plates in the form of a flower, and invert an almond mousse in the center of each flower. Sprinkle roasted flaked almonds on it and garnish with a rosette of whipped cream and mint leaves.

Sacher Parfait

Preparation time: 30 minutes
Cooking time: 15 minutes
Difficulty: ★

Serves 8

For the beaten egg mixture:
2 eggs
3¹/₂ tbsp / 50 g sugar

For the chocolate praline filling:
1³/₄ oz / 50 g chocolate coating
3¹/₂ tbsp / 50 ml nut nougat, liquid
2 tbsp / 30 ml milk

4 tsp / 20 ml brandy (or dessert wine)
1 cup / 250 ml whipping cream

To garnish:
10¹/₂ oz / 300 g strawberries
cocoa powder

Having existed only since 1954, the Sacher Parfait is brand new compared to more traditional recipes. At that time, the Sacher Hotel's pastry chef had the idea to make a torte using chocolate parfait and nougat parfait. It was immediately and enthusiastically received by Vienna's high society (who are well-versed in the art of pastries) and by the hotel's cosmopolitan clientele.

The Sacher Parfait, named after the hotel famous for its Sacher Torte, has met with considerable and enduring success. The pastry chefs at the Sacher Hotel are, in fact, genuine world masters of baking and, when demand is high, make up to 3,000 Sacher Tortes every day without any lapse in quality.

With this torte, the Sacher Hotel, which has propagated the Austrian art of baking worldwide, demonstrates its continuing ability to innovate. Not even a lawsuit with the rival Demel *konditorei*, over the production of the "genuine" Sacher Torte, has been able to bring its creativity to a standstill.

Helmut Lengauer is now the pastry chef at the Sacher Hotel, which has been spoiling its famous guests and heads of state for a hundred and fifty years. He views this parfait, truly deserving of its name, as an homage to Eduard and Anna Sacher, the amazing couple who founded the business, and he makes only a few minor adjustments to the original recipe, such as substituting forest fruits or Morello cherries for the strawberries used to garnish it.

1. Beat the eggs and sugar in a double boiler until foamy and firm. Melt the chocolate in a second double boiler and remove from the heat. Add the liquid nougat paste and combine thoroughly.

2. While stirring vigorously, add the milk and brandy to the chocolate praline mixture.

with Strawberries

3. Combine the chocolate praline mixture with the beaten eggs. Whip the cream until stiff, then carefully fold the praline mixture into the whipped cream.

4. Place a cake ring on waxed paper, fill it with the parfait and refrigerate for six hours. Before serving turn the parfait out onto a plate and remove the paper and cake ring. Dust with cocoa and garnish with a rosette of strawberry slices.

Preparation time: 45 minutes
Cooking time: 10 minutes
Difficulty: ★

Serves 4

For the quark dough:
1¼ cups / 140 g flour
1 pinch of salt
1 tsp vanilla sugar
1 egg
9 oz / 250 g quark
5 tbsp / 70 g butter

For the quark filling:
9 oz / 250 g quark
⅓ cup / 50 g confectioners' sugar

1 tsp / 5 g vanilla sugar
2 egg yolks
4 tsp / 10 g cornstarch
juice of ½ lemon
¼ cup / 50 g raisins
2 tsp / 10 ml rum

For the butter crumbs:
10 tbsp / 150 g butter
¾ cup / 100 g dry bread crumbs

For the rösti:
fresh or canned apricots (depending on the season)
clarified butter
confectioners' sugar

Some truly surprising experiences can occur in famous Austrian cafés. For example, while these turnovers are called ravioli in Vienna (probably due to the influence of nearby Italy), they are a typically Austrian specialty, if only because of their quark filling.

Austrians clearly think of ravioli as something quite different from the usual square affairs. Here, a round piece of dough is folded in the middle, giving the turnovers a half-moon shape – possibly yet another nod to the Turkish crescent.

Once this understanding of ravioli has been explained, it is a logical conclusion that the manner and composition of the fill-

ing are varied and allow for some inventive departures; whether sweet, savory, filled with fruit or other refreshing flavors, anything goes in giving the ravioli tastes that are both delicious and diverse. In this instance we concerned with the sweet version.

The ravioli are combined with a type of *rösti*, though in this case we are talking not about the familiar Swiss specialty, potato pancakes fried in a pan, but about apricot *rösti*, ideally made using very fleshy apricots. The apricots are caramelized in a pan with butter and sugar to give them an acidic flavor that is a beguiling flavor contrast to the ravioli.

1. To make the quark dough, combine the flour, salt, vanilla sugar, egg, butter, and quark in a bowl, mix everything thoroughly and then allow to rest for 20 minutes.

2. Marinate the raisins for the filling in the rum. Combine all the ingredients for the filling, except the raisins and rum, in a bowl and stir until the mixture is smooth. Then fold in the drained raisins.

Apricot Rösti

3. Roll out the quark dough thinly using a rolling pin. Cut out circles with a diameter of 2³/₄ in / 6 cm, put some quark cream in the center of each circle, and fold them together like turnovers. Press the edges together firmly with your fingers. For the butter crumbs, melt the butter in a saucepan, then stir in the bread crumbs to coat them evenly and brown them slightly.

4. Poach the ravioli for 8–10 minutes in boiling water, then drain. Place each ravioli in the buttered bread crumbs and coat both sides. For the rösti, cut the apricots into thin slices and caramelize in a pan with clarified butter and confectioners' sugar. Arrange three ravioli with apricot rösti on each plate, and dust with confectioners' sugar.

Quark Strudel with

Preparation time: 30 minutes
Cooking time: 1 hour
Difficulty: ★★

Serves 8

For the strudel dough:
2 cups / 250 g flour
2 tbsp / 30 ml oil
²/₃ cup / 150 ml water
a pinch of salt

For the filling:
6¹/₂ tbsp / 100 g butter, softened
3¹/₂ tbsp / 50 g each confectioners' sugar, sugar
1 tsp vanilla sugar
a pinch of salt
peel and juice of ¹/₂ lemon

4 eggs, separated
1 lb / 440 g quark
1 cup / 250 ml sour cream
¹/₂ cup / 60 g flour

¹/₄ cup / 50 g raisins marinated in 2 tsp / 10 ml rum

For the vanilla sauce:
2 cups / 500 ml milk
2 tbsp / 10 g each powdered cream, vanilla sugar
1 vanilla bean
6 egg yolks
¹/₃ cup / 80 g sugar
4 tsp / 20 ml rum

For the egg milk:
1 cup / 250 ml milk
2 tbsp / 30 g sugar
2 eggs

For dusting:
confectioners' sugar

The word strudel has, since the beginning of the 18th century, described a pastry rolled into a spiral shape. It probably derives from the verb *studan*, which, among other things, means "to wring out a cloth" or "rapidly turn in a circle." The latter refers to the spiraling movement of draining water as it forms a funnel. Perhaps another of its meanings, "to burn with passion," was coined to describe strudel's true fans …

During the 19th century, the citizens of Vienna made Sunday excursions into the Wienerwald, the Viennese forest, where they made a permanent institution of frequenting the cafés and eating strudel. This tradition lives on, and the Sacher Hotel continues to make and serve strudel.

All stages of work in making the strudel can take place the same day. No great instruction is necessary as to how to make the dough, except that rolling it out requires some skill; the dough has to be rolled out thin enough that, on a marble slab, the very veins of the marble can be seen through it.

When preparing the strudel filling, adhere strictly to the recommended ratio of sour cream to quark, and make sure the raisins are thoroughly marinated in rum before use. Once the filling is spread on the dough, roll it up tightly before baking. This is why, although it is wafer-thin, the dough must remain very pliable.

1. To make the strudel dough, knead the flour with the oil, water, and salt using the dough hook of an electric mixer. Shape the dough into a ball, brush its surface with oil and allow it to rest for one hour.

2. For the filling, beat the softened butter with the confectioners' sugar, vanilla sugar, salt, lemon peel, and lemon juice. Gradually add the egg yolks, quark, and sour cream. Beat the egg whites until stiff with the sugar, then fold them into the filling mixture. Finally, blend in the flour and the raisins marinated in rum.

Vanilla Sauce

3. Roll out the dough paper-thin on a floured pastry cloth, spread the filling over half its surface, and use the cloth to roll it up. To make the vanilla sauce, bring the milk, powdered cream, and vanilla bean to a boil in a saucepan. Using a whisk, beat the egg yolks with the sugar and vanilla sugar until foamy. Stir in a little hot milk, pour everything into the saucepan with the milk, and thicken over a gentle heat. Pass through a sieve and add the rum.

4. Prepare the egg milk in the same way: boil the milk, whisk the eggs and sugar together, then combine and thicken. Grease a rectangular baking form with butter, place the strudel in it and bake for 15 minutes at 355 °F / 180 °C. Pour the egg milk over it and bake for another 45 minutes. Finally, dust with confectioners' sugar and serve while still lukewarm with vanilla sauce.

Preparation time: 45 minutes
Cooking time: 45 minutes
Difficulty: ★★★

Serves 8

12 oz / 340 g strawberries
1–2 bananas
4½ tbsp / 100 g raspberry jam
2 cups / 500 ml whipping cream
confectioners' sugar

For the light génoise:
6 eggs
¾ cup / 175 g superfine sugar

1½ cups / 175 g flour
5 tbsp / 75 g butter, melted

For the syrup for soaking:
(see basic recipes)
⅔ cup / 150 ml Grand Marnier
2 cups / 500 ml water
1 cup / 250 g sugar

For the garnish:
roasted hazelnuts, crushed
green marzipan
several glazed whole strawberries

In this torte, strawberries and bananas unite in a combination pleasing both to the eye and the palate. From the outside, it looks mysterious and very enticing, raising curiosity as to what might lay inside.

Whipping cream is used here in two ways – firmly whipped for the filling, and then much more lightly whipped for spreading on the sides of the cake. For the filling, the cream must be whipped longer so that it is very stiff, to give the cake enough firmness to prevent sudden collapse. The cream for spreading, in contrast, is whipped only briefly (it must not become buttery) and crushed, roasted hazelnuts are pressed into it.

The strawberries for the garnish should be medium-sized, very red and fragrant; the Senga sengana variety is particularly suitable. But you can easily substitute other red berries, such as raspberries. In Britain, bananas are not particularly widely used, although the Cavendish variety ubiquitous in the United States is well known. Even so, the elegant combination of strawberries and bananas, further refined by the addition of the incomparable Grand Marnier, is held in high regard.

Southern European flavors also make an appearance in this recipe, if you use marzipan made with Spanish almonds and Italian hazelnuts for the garnish.

1. To make the génoise, beat the eggs and sugar in a double boiler until the mixture is creamy. Fold in the flour and then add the melted butter. Fill a greased cake pan three-quarters full with the sponge cake mixture, and bake for 40 minutes at 375 °F / 190 °C. Turn out the génoise onto a cooling rack to cool. Follow the basic recipe for the syrup for soaking. When the génoise is cold, slice it horizontally into three layers, and soak the bottom layer with syrup.

2. Spread raspberry jam on the soaked génoise. Place a second sponge cake layer on top, soak it with syrup and cover it with a thin layer of stiffly whipped cream. Wash the strawberries; peel the bananas and halve them lengthwise, then cut the long pieces again.

Banana Torte

3. Arrange the sliced banana and strawberries on the whipped cream. Dust the fruit with confectioners' sugar and cover with more whipped cream. Place the third soaked layer of sponge cake on top and press down a little so that the cake holds together firmly.

4. Spread the remaining cream, lightly whipped, on the top and sides of the torte, and press crushed roasted hazelnuts onto the sides. Then place a sheet of green marzipan on the top and garnish the torte with several whole glazed strawberries.

Apple and

Preparation time: 30 minutes
Cooking time: 60 minutes
Difficulty: *

Serves 8

3¹/₄ lbs / 1¹/₂ kg cooking apples (e.g. Bramleys)
12 oz / 350 g blackberries
³/₄ cup, 3 tbsp / 225 g sugar
water

For the pie crust:
1 cup, 2 tbsp / 280 g butter
4 cups / 500 g self-rising flour
1 pinch of salt

2 eggs
3¹/₂ tbsp / 50 g superfine sugar

For the glaze:
milk
superfine sugar

Pies can be either sweet or savory, and their honorable tradition in English and Scottish cooking dates back to the Middle Ages. Among the countless variations, this apple and blackberry pie is merely one classic example of this type of dessert. Michaël Nadell likes using Bramley apples for his, but any good cooking apple can be used. The alternatives that Michaël Nadell suggests include the sweeter, stronger flavored Granny Smiths or Golden Delicious, which also bake well.

While Bramley apples are too acidic to be eaten raw, they are excellent for baking. They are best used in autumn, also the time of year when marvelously juicy blackberries are available. The blackberries definitely complete this recipe and also infuse the apple pieces with a delicate hint of color.

While covering the pie dish with a sheet of pastry is not difficult, this stage of the process does need to be completed without putting the pastry down, so a steady hand is in order. Also, do not forget to make a small opening in the middle of the pie crust, so that the steam produced by the fruits can escape during baking. Take the pie out of the oven a few minutes before serving and allow it to rest and reach the correct consistency. It goes particularly well with crème anglaise, vanilla ice cream or simple whipped cream.

1. To make the pie crust, mix the butter, flour, and salt. Beat the eggs with the sugar. Work both mixtures together to form a smooth pastry. Refrigerate the pastry for one hour.

2. Peel, quarter, and core the apples, and combine with the blackberries. Place in a deep pie pan and sprinkle the fruit with sugar. Then pour in water to one-fourth of the height of the fruit.

Blackberry Pie

3. Roll out the pastry to a thickness of $1/3$ in / 7 mm. Moisten the sides of the pie pan with water and cover the fruit with the sheet of pastry. Press the sides of the pastry down with a knife and make a small hole in the middle.

4. Bake the pie for 45–60 minutes at 375 °F / 190 °C. Remove it from the oven and brush milk on the crust. Sprinkle it with superfine sugar and put the pie back in the oven for another five minutes to glaze the surface.

English

Preparation time: 40 minutes
Cooking time: 6 hours
Difficulty: ☆

Serves 8

1 cup / 125 g flour
2 cups / 160 g white bread, crumbled
$^1/_2$ cup, 2 tbsp / 125 g currants
$^1/_2$ cup, 2 tbsp / 125 g sultanas
1$^1/_4$ cups / 250 g raisins
1 cup / 250 g suet
$^1/_4$ cup / 50 g candied fruits, finely diced
    candied orange and lemon peel
1 pinch of salt
grated peel of 1 lemon
a pinch of nutmeg

1 tbsp 7 g mixed spices (e.g., cinnamon, cloves,
    ginger)
3 tbsp / 25 g almonds, crushed
3 eggs
$^1/_2$ cup / 125 g brown sugar
3$^1/_2$ tbsp / 50 ml cognac
5 tsp / 25 ml Guinness (stout beer)

For the brandy sauce:
1 cup / 250 ml milk
4 egg yolks
6 tbsp / 90 g sugar
4 tsp / 20 ml cognac

The pudding is a genuine, time-honored British institution that has been rapidly adopted by continental European cooks. It has managed, however, to keep its English name. Some orthographic variations were made in France, where the Comtesse de Ségur wrote pouding and probably pronounced it poudingue. There was one unsuccessful attempt to connect the word with the French *boudin* (a type of veal sausage or black pudding) by suggesting that it was originally used to describe a sausage skin filled with meat, a theory supported by virtue of the fact that puddings are cooked in a cloth.

The traditional English make the obligatory Christmas pudding, originally a country recipe, at least two to three months before Christmas. To give the extremely rich pudding a lighter consistency, suet is used instead of butter. This very delicate fat must be mixed in with the other ingredients carefully, without being squashed.

The bread used for the dough should be neither too fresh nor too stale. Yeast bread will not work because of its high proportion of eggs and butter; it is best to use white bread or whole grain bread.

The large quantities of candied fruits and raisins are the hallmark of the pudding, so be generous with them. Some bakers even add plums or carrots. But the secret of the pudding lies in the fact that it is slowly and gently steamed, for the sugar and especially the dried fruits must not have the chance to caramelize. When making the brandy sauce, add the cognac (or rum if you prefer) only at the last moment, so that it does not lose its bouquet.

1. On a large work surface, thoroughly mix the flour, crumbled white bread, currants, sultanas, raisins, chopped suet, candied fruits, salt, grated lemon peel, nutmeg, mixed spice, and crushed almonds.

2. Make a well in the center of this mixture. Pour the beaten eggs, sugar, cognac, and Guinness into the well and combine everything thoroughly to produce a smooth dough.

Christmas Pudding

3. Turn the pudding mixture into a pudding mold that has been greased with butter. Cover with greased paper, place a cloth on top and tie it down around the sides of the mold. Cook the pudding for four hours in a steamer, let cool and refrigerate. Before serving, reheat the pudding by cooking for another two hours in the steamer.

4. To make the brandy sauce, beat the egg yolks and sugar until creamy. Bring the milk to a boil, then pour a quarter of it onto the egg yolks. Pour this mixture into the saucepan with the milk and heat until the sauce thickens enough to coat a wooden spoon; do not let it boil! Pass through a sieve, then stir in the cognac. Keep the sauce warm. Turn the hot pudding out onto a plate, and serve the brandy sauce in a gravy boat.

Preparation time: 1 hour 30 minutes
Cooking time: 45 minutes
Difficulty: ✴✴✴

Serves 8

Strawberry and Banana Torte or Walnut Mazarin
   Torte: (see basic recipes)

sugar paste or marzipan

For the egg white icing:
2 egg whites
1²/₃ cups / 250 g confectioners' sugar
food coloring

For the spun sugar:
4 cups / 1 kg sugar
2 cups / 500 ml water
³/₄ cup / 200 ml glucose syrup
20 drops of tartaric acid
food coloring

Apart from the inevitable, somewhat strenuous ritual of drinking a long series of toasts to the guest of honor during birthday parties while dessert is eaten, there are other ways of expressing congratulations. One example is this delicious birthday cake. Michaël Nadell suggests choosing one of his other recipes, according to taste, such as the Walnut Mazarin Torte or Strawberry and Banana Torte as the basis and then decorating it as shown here.

The sugar paste and sugar rope can be bought ready-made in specialty stores, but it takes some skill to cover the cake with a paper-thin layer of sugar paste. If the egg white icing becomes too firm while you are piping the lettering, soften it again with a little water.

If you decide to make the sugar rope yourself, you will need to knead the sugar paste vigorously, which needs to be very warm, so that two even strands are produced. A pastry chef has specialized equipment to keep the sugar mixture at just the right temperature and consistency while making the sugar roses and ribbons, but they can also be placed on waxed paper in a warm oven.

Styling such a magnificent birthday cake is an excellent way for bakers to show off their capabilities and to give their creativity free reign. Michaël Nadell is proud to have presented this cake to members of Parliament, and even members of the Royal Family, to great acclaim.

1. Use the Strawberry and Banana Torte or Walnut Mazarin Torte as the basis for this cake, and prepare the chosen cake to the stage where it is garnished. Place it on a cake plate ¹/₂ in / 1 cm thick. Roll out the sugar paste ¹/₈ in / 3 mm thick, and carefully cover the cake with it. Trim the excess.

2. To make the sugar rope, evenly twist two strands of sugar paste (or marzipan). The rope must be long enough to reach all the way around the cake.

Cake

3. To make the egg white icing, add the unbeaten egg whites to the confectioners' sugar in a bowl. Stir with a wooden spatula until the mixture is firm, then add a few drops of food coloring. Decorate the cake with the icing using a small paper pastry bag. For the spun sugar, combine the sugar and water in a copper saucepan and bring to a boil, regularly skimming off the foam. Add the glucose syrup.

4. Boil the syrup at 310 °F / 155 °C, add 20 drops of tartaric acid and increase the temperature to 320 °F / 159 °C. Finish by placing the saucepan in ice cold water for one minute. Pour the sugar syrup onto an oiled marble slab and, using a metal spatula, continually fold it from the edge of the mass toward the center until it is firm. Then pull the sugar mass 30 to 40 times, folding back together each time, until it glistens. Color and make roses and ribbons for the garnish.

Macaroons with

Preparation time: 20 minutes
Cooking time: 10 minutes
Difficulty: ★★

Serves 8

For the lemon cream:
4 cups / 1 l heavy cream (48% fat)
5 sheets of gelatin
³/₄ cup, 3 tbsp / 230 g superfine sugar
peel and juice of 3 lemons

For the macaroons:
¹/₂ cup, 3 tbsp / 100 g almonds, very finely ground
2–3 egg whites
1 cup / 250 g sugar

This dessert dates back to the times of Henry VIII, the famous Tudor monarch whose father, Henry VII, came to the throne by defeating Richard III in battle. Toward the end of the 15th century it was discovered, quite accidentally, that lemons stabilized the boiled creams that were eaten in tremendous quantities at the time.

Michaël Nadell, an experienced collector, serves his lemon cream in glasses that date from the beginning of the 18th century; their stems contain hollow glass spirals. To be truly authentic in your presentation of the cream, try to find glassware appropriate for the period. To ensure that what is served in the stemware is equally authentic, use high fat heavy cream (48% fat), because the lemon cream might otherwise curdle. Be careful not to cook it longer than necessary.

Use only best-quality almonds when making the macaroon mixture, such as the slightly bitter and somewhat expensive Spanish Avolas. While it may seem old-fashioned to crush them in the traditional way, with a pestle and mortar, remember that the almonds and sugar need to be very thoroughly mixed; only then will the oil extracted from the almonds satisfactorily flavor the macaroons.

The macaroons should remain soft inside when baking; this can only be checked by taking one out and breaking it open.

1. To make the lemon cream, soak the gelatin in cold water. Bring the heavy cream to a boil, then add the gelatin, sugar, juice of three lemons and the peel of two lemons. Allow to cool. Cut the peel of one lemon into thin strips, blanch twice in water, and set aside.

2. Mix all the ingredients for the macaroons and beat until they form a smooth mixture. Using a pastry bag with a round tip, pipe small mounds, approximately 1¹/₂ in / 3 cm in diameter, onto a sheet lined with baking paper. Press the macaroons flat with a damp cloth and then bake for 15–20 minutes at 320 °F / 160 °C.

Lemon Cream

3. Take the macaroons out of the oven, remove the baking paper and allow them to cool. Quarter most of the macaroons, reserving a few to serve whole.

4. Put the broken macaroon pieces in the glasses and fill them halfway with the cooled lemon cream. Allow to set in the refrigerator for 20 minutes. Then fill the glasses with the remaining cream and refrigerate for another 20 minutes. Garnish with the lemon peel julienne and serve with the whole macaroons.

Walnut Mazarin

Preparation time: 1 hour 45 minutes
Cooking time: 15 minutes
Difficulty: ★★★

Serves 8

chocolate génoise, buttercream: (see basic recipes)

2/3 cup / 100 g walnuts

For the ganache:
1 cup, 2 tbsp / 280 ml milk
3¹/₂ cups / 850 ml crème fraîche (40% fat)
3 lb / 1¹/₃ kg chocolate coating

For the syrup for soaking:
(see basic recipes)
1¹/₄ cups / 300 ml rum
2 cups / 500 g sugar
2 cups / 500 ml water

To garnish:
chocolate
marzipan

This classic pastry is named for the famous Cardinal Mazarin (1602–1661), France's chief minister whose behavior sparked the civil wars known as the Fronde – he apparently enjoyed eating it between coups. There are almost as many different versions of Mazarin Torte as there are Mazarinades (pamphlets against the cardinal) in the Mazarin Library, and just as many variations of its garnish, including candied fruits, almonds, apricot jam, other jams and more. This recipe uses walnuts, which make the cake both rich and particularly aromatic.

Michaël Nadell has a personal avenue of supply, not readily available to others, from which he obtains the walnut paste that lends the buttercream its special flavor, but good walnut compounds are available from specialty stores.

France is famous for its walnuts, and some regions such as Dauphiné or Périgord, whose walnuts are noted for their high calorie and fiber content, are forever competing in this regard. The Briton Michaël Nadell has long been convinced of their delicate aroma and fine flavor, and this recipe is a sincere homage to them.

When applying the final layer of ganache, the temperature should be neither too high nor too low. Apply the layer both rapidly and generously, taking particular care to soak the sponge cake layer sufficiently in syrup beforehand; otherwise it will not remain soft.

1. Prepare the chocolate génoise and the syrup for soaking according to the basic recipes. Spread the sponge mixture ¹/₄ in / 5 mm thick onto a tray lined with baking paper. Bake for eight minutes at 445 °F / 230 °C. To make the ganache, bring the milk to a boil with the crème fraîche. Break the chocolate into small pieces and add it to the hot milk while stirring vigorously. Allow to cool.

2. Make the buttercream. Chop the walnuts finely and add them to the buttercream. Slice the chocolate génoise into four rectangular layers. Place the first layer on a cake round, soak it with rum syrup and coat it with buttercream. Place the second layer on top, soak it, and spread it with ganache. Place the third layer on top, soak it and cover it with buttercream, then place the final layer of génoise on top, soak it thoroughly, and spread the remaining ganache on it.

Torte

3. Melt the chocolate coating and spread it onto the Mazarin Torte. Refrigerate it for 20 minutes, then straighten the edges with a knife dipped into hot water.

4. Make two chocolate leaves and a marzipan walnut, and garnish one corner of the torte with them. Decorate the top with chocolate coating using a tiny pastry bag.

Preparation time: 2 hours 30 minutes
Cooking time: 1 hour 45 minutes
Difficulty: ★★★

Serves 8

ganache, Savoy sponge cake: (see basic recipes)

For the Piedmont sponge cake:
8 egg whites
2 cups / 500 g sugar
1¹/₂ cups / 200 g hazelnuts, very finely ground
3¹/₂ tbsp / 25 g cornstarch

For the syrup for soaking:
(see basic recipes)
1 cup 2¹/₂ tbsp / 280 ml rum

2 cups / 500 g sugar
2 cups / 500 ml water

For the meringue mixture:
4 egg whites
1 cup / 250 g sugar

For the buttercream:
1 cup / 250 g sugar
²/₃ cup / 150 ml water
3 eggs
2 cups / 500 g butter, softened
coffee extract

To garnish:
cocoa powder

Michaël Nadell has dedicated this torte, graciously adorned with a beautiful, generously mounded layer of meringue, to his wife Stella. Special care is required in the presentation and decoration of the cake, and Michaël Nadell acquired the necessary skill during the many years during which he practiced his art in the most renowned London hotels.

The meringue mixture will only succeed if it does not contain the slightest trace of egg yolk (more easily said than done). To make it especially firm, increase the amount of sugar by about a quarter, though this also makes the meringue somewhat heavier.

Because the ganache is spread directly onto the buttercream in the final step of assembly, the torte should be refrigerated

beforehand so that the buttercream is firm before the ganache is applied. This will avoid mixing the two creams, which would not only impair their individual flavors, but would also detract from the impressive visual effect created when the cake is cut, which is particularly important to Michaël Nadell.

This torte is a clear sign that peace reigns in the Nadell household; it can also, however, be considered a symbol of the reconciliation of the neighboring provinces of Savoy and Piedmont, which were enemies for a while. The sponge cake mixtures named after them combine here in sweet harmony, which shows that the art of baking knows neither borders nor prejudices.

1. To make the Piedmont sponge cake, beat the egg whites with half of the sugar until stiff. Sift the remaining sugar with the ground hazelnuts and cornstarch and fold into the beaten egg whites. Pipe two spirals of the sponge cake mixture onto a baking sheet lined with baking paper. Bake for one hour at 300 °F / 150 °C. Prepare the syrup for soaking according to the basic recipe.

2. Follow the basic recipes for the ganache and Savoy sponge cake. Slice the sponge cake into two layers when it has cooled. To make the meringue mixture, beat the egg whites with a quarter of the sugar until stiff, then add the remaining sugar. Draw a circle of the same diameter as the sponge cakes on waxed paper and use a pastry bag to pipe 13 oblongs (as a token of luck) and a large sphere in the middle. Allow to dry in the oven overnight at 150 °F / 65 °C.

Stella

3. To make the buttercream, boil the sugar and water until it is bubbling gently (250 °F / 121 °C). Beat the eggs until they have a zabaglione-like consistency. While stirring vigorously, slowly pour the syrup into the eggs, and continue to whisk until the mixture is completely cold. Add the pieces of softened butter and combine vigorously to achieve a light consistency. Stir in the coffee extract.

4. Assemble the torte: place a Piedmont sponge base on a cake round, and coat it with a thin layer of ganache. Top with a Savoy sponge cake layer, soak it with syrup, and spread with buttercream. Place the second Savoy sponge cake on top, soak it and cover it with ganache. Top with the second Piedmont layer, and spread with buttercream. Refrigerate for about ten minutes. Cover the torte with fluid ganache. Dust the meringue dome with cocoa and place on the torte.

Preparation time: 2 hours
Cooking time: 30 minutes
Difficulty: ✷✷✷

Serves 8

Joconde sponge cake, choux pastry:
(see basic recipes)

For the stencil mixture:
3¹/₂ tbsp / 50 g butter
¹/₃ cup / 50 g confectioners' sugar
2 egg whites
6¹/₂ tbsp / 50 g flour
¹/₂ oz / 12 g coffee extract

For the rum cream:
¹/₂ cup / 130 ml rum

2¹/₂ sheets of gelatin
5 tbsp / 70 g sugar
1¹/₂ cups / 350 ml whipping cream

For the coffee jelly:
2 cups / 500 ml sugar syrup (18 °Beaumé)
1 tbsp coffee extract
2¹/₂ sheets of gelatin

For the cappuccino mousse:
2 tbsp / 8 g instant coffee
4 tsp / 8 g dried milk
¹/₂ cup, 3 tbsp / 160 ml sugar syrup (18 °Beaumé)
¹/₂ cup, 1 tbsp / 140 g superfine sugar
15 sheets of gelatin
2 tbsp / 30 ml condensed milk
3²/₃ cups / 900 ml crème fraîche

Michaël Nadell is not particularly fond of tea, which is astonishing for an Englishman, and he likes strong coffee even less, for in his opinion it has too great an effect on the nervous system. For that reason he uses neither the fine Arabica highland coffee nor the simpler Robusta coffee in this recipe, instead using instant coffee to flavor the cappuccino mousse.

Michaël Nadell prefers mild and aromatic cappuccino, and he wanted this mousse to share its distinctive qualities. He was inspired to develop this recipe by the traditional jellies, or gelatin desserts, which have been made in England since the Middle Ages. Indeed, any discussion of English baking would seem incomplete without them.

The Joconde sponge cake must, as usual, be baked for just a short time in a hot oven so that it remains moist inside and soft overall. Once the layer of filled cream puffs and mousse has been applied, the dessert has to be refrigerated for a while so that it becomes firm and the cream puffs cannot move when you continue the assembly. Due to its high gelatin content, the mousse must be applied while it is still warm and pliable.

However, the mousse must have cooled completely before it is covered with the coffee jelly. Michaël Nadell even recommends freezing the mousse, taking it out of the freezer to glaze it, and then leaving it to defrost for four hours at room temperature before serving.

1. For the stencil mixture, cream the butter and confectioners' sugar. Add the egg whites one by one and finally fold in the flour with the coffee extract. Spread a very thin layer of the mixture onto waxed paper. Using a cake comb, draw a pattern of parallel stripes through the batter. Place in the freezer. To make the rum cream, heat the rum, dissolve the gelatin and sugar in it, then pass it through a sieve. When it is cool, fold in the stiffly whipped cream.

2. Prepare the Joconde sponge cake and choux pastry according to the basic recipes. Take the sheet with the stencil mixture out of the freezer and spread the Joconde sponge cake mixture onto it. Bake for ten minutes at 390 °F / 200 °C and allow to cool. Fill a pastry bag with the choux pastry and, using a wide round tip, pipe large cream puffs onto a baking sheet. Bake for 20 minutes at 355 °F / 180 °C. Fill the cream puffs with rum cream.

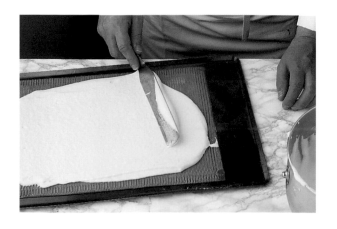

Cappuccino

3. To make the coffee jelly, bring the sugar syrup to a boil and add the coffee extract. Remove from the heat and add the gelatin. For the cappuccino mousse, dissolve the instant coffee and dried milk in the hot sugar syrup. Add the sugar and bring to a boil. Blend in the soaked gelatin and condensed milk and pass through a sieve. Beat the crème fraîche separately, then fold it in. Prepare the mousse immediately before assembling the dessert.

4. Line a high cake ring with waxed paper and then with a strip of Joconde sponge cake half as wide as the ring. Place a round Joconde sponge base inside, and cover it with a 1 in / 2 cm-thick layer of mousse. Place the cream puffs on top, one in the middle and the others in a ring around it. Fill the ring completely with mousse and refrigerate for four hours. Glaze the top with the coffee jelly and garnish with chocolate coffee beans.

Preparation time: 45 minutes
Cooking time: 50 minutes
Difficulty: ✷✷

Serves 8

4¹/₂ tbsp / 100 g apricot jam
4¹/₂ tbsp / 100 g raspberry jam
3 cups / 225 g fresh white bread, crumbled
grated peel of 2 lemons

For the custard mixture:
2 cups / 500 ml milk
2 cups / 500 ml crème fraîche (40% fat)
2 eggs

8 egg yolks
³/₄ cup / 175 g superfine sugar

For the red currant sauce:
3 cups / 500 g red currants
2 tbsp / 50 g red currant jelly
6¹/₂ tbsp / 100 g sugar

For the Swiss meringue:
8 egg whites
3¹/₃ cups / 500 g confectioners' sugar
lemon juice

Given that this pudding has been raised to a royal rank, should it perhaps be addressed as "Your Highness"? There is no provision for this in any of the books on etiquette. One can, however, easily imagine the types of engravings that Hogarth, for instance, might have made of this royal pudding's court: the Christmas Pudding would appear as the court chaplain, and a cluster of smaller plum puddings dressed as pages would take in the air in the arbors.

The meringue lattice should be dominated by shades of red, and the prettiest effect is achieved by using a combination of apricot and raspberry jam. As long as you use ripe and fleshy fruits and the correct quantity of sugar, it should not be difficult to achieve the desired shades.

In addition, this queen of puddings distinguishes itself by means of its lightness, for in contrast to the majority of its subjects, it contains no suet. It is also cooked in a double boiler instead of a steamer, lending it a different consistency.

Finally, the distinctive features of the Swiss meringue mixture deserve mention: it does not become hard immediately, and takes on a very pleasing color when baked in the oven. This all complements the custard nicely, which should only be heated gently so that it becomes creamy and aromatic.

1. To make the custard, bring the milk to a boil with the crème fraîche. Beat the eggs and egg yolks with the sugar until foamy. Add the hot milk and crème fraîche and pass through a sieve. Combine the bread crumbs with the grated lemon peel. For the red currant sauce, bring all the ingredients to a boil together until the mixture is creamy, pass through a sieve and allow to cool slightly.

2. Place the breadcrumbs in an ovenproof dish, and pour the egg and milk mixture over them. Allow to rest for ten minutes, then poach in a water bath in the oven for 30–40 minutes at 320 °F / 160 °C. Remove the custard from the oven as soon as it has set.

Puddings

3. Beat all the ingredients for the Swiss meringue in a round bowl in a double boiler until the mixture is nice and firm. Using a pastry bag with a star-shaped tip, pipe the meringue lattice and border decoration.

4. Bake the custard at 445 °F / 230 °C until the meringue has turned slightly golden-brown. Allow to cool. Then carefully fill the spaces between the meringue lattice alternately with apricot and raspberry jam. Serve the pudding with the red currant sauce.

Preparation time: 30 minutes
Cooking time: 2 hours 30 minutes
Difficulty: ★★

Serves 8

For the suet pastry:
4 cups / 500 g self-rising flour
1 tbsp / 15 g baking powder
3¹/₂ tbsp / 50 g sugar
1 cup / 250 g suet (or vegetable fat), chopped
1 cup, 2 tbsp / 280 ml water
1 pinch of salt

For the créme anglaise with honey:
2 cups / 500 ml milk
6 egg yolks
¹/₂ cup / 175 g honey

For the filling:
1 large lemon with a thin peel
1 cup, 2 tbsp / 280 g brown sugar
1 cup, 2 tbsp / 280 g butter

This dessert is not at all custard-like, but is a pudding in the British sense of the word, meaning sweet dishes in general. This recipe is a specialty of the county of Sussex to the south of London, and contains ingredients that were once imported via the port of Newhaven. It bears the promising name of Pond Pudding because of the liquid butter that pours out of the pudding when it is cut open. But this dessert is special mainly because of the contrast between the tart lemon and the sweet honey, which Michaël Nadell uses to very good effect here.

It is important that the pastry be made with suet, rather than other, heavier shortenings. This tender fat, which must not be crushed when used, is cut into small pieces that are rolled in the flour. If suet is not available, it can be replaced by a vegetable fat, but the resulting dough will have a heavier texture. Suet

plays an important role in English baking and there are many delicious sweets that would not be the same without it.

The lemon should be bright yellow and have a very thin peel (such as some of the Italian varieties, such as Primafiori and Feminello); it is pricked several times with a fork and placed in the center of the pudding. As it is cooked, the lemon's juice and flavor seeps out of the holes and combines with the brown sugar and butter to produce a delicious syrup.

The reverse also happens: the fat and sugar from the pastry slowly enter the lemon through the holes in the peel. This effect is particularly successful if the suet and flour have been very thoroughly combined. For suet causes the pastry to rise and press gently, but effectively, against the lemon.

1. To prepare the pastry, combine all the ingredients for the pastry, with the exception of the water, on a flat, smooth work surface. Make a well in the middle, slowly pour the water into the well, and knead everything to form a smooth dough.

2. Roll out three-quarters of the dough and line a pudding form with it. For the crème anglaise with honey, beat the egg yolks and honey until creamy. Bring the milk to a boil, and pour it onto the egg and honey mixture. Return to the heat and cook until the cream thickens, stirring continuously, but do not allow it to boil.

Pudding

3. Fill the form halfway with the butter, cut into small pieces, and the brown sugar. Prick the lemon several times with a fork and, leaving it whole, place it on the butter and brown sugar. Fill the form with the remaining butter and sugar.

4. Roll out the remaining pastry into a circle and cover the form with it, allowing the pastry to extend a little at the sides. Cover with buttered baking paper, tie a cloth around the form, and cook the pudding for 2¹/₂ hours in a steamer. Serve hot accompanied by crème anglaise with honey.

Preparation time: 1 hour
Cooking time: 20 minutes
Difficulty: ✲✲

Serves 12

striped Joconde sponge cake: (see basic recipes)

For the milk chocolate ganache:
1 lb / 500 g milk chocolate
¹/₂ cup / 125 ml unsweetened condensed milk

For the Duchess sponge cake:
9 eggs
3 egg yolks
1 cup / 250 g sugar
2 cups / 250 g flour
3¹/₂ tbsp / 50 g butter

For the sweet chestnut cream:
4¹/₂ oz / 125 g canned glazed sweet chestnuts
2 tsp / 10 ml brown rum
1 cup / 250 ml crème frâiche

For the rum syrup:
(see basic recipes)
³/₄ cup / 200 ml water
6¹/₂ tbsp / 100 g sugar
²/₃ cup / 150 ml rum

To garnish:
phyllo pastry
glazed sweet chestnuts

The use of glazed sweet chestnuts has long been tradition in Belgian pastry-making, and the Nihoul family has close to 100 years of experience in this field. Christian Nihoul's grandfather created *Dijonnaises*, a meringue garnished with whipped cream and chopped sweet chestnuts. The *Merveilleux* (French for "marvel") is another Belgian variation of this delicacy that includes chocolate cream. Whichever he is making, Christian Nihoul always chooses his basic ingredients with the greatest of care.

In just the last few generations, a fundamental change has taken place. Rather than preparing each element of their recipes themselves, pastry chefs can now buy their ground nuts, fondant, nougat, marzipan, and so forth from wholesalers;

however, their standards for quality remain as strict as always. The chopped sweet chestnuts, even if they do not look particularly promising, must likewise be first class.

A puree of glazed sweet chestnuts, combined with a dash of brown rum and unsweetened whipped cream, form an ideal topping for this torte, without any need for additional sugar.

For the ganache, choose a chocolate with a high milk content and very little sugar, such as that made by Belgian manufacturers. The Sweet Chestnut Torte is a very rich dessert, and is particularly popular during the cold winter months. Christian Nihoul tells us that it has also been a favorite in the Japanese branches of his *pâtisserie* for several years.

1. Make the ganache a day in advance by melting the chocolate, bringing the condensed milk to a boil and stirring it into the chocolate. Refrigerate until needed. To prepare the sponge cake, beat the eggs, egg yolks, and sugar with a mixer over low heat. Remove from heat and beat until cooled. Use a skimmer to add the sifted flour and warm melted butter. Pipe the sponge cake mixture onto a baking sheet and bake for 20 minutes at 355 °F / 180 °C.

2. To make the sweet chestnut cream, puree a can of chopped sweet chestnuts, including the syrup, in a blender and stir in the rum. Refrigerate. Whip the cream until stiff and fold it into the sweet chestnut puree. Make the rum syrup according to the basic recipe.

Chestnut Torte

3. Cut the sponge cake into three layers with the same diameter as a cake ring. Fill the ring with alternating layers of sponge cake (each soaked with rum syrup) and sweet chestnut mousse. Refrigerate the torte for 24 hours. Warm the ganache in a double boiler and use it to evenly coat the top and sides of the torte.

4. Place a strip of striped Joconde sponge cake around the outside of the torte. Cut chestnut leaves out of the phyllo pastry and brown them in the oven. Garnish the cake with the chestnut leaves and a few whole glazed sweet chestnuts.

Preparation time:	1 hour
Cooking time:	20 minutes
Difficulty:	★★

Serves 12

For the Montmorency sponge cake:
12 oz / 375 g marzipan
4 eggs
¹/₃ cup / 40 g flour
8 egg whites
8 tsp / 40 g sugar
8 tsp / 40 g butter, melted

For the pastry cream:
2 cups / 500 ml milk

¹/₄ cup / 60 g sugar
5 egg yolks
¹/₃ cup / 40 g cornstarch

For the coffee cream:
2 sheets of gelatin
2 cups / 500 ml cream, stiffly whipped
2 cups / 500 ml pastry cream
3¹/₂ tbsp / 50 ml coffee extract

To garnish:
white chocolate
milk chocolate
cocoa

There are many legends concerning the origins of coffee, one being that it was a gift from the ancient gods to the pitiable mortals. A similar legend originates in Yemen, where trade flourishes between the small harbor town of Mocha and Ethiopian coffee farmers – those in the small kingdom of Kaffa, to be more precise, from whose name the word "coffee" is thought to be derived.

Of the hundreds of species of coffee plants, Arabica and Robusta are the two varieties of beans most widely available on the market. Robusta is a hearty variety with a straightforward flavor, while the more sensitive Arabica grows at higher altitudes and yields coffee with more subtle nuances of flavor.

When making the pastry cream, omit the vanilla bean that would ordinarily be used, for its flavor would clash with that of the coffee. For this recipe, Christian Nihoul recommends using the high-quality Trablit coffee extract, which gives the pastry cream an exquisitely intense flavor. Some brave souls may prefer to make the coffee extract themselves. To do so, pour boiling coffee, complete with the coffee grounds, onto melted sugar. Be aware that the gases and steam released in the process will send glowing particles shooting in all directions! If you are not particularly enamored of volcanoes, you will probably prefer to stick to the more peaceful Trablit.

Use particular care when preparing the Montmorency sponge cake. Do not expect to find the cherries of the same name in it; the sponge cake's name derives from the Duke of Montmorency-Laval, foreign minister to King Louis XVIII.

1. To make the Montmorency sponge cake, beat the marzipan and whole eggs until smooth, then fold in the flour. Whip the egg whites and sugar until stiff, fold them into the marzipan mixture and finally blend in the warm melted butter. Spread the mixture onto a baking sheet and bake at 355 °F / 180 °C. When the sponge cake has cooled, cut out three round layers with the same diameter as a cake ring.

2. For the pastry cream, bring the milk to a boil with some of the sugar. Beat the egg yolks with the remaining sugar until they are creamy and white, then add the cornstarch. Stir a little hot milk into the egg yolks, pour the mixture into the pan with the milk, and return to a boil. Allow to cool. For the coffee cream, add the soaked gelatin together with the stiffly whipped, sweetened cream to 2 cups / 500 ml of the pastry cream. Flavor with coffee extract.

Cream Torte

3. To assemble the torte, using a cake ring if desired, alternate layers of Montmorency sponge cake and coffee cream, using a pastry bag to pipe the cream onto the sponge cake. Refrigerate.

4. Use white chocolate and milk chocolate to form a striped band, and place this around the torte. Form milk and white chocolate rolls and garnish the cake with them. Dust the top with cocoa.

Preparation time: 30 minutes
Cooking time: 15 minutes
Difficulty: ☆

Serves 10 to 12

For the pistachio mixture:
1 cup / 125 g pistachios
½ cup / 125 g sugar

For the cake batter:
pistachio mixture
6 egg whites
1¼ cups / 210 g confectioners' sugar
½ cup plus 3 tbsp / 85 g flour
1 cup / 250 g butter

Since Californian almonds are the ones most frequently used in baking, Christian Nihoul was taken by surprise when, during a festival in the United States, he was unable to gather enough to put together an almond mixture. Understandably in despair, he finally turned necessity into virtue and substituted pistachios that were ground almost as finely as sugar. The resulting recipe makes it fair to say that the journey was worth it on that account alone!

Small Flexipan tins are ideal for baking these cakes (also ideal for rum babas or little quiches). If no Flexipan tins are available, the cake batter can just as easily be poured into miniature muffin pans or carefully buttered individual forms, but keep a careful eye on them during baking.

To prevent the egg white from sticking, prepare the batter in a copper bowl and make sure it experiences even heat, best achieved over an electric source. The cakes should rise by a third when baked and resemble mushrooms about to open. After baking, place the Flexipan tins in the refrigerator and let the cakes cool completely before removing them. If you use metal tins, however, you will need to turn the cakes out onto a cooling rack immediately after baking.

The cakes are best served with coffee, or perhaps a glass of sweet wine such as a Sauternes or Monbazillac. True connoisseurs will take advantage of the opportunity to drink a nice amber, ten-year-old tawny port.

1. Combine the pistachios and sugar in the bowl of a food processor and grind them until the pistachios are very fine.

2. To make the batter, combine the pistachio mixture with the confectioners' sugar and egg whites in a copper bowl. Heat the mixture gently and evenly while stirring constantly until it binds. Remove from the heat. Heat the butter until it turns a golden color. Stir the melted butter and flour into the pistachio mixture.

Pistachio Cakes

3. Fill Flexipan tins or muffin pans four-fifths full with the batter. Bake for 10–15 minutes at 355 °F / 180 °C, then reduce the temperature to 300 °F / 150 °C and continue baking until done.

4. Take the cakes out of the oven, allow them to cool and turn out onto a plate or cooling rack.

Brussels Waffles

Preparation time: 1 hour
Cooking time: 7–10 minutes
Difficulty: ✶

Makes 40

1²/₃ cups / 400 ml water
2³/₄ cups / 675 ml milk
3²/₃ cups / 900 ml Leffe (Belgian beer)
5¹/₂ cups / 675 g flour

6 cups / 350 g sponge cake crumbs
1³/₄ oz / 50 g fresh yeast
2 cups plus 3 tbsp / 540 g butter
2 tsp / 10 g vanilla sugar
8 eggs

For dusting:
confectioners' sugar

In the original version of the *Tintin and Snowy* comics wildly popular in the 1930s and 1940s, Captain Haddock insults his opponent by calling him a *moules à gaufres* (waffle iron), an indication of the Belgian origins of Georges Rémi, better known as Hergé, the spiritual father of the comic book heroes. Every town in Belgium has its own recipe for waffles. In Liège, for example, they are made out of a kind of bread dough sweetened with cane sugar, while the waffles in Brussels are finer and lighter. Throughout winter, the baking (and eating) of waffles is almost a Belgian national pastime.

The addition of beer causes the mixture to rise when baked, preventing its collapse in the waffle iron, which should not be pressed together too firmly in any case. Ideally, the batter should completely fill the waffle iron, and the waffles will be easy to remove after baking. Waffle irons are easy to clean with water to which a little cornstarch has been added.

Freshly baked waffles should always be light and crunchy, since contact with the hot waffle iron dries out the moist ingredients in the mixture. Soft waffles have not been allowed to bake through completely.

Beer is another national passion in Belgium: the Belgians consume an average of 28.5 gallons / 108 liters of beer per capita each year, more than in any other European country, and nearly a thousand different beers are brewed in Belgium. Any number of them would be an excellent addition to this waffle batter, though Christian Nihoul prefers to use the beer brewed in the Leffe monastery for this recipe.

1. Dissolve the yeast in some of the water and milk, slightly warmed. In a mixing bowl, combine the yeast mixture with the other ingredients, adding the melted butter last. Stir until a smooth batter has been produced. Refrigerate the mixture for one hour.

2. Preheat the waffle iron. Use a pastry brush to carefully brush butter onto its entire surface.

à la Leffe

3. Use a ladle to pour the waffle batter onto one half of the waffle iron. Close the waffle iron, turn it over, and bake the waffles for 6–7 minutes.

4. Take the waffles out of the waffle iron and dust them with confectioners' sugar. Serve hot and crunchy with tea, coffee or hot chocolate. Serve with cream or (best in summer) fresh strawberry jam.

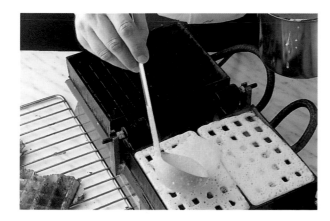

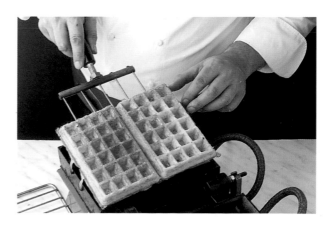

Buttercream Sponge

Preparation time: 45 minutes
Cooking time: 30 minutes
Difficulty: ★★

Serves 12

For the sponge cake:
8 egg whites
6¹/₂ tbsp / 100 g superfine sugar
6¹/₂ tbsp / 50 g flour

For the buttercream:
³/₄ cup / 175 ml water
1 cup plus 7 tbsp / 350 g superfine sugar
¹/₂ vanilla bean
5 egg yolks
1¹/₂ cups / 375 g butter

Almond and sugar mixture:
1 cup plus 2 tbsp / 275 g sugar
1¹/₂ cups / 275 g finely ground almonds

To garnish:
confectioners' sugar
cocoa powder

Because it needs to be prepared well in advance, the time it takes to prepare *le Misérable* (the French name for this pastry) is almost as long as the Victor Hugo novel after which it is named. Traditionally one began working on Wednesday if this cake, based on the simple idea of cleanly separating egg whites from egg yolks, was to grace the dessert table on Sunday. The sponge cake and cream were prepared on Wednesday, the cake was assembled on Thursday, and then refrigerated for 48 hours. The final touches were added to it on Saturday, and the fruits of those efforts enjoyed on Sunday.

In spite of its name, which means "the miserable one," *le Misérable* is quite rich, consisting primarily of finely ground,

highly nutritious almonds. Here, the almond and sugar mixture is made up of equal parts (by weight) almonds and sugar; to prevent it from turning into marzipan, make sure that the powdery consistency is retained if you decide to grind the almonds yourself. The same applies if you use a ready-made mixture.

The butter cream (more precisely, a sugar syrup cream) should be just slightly flavored with vanilla, so that its taste remains light. The vanilla bean can be used afterward to make vanilla sugar by drying it and storing it in a jar full of sugar. Serve the pastry well-chilled, for its flavor is lessened if allowed to reach room temperature.

1. For the sponge cake, beat the egg whites and sugar until stiff. Thoroughly combine the flour and the almond and sugar mixture. Use a wooden spatula to fold the dry ingredients into the meringue. Spread the mixture onto a tray lined with baking paper and bake for 30 minutes at 230 °F / 110 °C. Remove from the oven and place on a cooling rack in a cool, humid spot.

2. To make the buttercream, bring the water to a boil with the sugar and the vanilla bean, which has been slit open. Beat the egg yolks in a copper bowl until they are creamy and white. Once the syrup is boiling, remove the vanilla bean, scrape out the pulp and add it to the syrup. Pour the syrup onto the egg yolks while stirring vigorously, and heat until the mixture thickens. Refrigerate.

Cake Slices

3. Knead the butter until it is soft and combine with the syrup and egg yolk mixture; refrigerate the cream. Remove the baking paper from the sponge cake and cut it horizontally into two equally thick layers.

4. Spread a generous layer of buttercream onto one sponge cake base. Place the second layer of sponge cake on top and press down. Refrigerate for 24 to 48 hours. Using a knife dipped in hot water, straighten the edges. Dust with confectioners' sugar before serving.

Wedding Cake

Preparation time: 1 hour
Cooking time: 20 minutes
Difficulty: ★★

Serves 12

For the sponge cake:
3¹/₂ oz / 100 g marzipan
9 eggs
5 egg yolks
1 cup / 250 g sugar
2¹/₂ cups / 315 g flour
6¹/₂ tbsp / 100 g butter, melted

For the syrup for soaking:
(see basic recipes)
6¹/₂ tbsp / 100 g sugar

³/₄ cup / 200 ml water
²/₃ cup / 150 ml Cointreau

For the filling:
whipping cream

For the buttercream:
3 cups / 750 kg butter
1 lb 9 oz / 750 g Italian meringue (see basic recipes)

To garnish:
fresh fruit (pineapple, raspberries, strawberries,
   grapes)
confectioners' sugar

Goodwill alone is not enough here; acquaintance with two people determined to say "I do" is vital to the successful presentation of this cake. Although the statistics might lead one to think otherwise, this particular species is far from extinct.

Christian Nihoul assures us that this wedding cake is as easy to make as any cream-filled sponge cake. The purpose of the cream decoration is to conceal what lies beneath it, and the artistic pattern created with the aid of a pastry bag gives it an extraordinary look befitting such an important occasion. Bakers generally use fondant glazes or very smooth coatings of white marzipan to give wedding cakes their immaculate, virgin-white appearance, but Christian Nihoul has found an

alternative considerably lower in sugar, not to mention much easier to cut. A wedding cake is usually not cut until toward the end of the wedding meal, by the bride and groom themselves, and the general commotion makes it a challenge to concentrate on the task. If you like, add further decorations to the cake, perhaps a pair of turtle doves out of porcelain or sponge cake.

Many variations are possible with the syrup used for soaking the sponge cake layers, as long as the flavor of the syrup and the fruits used to garnish the finished cake complement each other. Possibilities include kirsch and red berries, Grand Marnier and oranges, or even pieces of pineapple, banana, or other exotic fruits.

1. To make the sponge cake, beat the marzipan, eggs, egg yolks, and sugar over an electric source of heat until smooth. Stir in the flour and melted butter. Spread on a baking sheet and bake for 20 minutes at 340 °F / 170 °C. When the sponge cake is cool, cut out three round layers with the diameter of the cake ring. Prepare the syrup according to the basic recipe. Place one of the layers in the cake ring, soak it with Cointreau syrup, spread it with whipped cream and garnish with fresh fruit.

2. Place the second sponge cake layer on top, drench it with the syrup, spread it with whipped cream and arrange fresh fruit on it, then cover with the third sponge cake layer. Prepare the Italian meringue according to the basic recipe.

with Fresh Fruits

3. To make the buttercream, cream the butter for several minutes until it is light and fluffy, then combine it with an equal amount of Italian meringue. Spread some of this in a dome shape on the cake.

4. Fill a pastry bag with the remaining buttercream and, using a flat, waved tip, pipe a lattice pattern onto the cake. Garnish with fresh fruit before presenting.

Preparation time: 1 hour
Cooking time: 30 minutes
Difficulty: ★★★

Serves 12

striped Joconde sponge cake, Italian meringue:
 (see basic recipes)

For the marzipan sponge cake:
12¹/₂ oz / 360 g marzipan
4 eggs
8 egg whites
8 tsp / 40 g sugar
¹/₃ cup / 40 g flour
8 tsp / 40 g butter, melted

For the hazelnut cream:
3¹/₂ oz / 100 g hazelnut paste
3¹/₂ oz / 100 g Italian meringue
3 sheets of gelatin
³/₄ cup / 200 ml cream

For the glaze:
coffee extract
cake glaze

Ever since 1896, the Nihoul family has been making its own praline pastes for a variety of cakes, tortes, and pastries. They begin by roasting almonds, hazelnuts or a combination thereof with a vanilla bean, and then add an equal part of confectioners' sugar and press the mixture through a mill with marble rollers. The intensely flavored paste made in this way, in this case with hazelnuts, gives this *Piémontais* torte a delicious flavor. The cake owes its name to hazelnuts from the Piemont region in northwestern Italy, which, due to their exceptional quality, are ideal for making praline.

Exquisite hazelnut paste is not always easy to find. The best solution, then, is to make it yourself in a food processor, using blanched hazelnuts that have been roasted in the oven.

Since every household has a refrigerator, it is no problem to try out recipes like this one. And if the preparation of the torte is spread out over three days, it need not be a daunting task. You can make the sponge cake on the first day, the creams for the filling on the second, and assemble the torte on the third. After each stage of the work, refrigerate it overnight.

To reward yourself after such a display of patience, try a glass of well-chilled wine – perhaps a golden dessert wine, or even the famous sherry-like *Vin jaune* (yellow wine) from the French Jura, which is sold in a clavelin, its own uniquely-shaped bottle.

1. To make the sponge cake, beat the marzipan and eggs until smooth. Whisk the egg whites and sugar until stiff. Fold the beaten egg whites together with the flour into the marzipan mixture, then add the melted butter. Turn the mixture into a greased cake pan and bake. Prepare the striped Joconde sponge cake according to the basic recipe. When it has cooled, cut a strip and line a cake ring with it.

2. Follow the basic recipe for the Italian meringue. To make the hazelnut cream, carefully blend the hazelnut paste into the Italian meringue. Then add the gelatin, which has been dissolved in a little water, and carefully fold in the stiffly whipped cream.

Cream Torte

3. Slice the marzipan sponge cake through once horizontally to make two layers. Place one layer in the cake ring, spread it with hazelnut cream, and place the second sponge cake layer on top. Fill the cake ring completely with the remaining cream. Freeze.

4. Take the dessert from the cake ring and use a pastry brush to carefully cover its entire surface with coffee extract. Cover the torte with cake glaze and garnish with a chocolate roll.

Preparation time: 45 minutes
Cooking time: 3 hours
Difficulty: ★★

Serves 8 to 10

Vanilla ice cream: (see basic recipes)

For the meringue:
16 egg whites
4 cups / 1 kg sugar
$^1/_2$ cup / 125 ml water

To garnish:
whipped cream
fresh berries (raspberries, blueberries, blackberries and cherries)
crushed pistachios
roasted flaked almonds
mint leaves

Now that most households boast freezers, we can eat whatever our hearts desire at any time of year. Things were not so convenient for Christian Nihoul's grandfather, the inventor of this recipe. He never regretted his efforts in creating this uncomplicated but irresistible ice cream cake in spite of the drama required to obtain enough fresh red berries to make it. The rapid methods of transport needed to make this possible were prohibitively expensive.

Nowadays, there is no need to go for a walk in the woods to find an assortment of delectable fresh berries – raspberries, wild strawberries, blackberries, blueberries, red currants and black currants are all wonderful selections – for decorating this cake. If you like, use berries to give the vanilla ice cream, which is already flavored with chopped mint, an even more refreshing touch.

For the meringue mixture, use egg whites that have been gathered and refrigerated together or frozen in a plastic container. Bake the meringue mixture very slowly, ideally in a convection oven, to dry the egg whites rather than bake them. This allows the meringue to be firm and crispy outside but still soft on the inside. If it is overbaked, the meringue becomes brittle inside. When baked properly, the meringue separates from the baking paper by itself, and it will keep for quite a while in a metal tin.

1. To make the meringue, beat the egg whites with a quarter of the sugar in a mixer until stiff. Heat the remaining sugar and the water to 250 °F / 121 °C, and slowly pour this syrup onto the egg whites, beating continuously until cooled.

2. Using a pastry bag, pipe a meringue base and three equally large rings of meringue onto a tray lined with baking paper. Bake for two hours at 300 °F / 150 °C. Make the vanilla ice cream according to the basic recipe.

Berries Cake

3. Place the meringue rings on top of each other on the meringue base, spread meringue mixture onto them and garnish with chopped pistachios and roasted flaked almonds. Dry briefly in the oven.

4. Fill the assembled meringue ring with vanilla ice cream, which has been flavored with fresh chopped mint, and fruit, if desired. Garnish the cake with whipped cream and fresh, perfect fruits and berries.

Preparation time: 1 hour 30 minutes
Cooking time: 15–20 minutes
Difficulty: ★★

Serves 12

For the chocolate sponge cake:
5 eggs
1 egg yolk
$^1/_2$ cup plus 1 tbsp / 135 g sugar
$^3/_4$ cup / 90 g flour
$^1/_3$ cup / 40 g cornstarch
$3^1/_2$ tbsp / 25 g cocoa powder

For the basic cream:
$^1/_2$ cup / 125 g sugar
5 tsp / 25 ml water
5 egg yolks

For the chocolate mousse:
$4^1/_2$ oz / 125 g chocolate coating, very bitter
2 oz / 60 g basic cream
2 sheets of gelatin
2 cups / 500 ml whipping cream
10 egg whites
$3^1/_2$ tbsp / 50 g sugar

For the ganache coating:
1 lb / 500 g bittersweet chocolate
$1^1/_2$ cups / 350 ml unsweetened condensed milk

To garnish:
chocolate wafers and truffles

Christian Nihoul introduced this recipe at Expo '92 in Seville, aiming it at fans dedicated to extra-bitter chocolate – not sour, but with a flavor definitely more intense than regular bitter-sweet chocolate. The chocolate used for this cake produces a long, intense aftertaste. It should be used fresh and not melted until just before it is used. Christian Nihoul cautions us to heat it gradually and carefully; it does not tolerate sudden changes of temperature. A night in an electric oven at 100–120 °F / 40–50 °C will give it the right consistency.

Some of chocolate's ingredients react in different ways to changes in temperature. As is sometimes the case with the

chocolate sauce for the classic poire Hélène dessert, too-rapid heating can cause it to separate into its original components.

To simplify the preparation of the Seville Torte, make the sponge cake and ganache a day in advance, and refrigerate them separately. Wait until the last possible minute to coat the torte with the ganache.

Using condensed milk in the ganache makes it softer and much shinier than that made in the usual way, and thus perfectly suited for use as a chocolate coating or glaze.

1. Prepare the chocolate sponge cake by beating the egg yolks and eggs in a copper bowl until the mixture falls from the spoon in long ribbons. Sift the flour with the cornstarch and cocoa, and use a wooden spatula to fold it into the eggs. Pour the mixture into a greased and floured springform pan $1^1/_2$ in / 3 cm high. Bake for 15–20 minutes at 355 °F / 180 °C.

2. To make the basic cream, proceed as for an Italian meringue. While the sugar and water are heating to 250 °F / 121 °C, beat the egg yolks in a food processor until they are creamy and white. Beating at low speed, slowly pour the hot sugar syrup onto the egg yolks. Stir continuously until the mixture has cooled completely. Measure 2 oz / 60 g of the cream for use in the chocolate mousse.

Torte

3. For the chocolate mousse, melt the chocolate coating and combine it with the basic cream. Soak the gelatin in cold water, drain, dissolve and add it to the chocolate cream. Whip the cream until stiff, and beat the egg whites and sugar until stiff. Carefully blend the three mixtures. To make the ganache, melt the chocolate and, in a separate pan, bring the condensed milk to a boil. Combine the two, cool, and put in the freezer until needed.

4. Place a ¹/₂ in / 1 cm-thick layer of chocolate sponge cake inside a cake ring and coat it with chocolate mousse. Place a second sponge cake layer, soaked with a little sugar syrup, on top and fill the ring with the remaining mousse. Allow to set in the refrigerator. Heat the cake ring briefly to release the torte, and refrigerate it. Warm the ganache in a double boiler and cover the torte with it. Garnish with chocolate wafers and truffles.

Spekulatius

Preparation time: 30 minutes
Cooking time: 30 minutes
Difficulty: ★★

Serves 8

2 cups / 500 g butter
3 cups / 750 g brown cane sugar
1 cup / 250 g white cane sugar
¹/₂ cup / 125 ml milk
2 eggs
8 cups / 1 kg flour
3¹/₂ tbsp / 25 g cinnamon
1 tbsp / 7 g spices (nutmeg, cloves, allspice, coriander)
2 tbsp plus 1 tsp / 30 g baking powder
1 pinch of salt

While the people of Brussels are convinced that *spekulatius* are a Brussels specialty, its origins are disputed. The term *spéculoos* (or its variation *spéculos*), which first appeared early in the 20th century, is apparently derived from the Dutch *speculaas*, the name for a similar cookie. Those supporting the Brussels origin theory maintain that a pastry chef named Van den Spigel (*spiegel* = mirror in Dutch) created *spekulatius*, obliquely naming it for himself (mirror in Latin is *speculum*). Yet another possible etymology traces back to the Latin word *species*, used in the Late Roman Empire to describe spices, which *spekulatius* certainly contain in abundance.

The mystery of the word's etymology, however, in no way diminishes the pleasure of eating the cookies, especially if they have been made from this recipe handed down by Christian Nihoul's grandfather. *Spekulatius* are typically winter cookies, given to children on St. Nicholas' feast day, or enjoyed by grown-ups with coffee or tea.

Once the finished dough has become nice and firm in the refrigerator, it takes some force to roll it out; it is very compact and only yields to vigorous "guidance" from a rolling pin. Spekulatius remain fresh for a long time without losing their flavor.

The wooden molds used for forming *spekulatius* have a well-known shape, and in Brussels it is even said of a person with a protuberant nose that they "would make a good model for a *spekulatius* mold!"

1. Mix all the ingredients for the spekulatius dough on a large, smooth work surface and knead them carefully until everything is thoroughly combined and the dough is smooth. Allow the dough to rest for 24 hours in a cool place.

2. Roll out the dough on a floured work surface, using a rolling pin. Then dust a wooden mold lightly with flour and drape a section of the rolled-out dough over it.

3. Press the dough into the mold and, using a cheese slicer, cut off the excess. Preheat the oven to 355 °F / 180 °C.

4. Turn the unbaked spekulatius out of the mold onto a baking sheet that has been lightly greased with butter. Bake for 30 minutes. Remove from the tray and allow to cool. The perfect accompaniment for spekulatius is a cup of hot coffee.

Meringue Cake with

Preparation time: *1 hour*
Cooking time: *2 hours*
Difficulty: *★*

Serves 10

Génoise, pastry cream: (see basic recipes)

For the raspberry syrup:
3¹/₂ oz / 100 g raspberries
6¹/₂ tbsp / 100 g sugar
³/₄ cup / 200 ml water

For the raspberry cream:
pastry cream
2 tbsp / 30 ml raspberry liqueur
2¹/₂ cups / 600 ml cream

For the meringue cylinders:
4 egg whites
1 cup / 250 g superfine sugar

For the filling and garnish:
¹/₃ cup / 50 g raspberries
¹/₂ cup / 80 g blueberries

This recipe is not one of the liqueur cakes typically found in Italy; it is a simple, no-frills dessert that combines the tart flavor of raspberries and blueberries with the sweeter meringue, here in the form of an intriguing and appealing garnish of meringue cylinders. The shape of the cake makes it easy to put into an airtight container, where it will keep well.

With regard to altitude and climate, raspberries and blueberries require almost identical growing conditions. While they differ in terms of color and flavor, they do complement each other well and are both high in vitamin C.

The names of the many raspberry varieties often sound poetic, such as Belle de Fontenoy, Malling Promise, Zeva Remontante and others. The best-known of the cultivated blueberries are Ama, Heerma, Earliblue, and Bluetta.

Since raspberries and blueberries are available only at certain times of year and many months pass before they are in season again, it is good to know that you can, if necessary, substitute pieces of banana or passion fruit in this dessert to flavor the syrup.

1. Prepare the génoise according to the basic recipe. Pour it into a greased and floured cake pan with a diameter of 9 in / 20 cm and bake for 30 minutes at 390 °F / 200 °C. Allow it to cool and then slice the génoise horizontally to form two layers. For the raspberry syrup, puree the raspberries with the sugar in a blender, add the water and bring to a boil. Allow to cool, then pass through a sieve. Follow the basic recipe for the pastry cream, reserving the egg whites for the meringue.

2. For the raspberry cream, whip the cream until stiff. Beat the pastry cream slightly in a bowl, add the raspberry liqueur, and fold in the whipped cream. To make the meringue, beat the egg whites until stiff and carefully add the sugar. Pipe small cylinders of the meringue, 1¹/₂–2 in / 3–4 cm long, onto a tray lined with baking paper. Bake them for 1¹/₂ hours at 275 °F / 140 °C.

Raspberries and Blueberries

3. To assemble the cake, place a layer of génoise on a cake round and soak it with raspberry syrup. Spread some pastry cream onto the génoise and arrange raspberries and blueberries on the cream. Place the second, somewhat smaller génoise on top, and soak it with syrup. Spread the remaining cream in a dome shape over the entire cake.

4. Cover the cake all over with the meringue cylinders, and garnish with raspberries and blueberries. Refrigerate before serving.

Meringue Torte

Preparation time: 20 minutes
Cooking time: 2 hours
Difficulty: ★

Serves 10

For the meringue:
3 egg whites
6¹/₂ tbsp / 100 g superfine sugar
¹/₂ cup plus 2 tbsp / 100 g confectioners' sugar
 ground vanilla pulp (optional)

For the Gianduja cream:
1³/₄ oz / 50 g hazelnut paste
1³/₄ oz / 50 g chocolate coating
2¹/₂ tbsp / 20 g bitter cocoa

¹/₃ cup / 50 g roasted hazelnuts
2¹/₂ cups / 600 ml whipping cream

To garnish:
cocoa powder
roasted chopped almonds

Gianduia or Gianduja is a particularly smooth type of chocolate, a fine paste made of chocolate and hazelnuts. It is also the term for a traditional Piemontese mask. Piemonte (or Piedmont), in northern Italy, is home to wonderful hazelnuts like Avellinos or the round Piedmont hazelnuts. Naturally, the cakes and tarts typical to this region, which usually contain hazelnuts, are also referred to as gianduja.

Flavio Perbellini recommends using small, fragrant hazelnuts, which should be thoroughly roasted before being mixed into the cream. The cream itself is very mild and contains no sugar. It is bound with chocolate coating, which must contain at least 60% cocoa.

When preparing the gianduja cream, proceed delicately. Fold the whipped cream in very carefully to prevent the cream from collapsing and becoming too soft. The meringue also must be made with care and dried in a very low oven, so that steam does not develop – can even be left to dry overnight.

To give the meringue a significantly better consistency, use egg whites that have been stored for about 15 days at 40 °F / 4 °C. This should not cause any problems and is of no concern health-wise. As a finishing touch, the torte is topped with a decorative dusting of cocoa powder, applied with the aid of a stencil.

1. To make the meringue, beat the egg whites and superfine sugar in a bowl until stiff. Using a small skimmer, fold in the sifted confectioners' sugar and a little ground vanilla pulp, if desired. Retain a quarter of the meringue for spreading on the torte.

2. Grease a baking sheet with butter and dust it with flour (or line it with waxed paper). Pipe two round meringue layers with a diameter of 9 in / 20 cm onto it. Bake the meringues for two hours at 250 °F / 120 °C (or overnight at a lower temperature).

with Gianduja Cream

3. To make the Gianduja cream, melt the hazelnut paste, the chocolate coating, and bitter cocoa in a double boiler. Add the crushed roasted hazelnuts. Allow the mixture to cool, then fold in the stiffly whipped cream.

4. To assemble the cake, place one of the meringue bases on a cake round, spread it with Gianduja cream, then place the second meringue layer on top. Spread the remaining meringue all over the torte. Use a stencil to sift a cocoa powder pattern onto the top and press chopped roasted almonds into the sides.

Preparation time: 30 minutes
Cooking time: 30 minutes
Difficulty: ★★★

Serves 10

puff pastry: (see basic recipes)

For the stracchin vanilla cream:
6 egg yolks
³/₄ cup / 180 g sugar
¹/₄ cup / 60 g butter
a pinch of cornstarch
1 vanilla bean

For the meringue:
7 egg whites
¹/₄ cup / 60 g sugar

For the amaretti (almond macaroons):
¹/₂ cup / 75 g bitter almonds
³/₄ cup plus 3 tbsp / 225 g sugar
1 egg white
a pinch of baking soda

To garnish:
3¹/₂ oz / 100 g bittersweet chocolate
ganache (see basic recipes)
confectioners' sugar

Stracchin, a word from the Venetian dialect, means "losing a little vitality." In this case, the word is used in reference to the cream, which is spread onto an exquisite puff pastry base and has a very short shelf-life. Since the cream rapidly loses its consistency and lightness, it is important to serve the cake promptly; it has to be made relatively shortly before serving.

Obviously, the puff pastry should be prepared first since it must be allowed to rest for a while in the refrigerator so it remains firm. Then fold it like a handkerchief and put it into the oven to bake at a fairly low temperature. This way, both the edges and the center will bake through evenly, and the pastry will be crisp.

Then begins the lengthy procedure of making the stracchin cream. Prepare it over high heat in a copper saucepan or a

double boiler inside a stainless steel pan. Once the cream has reached 180–182 °F / 82–83 °C, its consistency becomes somewhat thick, but continue stirring it until it has cooled.

Flavio Perbellini recommends sprinkling the cake with amaretti crumbs, as is traditional. Since the bitter almonds used to make the amaretti are not available in the United States, you may need to substitute bitter almond paste, or use some of the excellent store-bought amarettini available in gourmet stores. Crumbled and pressed into the sides of the torte, the macaroons make it even more difficult to cut, so use a serrated knife with a very thin blade. One can imagine the difficulties Flavio Perbellini must have encountered when he served the *mille-foglie* (Italian for puff pastry, literally "thousand leaves") to one hundred people at a reception in honor of the Prince of Denmark.

1. Prepare the ganache and puff pastry according to the basic recipes. Bake the puff pastry and then cut out three round layers of equal diameter. For the stracchin cream, beat the egg yolks with the sugar, softened butter, cornstarch, and vanilla pulp. While stirring constantly, slowly heat the mixture to 185 °F / 85 °C. Allow to cool slightly.

2. To make the meringue, beat the egg whites and sugar until stiff. Combine the two mixtures carefully, and assemble the torte immediately afterwards.

Stracchin Vanilla Cream

3. For the macaroons, mix the bitter almonds and sugar in a food processor and grind them until they are very fine. Stir in the unbeaten egg white and pinch of baking soda.

4. Pipe the amarettini onto a baking sheet and bake for 30 minutes at 350 °F / 175 °C. Allow to cool, then crush in a food processor and fold two-thirds of the crumbs into the cream. To assemble the torte, place a puff pastry base on a cake round and spread cream on it. Repeat with the next two layers. Press the reserved amaretti crumbs into the sides of the cake, decorate the top with ganache, and dust with confectioners' sugar.

Preparation time: 3 hours
Cooking time: 1 hour 5 minutes
Difficulty: ★★★

Serves 30

1 oz / 30 g compressed fresh yeast
1 oz / 30 g brewer's yeast
4¹/₂ tbsp / 70 ml milk

8 cups / 1 kg flour
12 eggs
1²/₃ cups / 400 g sugar
1 cup plus 13 tbsp / 450 g butter
3¹/₂ tbsp / 50 g cocoa butter
2 pinch of salt
1 drop vanilla extract
1 drop orange extract

This yeast star – called *Pandoro* in Italian – is baked at Christmas in the region around Verona, in accordance with a tradition just as enduring as the story of the Capulets and Montagues. The Pandoro looks like an eight-pointed star and is reminiscent of another cake, the Madalin, which is flatter, less moist, and contains less butter.

To minimize difficulty in making the dough, Perbellini suggests using gluten-rich flour. To be truly authentic, one would have to incorporate a small piece of sourdough from a previous baking or bought at a bakery into the dough along with the fresh yeast, a method occasionally practiced in France and Italy.

An expert hand is required when working the butter into the dough. Flavio Perbellini recommends allowing the dough to rest a few hours beforehand in a cool place (40 °F / 4°C). Then it is worked like a puff pastry – folded and turned three times. All stages of the work must be carried out the same day; any interruption could destroy the final result. During baking, make sure that the top does not darken too much.

It may not be easy to find a eight-pointed, star-shaped cake pan, especially given the fact that the Veronese claim that the authentic form exists only in Verona. So you may have no choice but to travel to Verona and buy one there ... or you could settle for a different star-shaped tin instead.

1. Dissolve the compressed yeast and combine it with the brewer's yeast, milk and 1 cup plus 2 tbsp / 140 g flour. Allow the dough to rise in a warm place (85 °F / 30 °C) until it has doubled in size. To this dough, which should weigh approximately 9¹/₂ oz / 270 g, add 2 cups plus 6 tbsp / 300 g flour, 3 eggs, 3¹/₂ tbsp / 50 g sugar, 3¹/₂ tbsp / 50 g butter and the cocoa butter. Knead thoroughly and allow it to rise until it has doubled in size again.

2. To the dough (which now weighs 1 lb 13 oz / 820 g) add 4¹/₂ cups / 560 g flour, 7 eggs and 3¹/₂ tbsp / 50 g melted butter. Knead to form a smooth dough, then add 1 cup plus 7 tbsp / 350 g sugar, 2 eggs, and the salt, vanilla extract, and orange extract. Using the technique for puff pastry, incorporate 1 cup plus 7 tbsp / 350 g butter. Divide the dough into three sections, each weighing 1 lb 10 oz / 750 g.

Star

3. Shape each of the three portions of dough into a ball.

4. Place each dough ball into a greased tall star-shaped cake pan. Allow to rise for ten hours at a temperature of 75 °F / 24 °C (or 12 hours at 70 °F / 21 °C) until they have doubled in size. Bake for 65 minutes at 350 °F / 175 °C. Dust with confectioners' sugar before serving.

Panettone

Preparation time: 3 hours
Cooking time: 1 hour 5 minutes
Difficulty: ★★★

Serves 30

1 oz / 30 g fresh compressed yeast
1 oz / 30 g brewer's yeast
4¹/₂ tbsp / 70 ml milk
8 cups / 1 kg gluten rich flour
10 eggs

2 cups / 500 g butter
1²/₃ cups / 400 g sugar
2 tsp / 10 g salt
vanilla extract
lemon extract
orange extract
1¹/₂ cups / 300 g raisins
³/₄ cup / 140 g candied orange peel
³/₄ cup / 140 g candied lemon peel

In Milan, they say that *panettone*, now known and highly regarded throughout the world, was invented by a poor Milanese baker who made his fortune baking it. The exact combination of ingredients in panettone vary from town to town: the Veronese, for example, make it using a yeast starter specially enriched with brewer's yeast, a method of preparation completely foreign to the Milanese. The Perbellini family, with four generations of pastry chefs, has kept its *panettone* recipe a secret since 1852. Here Flavio Perbellini presents a popular recipe for this yeast cake, originally baked at Christmas time.

In accordance with tradition, this *panettone* contains both dried and candied fruits. You should not use too much of either, for dried fruits soak up the cake's moisture, and candied fruits may make it overly sweet, impairing its distinctive delicate flavor. The Venetian version of *panettone*, interestingly, includes a fairly intense orange essence instead of candied fruits.

To help the dough rise perfectly, Perbellini incorporates a bit of dough reserved from a previous baking into the yeast starter; he and his forefathers have kept their starter in continuous use in this fashion for thirty years already, carefully stored wrapped in a thick cloth. This, combined with baking the dough wrapped in the famous Pizotino baking paper (much more practical than a metal cake ring), keeps the *panettone* in line with the best gastronomic tradition.

1. Dissolve the fresh compressed yeast and combine it with the brewer's yeast, milk and 1 cup plus 2 tbsp / 140 g flour. Allow the dough to rise at 85 °F / 30 °C until it has doubled in size.

2. To the dough produced in step one, which should weigh approximately 9¹/₂ oz / 270 g, add 2 cups plus 6 tbsp / 300 g flour, 3 eggs, 3¹/₂ tbsp / 50 g butter and 3¹/₂ tbsp / 50 g sugar, and knead thoroughly. Allow the dough to prove until it has doubled in size again.

3. To the dough that now weighs approximately 1 lb 13 oz / 820 g, add 4¹/₂ cups / 560 g flour, 7 eggs, 1 cup plus 7 tbsp / 350 g sugar, 1 cup plus 13 tbsp / 450 g butter, salt, one drop each of vanilla, lemon, and orange extract, and knead until the dough is smooth.

4. Add the finely diced candied fruits (orange and lemon peel) and the raisins and work them into the dough. Divide it into portions weighing 2 pounds / 1 kg each, shape them into balls and then place them inside paper baking forms. Allow the dough to rise for ten hours at 75 °F / 24 °C until they have doubled in size, and then bake for 65 minutes at 350 °F / 175 °C.

Preparation time: 1 hour
Cooking time: 30 minutes
Difficulty: ★★

Serves 10

génoise, Italian meringue: (see basic recipes)

For the basic cream:
2¼ cups / 560 ml whipping cream
5 oz / 140 g Italian meringue
5 sheets of gelatin
ground vanilla

For the pistachio cream:
1 oz / 25 g pistachio paste
9 oz / 250 g basic cream

For the chocolate cream:
1 oz / 30 g chocolate coating
7 oz / 200 g basic cream

For soaking:
6½ tbsp / 100 ml mandarin liqueur, 36 Proof

Since the world is full of pizzerias and Italian restaurants, people think they are well-acquainted with the most familiar Italian desserts, such as zabaglione and tiramisu. *Semifreddo*, Italian for "half-cold," actually designates a wide variety of chilled sweets including cakes and puddings. Unfortunately, along with the traditional recipes consistently made with loving care by master pastry chefs, there are also many lower quality, mass-produced versions.

Italy offers a great variety of dried fruits, including the well-known Avola almonds (used to make delicious sugared almonds) and Piedmont hazelnuts. In this recipe, Flavio Perbellini showcases pistachios, rich in vitamin A and minerals, in the concentrated green paste that gives the *semifreddo* its distinctive flavor.

The semi-frozen torte is composed of three layers. The génoise is generously soaked in a special 36 proof mandarin liqueur, distilled from macerated mandarin peel. The meringue (the Italian version, of course) requires concentration and a steady hand when the hot sugar syrup is poured onto the beaten egg whites. And then there is the basic cream, which appears in three flavors: vanilla, chocolate, and pistachio.

This *semifreddo*, which should be neither too light nor too firm, pays homage to the art of the nuance. This aesthetic has a long tradition, dating all the way back to the 16th century and the work of another son of Verona, Paolo Caliari, better known as Veronese, who painted the famous *Marriage at Cana*.

1. Prepare the Italian meringue and the génoise according to the basic recipes. Pour the génoise mixture into a greased and floured cake pan with a diameter of 9 in / 20 cm, and bake for 30 minutes at 390 °F / 200 °C. After it has cooled slice the génoise through horizontally. To make the basic cream, stiffly whip the cream and gently combine it with the Italian meringue, the soaked gelatin, and the ground vanilla. Divide the basic cream into three bowls.

2. To make the pistachio cream, stir the pistachio paste in a bowl with a whisk, and then add it to one bowl of basic cream a little at a time.

Torte

3. For the chocolate cream, melt the chocolate coating in the top of a double boiler. Allow it to cool slightly and then carefully fold it into the a second bowl of basic cream.

4. Place a layer of génoise onto a cake round, soak it with half of the mandarin liqueur and spread it with pistachio cream. Put the second layer on top, and soak it with the remaining mandarin liqueur. Apply the remaining pistachio cream and smooth the surface. Refrigerate. Using a pastry bag with a star-shaped tip, garnish the sides with chocolate cream. Use another pastry bag to decorate the top with the vanilla-flavored basic cream. Serve the torte well-chilled.

Preparation time: 25 minutes
Cooking time: 30 minutes
Difficulty: ✦✦

Serves 10

For the Savoy sponge cake:
4 eggs
2 egg yolks
$^1/_2$ cup / 125 g sugar
$^3/_4$ cup / 90 g flour

For the tiramisu cream:
7 egg yolks
1 cup / 150 g confectioners' sugar
14 oz / 400 g mascarpone cheese

8 egg whites
1 cup / 250 g sugar

For the coffee syrup:
$^1/_2$ cup / 30 g instant coffee
1$^2/_3$ cups / 400 ml water
$^3/_4$ cup plus 1 tbsp / 200 g sugar

For the roasted flaked almonds:
2 cups / 300 g flaked almonds
a pinch of ground vanilla
orange petal water
sugar syrup (30 °Beaumé)

To garnish:
confectioners' sugar

Tiramisu Bianco, a very rich dessert, has three components – mascarpone cheese, coffee, and the Savoy sponge cake. It is popular throughout Italy, especially in Verona where it is prized for its distinctive coffee flavor (very strong, very Italian) and creaminess. This classic, fortifying egg dessert also has a devoted following outside Italy. Flavio Perbellini, in his determination to maintain superb quality, continues to use an old family recipe.

The Savoy sponge cake (the dukes of Savoy later became the kings of Italy) differs from the classic Genoese sponge cake, or génoise, in that it contains more egg yolk and less egg white and flour. It should not be confused with the Savoy gâteau, which is made in a completely different way.

The choice of the mascarpone, which should be fresh, mild and creamy, almost like a very high-fat cream, plays a decisive role in the flavor of the dessert. Mascarpone is now available all year round, rather than just in winter as used to be the case; there is even a pasteurized version that keeps well for a few days in the refrigerator. Be sure the mascarpone used for this tiramisu has no trace of bitterness.

If the tiramisu is not sweet enough for your taste, a light, frothy zabaglione is a wonderful accompaniment to this dessert.

1. Prepare the Savoy sponge cake with the ingredients given above, using the basic recipe for génoise as a guide, and pour the mixture into a greased and floured 9 in / 20 cm cake pan. Bake for 30 minutes at 390 °F / 200 °C. Allow the cake to cool and then slice it horizontally into three layers. To make the tiramisu cream, vigorously whisk the egg yolks and confectioners' sugar until the mixture is thick and foamy, then add the mascarpone. Finally, beat the egg whites until stiff with the sugar.

2. Carefully fold the mascarpone and egg mixture into the very stiffly beaten egg whites. For the coffee syrup, bring the sugar and water to a boil. Remove from the heat and stir in the instant coffee powder.

Bianco

3. Place a layer of Savoy sponge cake on a cake round, soak it with coffee syrup and spread it with tiramisu cream. Place the second layer on top, soak it with coffee syrup and cover it with a layer of tiramisu cream. Top it with the third layer of sponge cake, and cover it with the remaining cream.

4. Spread out the flaked almonds on a tray and drizzle over them a mixture of orange petal water and sugar syrup (which has been flavored with a pinch of ground vanilla). Roast the nuts in the oven or with a salamander. Sprinkle them all over the cake and dust with confectioners' sugar. Refrigerate.

Preparation time: 25 minutes
Cooking time: 40 minutes
Difficulty: ★★

Serves 10

pastry cream, génoise: (see basic recipes)

For the maraschino cream:
10¹/₂ oz / 300 g pastry cream
1 tbsp / 15 ml Maraschino liqueur

For the almond paste:
3¹/₃ cups / 500 g blanched almonds
1³/₄ cups plus 2 tbsp / 450 g sugar
3¹/₂ tbsp / 50 g invert sugar
1 egg white
grated orange peel

For the syrup for soaking:
6¹/₂ tbsp / 100 g superfine sugar
6¹/₂ tbsp / 100 ml water
3 tbsp / 45 ml maraschino liqueur

To glaze:
sugar syrup (30 °Beaumé)
or clear cake glaze (see basic recipes)

The recipe for this almond cake is familiar to all Italian pastry chefs, who make it with varying degrees of success. Flavio Perbellini prepares this *torta delizia* in accordance with long Perbellini family tradition, using pastry cream and a génoise soaked with maraschino liqueur. Maraschino liqueur, which originated in the region around Zara (now Zadar) in Dalmatia, is made from a fruit schnapps distilled exclusively from wild Marasca cherries, a sour cherry also native to this area.

Marasca cherries are also used for other desserts, such as ice cream – like Amarena cherries, they go very well with vanilla. Flavio Perbellini also notes the Amarcine, a dessert made of Marasca cherries, which are steamed in sugar with cloves, cinnamon, and a concentrated syrup.

There are several types of almonds you could choose from, but Flavio Perbellini names the Sicilian Marri as most suitable for this recipe. The almond paste must be very fine, so use an almond mill or food processor for grinding the almonds. If neither is available, crush the almonds with a mortar in a wooden pestle, which is time-consuming, but the results are worth the extra effort.

In the unlikely event that some of the cake is left over, it will keep at room temperature for two days or, if need be, for five to six days in the refrigerator.

1. Prepare a classic pastry cream according to the basic recipe, allow it to cool and flavor it with maraschino liqueur. Make the génoise, again following the basic recipe, and pour it into a greased and floured cake pan with a diameter of 9 in / 20 cm. Bake for 30 minutes at 390 °F / 200 °C, and after it has cooled slice it through horizontally.

2. To make the almond paste, grind the blanched almonds with the sugar and invert sugar in a food processor and mix thoroughly, then add the egg white and grated orange peel. Follow the basic recipe for the syrup for soaking.

Cake

3. To assemble the cake, place a layer of génoise on a cake round, soak it with maraschino syrup and spread pastry cream on it, then place the second génoise layer on top.

4. Using a pastry bag with a flat, ribbed tip, decorate the top of the cake with woven strips of almond paste. Put in the oven for 8–10 minutes at 480 °F / 250 °C until the surface has browned slightly. Remove it from the oven and coat the cake with clear glaze or sugar syrup.

Preparation time: 45 minutes
Cooking time: 30 minutes
Difficulty: ★★

Serves 10

For the puff pastry:
4 cups / 500 g flour
1 tbsp / 15 g salt
1 cup / 250 ml water
1²/₃ cups / 400 g butter

For the pastry cream:
1¹/₄ cups / 300 ml milk
2 egg yolks
6¹/₂ tbsp / 100 g sugar
6 tbsp / 45 g flour

4 tsp / 10 g cornstarch
5 tsp / 25 ml Marsala
5 tsp / 25 ml Alchermes

For the génoise:
(see basic recipes)
4 eggs
¹/₂ cup / 125 g brown sugar
1 cup / 125 g flour
5 tsp / 25 ml rum, for soaking

For the ganache:
(see basic recipes)
3¹/₂ oz / 100 g bittersweet chocolate
¹/₂ cup / 125 ml cream

To garnish:
crushed amaretti (almond macaroons)
confectioner's sugar

This classic torte consists of puff pastry, génoise, and pastry cream, and is in every respect worthy of the legacy of Luigi Perbellini, founder of the Pasticceria cake shop in Verona. One should be calm and focused when making it, and the individual stages of work up through the assembling of the torte, which will require some skill, need to be well-coordinated.

The pastry cream, based mainly on the traditional recipe, contains no gelatin. Make the puff pastry and the génoise (also known as *pan de Spagna*, or "Spanish bread," in Italy) on the same day, so that they remain crunchy and soft respectively. Ganache and the typically Italian amaretti biscuits complete the torte.

Though this Torta Italiana is soaked with three different spirits, it can nonetheless be enjoyed by children at family celebra-

tions. First, there is the well-known brown rum. Second, Marsala, probably less well known, is the pride of Sicilian wine growers. It is a fortified wine consisting of sweet white wine, alcohol and grape must and contains 18% alcohol. Third, the red Alchermes, an herbal liqueur flavored with rose, iris, and jasmine extracts, is also quite extraordinary. These three spirits should not be mixed.

The amaretti biscuits are not difficult to make (see p. 232 for recipe), but because the bitter almonds they call for contain small quantities of prussic acid, which is used to make cyanide, their sale is banned in the United States. Bitter almond paste is available, however, and ready-to-enjoy amaretti are increasingly available in stores.

1. For the puff pastry, knead the flour with the salt, water and 5 tbsp / 75 g soft butter, shape into a ball, and refrigerate for 30 minutes. Roll out the pastry in a star shape, place the rest of the butter in the middle, cover it with the points of the star, and fold and turn twice. Refrigerate for 20 minutes, fold and turn twice more, and repeat after another 20 minutes. Roll out the pastry ¹/₄ in / ¹/₂ cm thick, place it on a baking sheet and bake at 445 °F / 230 °C. When cool, cut out two circles with a diameter of 9 in / 20 cm.

2. To make the pastry cream, bring the milk to a boil. Beat the egg yolks and sugar until foamy, sift the flour and cornstarch, and add to the egg yolks. Pour the boiling milk over the egg mixture, return to the heat, and boil for two minutes. Allow to cool, then flavor with the Marsala and Alchermes.

Torte

3. Prepare the génoise using the basic recipe as a guideline, but with the ingredients listed above. Pour the mixture into a greased and floured cake pan with a diameter of 9 in / 20 cm, and bake for 30 minutes at 390 °F / 200 °C.

4. Place a layer of puff pastry on a cake round and spread it with pastry cream. Place the génoise on the cream, soak it with rum, and coat it with pastry cream. Place the second puff pastry layer on top. Spread pastry cream all over the torte and press amaretti crumbs onto the sides. Garnish the top with the ganache and dust with confectioners' sugar. Refrigerate for 30 minutes before serving.

Preparation time: 1 hour
Cooking time: 30 minutes
Difficulty: ★★★

Serves 10

génoise, pastry cream, Italian meringue:
  (see basic recipes)

For the pistachio cream:
5¼ oz / 150 g pastry cream
4½ oz / 125 g Italian meringue
1 oz / 30 g pistachio paste

For the rum cream:
5¼ oz / 150 g pastry cream
4½ oz / 125 g Italian meringue
3½ tbsp / 50 ml rum

For soaking the génoise:
3½ tbsp / 50 ml rum
3½ tbsp / 50 ml Alchermes
3½ tbsp / 50 ml Marsala

The typically Italian dessert Zuppa inglese was actually created by Neapolitan pastry chefs and has nothing to do with England, in spite of its somewhat misleading name. Zuppa inglese does not mean English soup (*minestra* is the Italian word for soup), but would be better translated as English pudding, and thus perhaps derives its name from the well-known British fondness for puddings of all sorts.

Keen observers cannot fail to notice that the three colors of the Italian flag are used here. As in the Torta Italiana, three spirits are used – brown rum, Marsala – and Alchermes. Other combinations are also possible, however; for example, the Marsala can be replaced by Madeira or port, and the Alchermes by Grand Marnier.

The hallmark of the Zuppa inglese is that each of the three génoise layers is soaked in a different spirit, and three different creams (actually two creams and an Italian meringue) are also spread between those layers. You can further refine the creams with the addition of chopped hazelnuts, bits of chocolate or marinated fruits, but be careful not to overdo it.

One final point worthy of note is the Italian meringue, which should not be prepared until you are ready to use it, as the cake's final touch. Flavio Perbellini insists that it must be absolutely smooth, without any lumps. Browning the torte slightly with a Bunsen burner makes the presentation even more elegant.

1. Prepare the pastry cream and Italian meringue according to the basic recipes. Follow the basic recipe for the génoise, pour into a greased and floured cake pan with a diameter of 9 in / 20 cm, and bake for 30 minutes at 390 °F / 200 °C. Allow the génoise to cool and then slice it into three layers. To make the pistachio cream, mix the pastry cream with the Italian meringue and pistachio paste.

2. To make the rum cream, again combine pastry cream and Italian meringue, replacing the pistachio paste with the rum.

Inglese

3. To assemble the torte, place a layer of génoise onto a cake round, soak it with Alchermes and cover it with rum cream. Place the second layer on top, soak it with rum and spread pistachio cream on it. Put the third layer on top and soak it with Marsala.

4. Spread Italian meringue on the top of the torte, smooth the surface and use a pastry bag to apply a meringue decoration. Then garnish with fresh fruits and refrigerate the torte until served.

Preparation time: 1 hour 30 minutes
Cooking time: 50 minutes
Difficulty: ★★★

Makes 12

puff pastry, cocoa sponge cake: (see basic recipes)

For the orange-flavored crème brûlée:
1 cup / 250 ml cream
3¹/₂ tbsp / 50 g sugar
4 egg yolks
2 tbsp / 30 ml orange juice
grated peel of 1 orange

For the mousse Caraïbe:
4 egg yolks
²/₃ cup / 150 ml sugar syrup (30 °Beaumé)

9 oz / 250 g Caraïbe chocolate coating (70% cocoa content)
2 cups / 500 ml whipping cream

For the puff pastry wafers:
2¹/₂ oz / 75 g puffed rice
4 oz / 120 g puff pastry, chopped
3¹/₂ oz / 100 g milk chocolate coating, melted
8 oz / 230 g sweet almond praline paste

For the cocoa glaze:
1 cup / 240 ml water
1¹/₄ cups / 300 g sugar
³/₄ cup plus 3 tbsp / 100 g cocoa powder
³/₄ cup / 200 ml cream
6 sheets of gelatin

To garnish:
milk chocolate coating
chocolate wafers

In 1993, the Belgian team already achieved second place in the pastry chef world championship, and in 1995 the team of Rik de Baere, Pierre Marcolini, and Gunther van Essche (now Bernard Proot's closest colleague) finally achieved the world title with their creations on the given theme of "lift off." This Caraïbe was one of the desserts with which the Belgians convinced the jury of their expertise.

Some skill is required for the masterful combination of ingredients called for in this exciting, unique recipe. The puff pastry, for example, must be especially crunchy and is combined with a sweet almond praline and puffed rice. This sweet, crispy mixture cannot fail to impress even the most discriminating guests.

For the mousse Caraïbe, it is essential to use bitter chocolate with a cocoa content of at least 70% (the usual chocolate coating contains between 50% and 55%). And one additional tip, for those inexperienced in making cocoa glaze: all the ingredients, with the exception of the gelatin, must be combined on the stove top over low heat. Cool the mixture to 145 °F / 60 °C before folding in the gelatin.

Under no circumstances should you bake the crème brûlée in a convection oven, for this will not achieve the desired effect. Also, carefully balance the quantities of crème brûlée and chocolate, so that the chocolate's bitterness does not overpower the mild flavor of the custard.

1. Prepare the cocoa sponge cake according to the basic recipe. For the crème brûlée, combine all the ingredients, without heat, and pass through a sieve. Pour into mini Flexipan tins and bake for 50 minutes at 210 °F / 100 °C. Remove the crèmes from the tins, cool, and place in the freezer. To make the mousse Caraïbe, whisk the egg yolks and sugar syrup over a double boiler until foamy and thick. Melt the Caraïbe chocolate coating at 105 °F / 40 °C, add it to the egg yolks, and fold in the stiffly whipped cream.

2. For the puff pastry wafers, combine all the ingredients with the melted milk chocolate coating. Spread the mixture ¹/₄ in / ¹/₂ cm thick on a tray and freeze. When set, cut out circles slightly smaller than large Flexipan tins. To assemble the tarts, fill large Flexipan tins half full with mousse Caraïbe. Place small slices of cocoa sponge cake and a frozen slice of crème brûlée in the center of each and fill with more mousse Caraïbe. Complete each tart with a frozen puff pastry wafer, then refrigerate.

Caraïbe

3. Make the cocoa glaze by heating all the ingredients, except the gelatin, to 150 °F / 65 °C. Allow to cool slightly and then add the soaked gelatin. Turn the tarts out of the tins, place them on a tray and cover with cocoa glaze.

4. For the final touches, melt the milk chocolate coating in a double boiler. Fill a tiny paper pastry bag with it and use it to garnish the Caraïbes, then place a border of chocolate wafers around each one.

Preparation time: 45 minutes
Cooking time: 1 hour 30 minutes
Difficulty: ★★

Serves 8

For the chocolate sponge cake:
5 eggs
$^1/_4$ cup / 60 g sugar
$6^1/_2$ tbsp / 50 g flour
1 oz / 30 g stabilizer
$^1/_3$ cup / 80 g butter
$5^1/_4$ oz / 150 g milk chocolate coating, melted

For the mousse Jivara:
$2^1/_2$ tbsp / 40 ml sugar syrup
4 egg yolks
$^1/_4$ cup / 60 g sugar

$1^3/_4$ cups / 420 ml cream
7 oz / 200 g milk chocolate coating, melted

For the ganache with forest berries:
$1^1/_4$ cups / 200 g forest berries
$2^1/_4$ oz / 70 g bittersweet chocolate coating
8 tsp / 40 g sugar
$1^1/_2$ sheets of gelatin

For the crème brûlée:
1 cup / 250 ml cream
$3^1/_2$ tbsp / 50 g sugar
4 egg yolks
$^1/_2$ vanilla bean

To garnish:
chocolate discs

The derivation of this specialty's name, also the name of the *pâtisserie* owned by Bernard Proot, is not exactly clear. In Spanish, it means "belonging to the King," but its meaning contains another small spin, a discreet homage to the former owner of the shop, Adèle Reymacckers, who was more than happy to go along with this word play.

As far as the preparation of the torte bearing the name is concerned, the mousse Jivara is best made a day in advance. Be sure to fold the stiffly whipped cream into the caramel and chocolate mixture at exactly the right moment; to ensure that the cream does not collapse, this mixture should be only lukewarm. The mousse develops the flavor of milk chocolate with a slightly fruity aftertaste.

For the ganache, select only fully ripe, aromatic berries of the highest quality. Even though they will not function as garnish, do not use any bruised or damaged berries, which would impair the flavor of the whole. Gourmets prefer to use bittersweet chocolate with a cocoa content of 50% to 55% for the ganache. Use it sparingly so that the taste of the berries is neither overpowered nor adulterated.

Garnish this dessert in whatever way you like. Use your imagination, and perhaps the inspiration of a special occasion, to create decorations worthy of this torte's royal name.

1. To make the sponge cake, beat the eggs and sugar until foamy, then add the flour and stabilizer. Melt and combine the butter and chocolate coating. Use a pastry bag to pipe two spirals onto a baking tray, and bake for 40 minutes at 210 °F / 100 °C. For the mousse Jivara, whisk the egg yolks, pour the hot sugar syrup onto them and beat until cooled. Caramelize the sugar and carefully add $^1/_4$ cup / 60 ml cream. Whip the remaining cream. Pour the melted chocolate coating onto the egg yolk mixture, add the caramel, and fold in the stiffly whipped cream.

2. Prepare the ganache with forest berries by melting the chocolate coating. Boil the berries with the sugar, allow them to cool slightly, then add the soaked gelatin and the melted chocolate coating. To make the crème brûlée, mix all the ingredients without heating them. Pass the mixture through a sieve, pour into large, flat Flexipan tins and bake for 50 minutes at 210 °F / 100 °C.

Rey

3. After it has cooled, spread a thin layer of the ganache with forest berries onto the crème brûlée, and place in the freezer.

4. To assemble the torte line a cake ring with a strip of baking paper and spoon in some mousse Jivara. Top it with a layer of chocolate sponge cake, then a slice of frozen crème brûlée. Fill the cake ring with the remaining mousse and finish off with the second layer of sponge cake. Then turn out the torte and remove the baking paper. Garnish the top of the cake, and arrange a border of chocolate wafers around the outer edge.

Preparation time: 40 minutes
Cooking time: 5 minutes
Difficulty: ★★

Serves 8

For the Joconde sponge cake:
2 egg whites
2 tbsp sugar

Almond and sugar mixture:
¹/₃ cup / 80 g sugar
¹/₂ cup / 80 g finely ground almonds
6 eggs
3 tbsp / 25 g flour
1 oz / 25 g praline
1 oz / 25 g mocha coating
 melted butter

For the orange mousse:
5 egg yolks
¹/₂ cup / 120 ml sugar syrup (35 °Beaumé)
6 oz / 175 g orange chocolate
4¹/₂ oz / 125 g bittersweet chocolate coating
3¹/₂ oz / 100 g sweet almond praline
1³/₄ cups / 450 ml whipping cream, unsweetened

For the chocolate mousse with almond milk:
²/₃ cup / 150 ml almond milk
4 egg yolks
4 oz / 120 g bittersweet chocolate coating
5¹/₄ oz / 150 g mocha coating
2 cups / 500 ml unsweetened whipping cream

For the cocoa glaze:
³/₄ cup plus 3 tbsp / 225 g sugar
³/₄ cup / 180 ml water
²/₃ cup / 150 ml cream
³/₄ cup / 75 g cocoa
4 sheets of gelatin
 clear cake glaze

To garnish:
white chocolate coating
marbled chocolate

It was for this recipe that Gunther Van Essche, Bernard Proot's brilliant assistant, was named best pastry chef in Belgium of 1995 and awarded the Prosper Montagné Prize, the most respected in Belgium. So translate the "Victoria" in the name of this torte as "victory." Other interpretations, such as it being a reference to the indefatigable English queen, do not merit serious consideration.

The Victoria Torte is an imaginative variation of two mousses with similar, yet distinctive flavors. Gunther Van Essche contends that for this recipe, only chocolate with a 50% cocoa content will meet the most discerning standards. It is used as bittersweet chocolate coating in both the orange and almond milk mousses. Both should be light and have a melt-in-the-mouth consistency. To achieve this, along with a perfect visual effect, combine the ingredients with great care.

If you prefer to make the orange chocolate yourself, you can prepare a concentrated infusion that is flavored with orange peel and then mixed with the mousse. So that the cocoa glaze has a nice sheen, use very finely ground cocoa.

1. To make the Joconde sponge cake, beat the eggs until foamy with 1 tbsp / 5 g sugar, and beat the egg whites and remaining sugar until stiff. Combine both mixtures. Blend the flour with the almond and sugar mixture, and fold the dry ingredients into the eggs. Stir in the melted chocolate and praline, and finally add the melted butter. Pipe spirals with a diameter of 10 in / 22 cm onto a tray and bake for five minutes at 445 °F / 230 °C. When cool, slice through horizontally.

2. For the orange mousse, warm the egg yolks and sugar syrup in a double boiler and beat until cool. Melt the orange chocolate and chocolate coating, stir in the praline, and add to the egg yolks. Cool slightly, then carefully fold the mixture into the whipped cream. Place a layer of Joconde sponge cake in a cake ring 1 in / 2 cm high. Fill the ring with mousse and place it in the freezer. Prepare the marbled chocolate for the garnish.

Torte

3. To make the chocolate mousse, beat the almond milk and egg yolks in a double boiler. Add the melted chocolate and mocha coatings and carefully fold in the whipped cream. Line a 11 in / 24 cm cake ring, 2 in / 4 cm high, with a strip of baking paper and spread some chocolate mousse in it. Place the frozen orange mousse in the ring, centered, and cover it with the remaining chocolate mousse. Top it with a layer of Joconde sponge cake and freeze.

4. Prepare the cocoa glaze by combining all the ingredients, except the gelatin, in a saucepan and heating to 150 °F / 65 °C. Allow to cool, then dissolve the soaked gelatin in it. Thicken with clear cake glaze until it reaches the desired consistency. Remove the torte from the ring. Spread cocoa glaze over its entire surface, and line the edge with chocolate wafers. Use a tiny paper pastry bag to apply a garnish of white chocolate and decorate with marbled chocolate.

Preparation time: 1 hour
Cooking time: 10 minutes
Difficulty: ★★

Makes 10

Joconde sponge cake: (see basic recipes)

For the quark mousse:
2 lb 3 oz / 1 kg quark
8 egg yolks
$^{1}/_{4}$ cup / 60 g sugar
4 tsp / 20 ml water
$4^{1}/_{2}$ cups / 1.1 l whipping cream
21 sheets of gelatin

For the chocolate mousse:
4 egg yolks
$^{1}/_{2}$ cup / 125 ml sugar syrup
8 oz / 225 g milk chocolate coating
$1^{3}/_{4}$ cups / 430 ml whipping cream

For the cigarette batter:
$6^{1}/_{2}$ tbsp / 100 g butter
$^{1}/_{2}$ cup plus 2 tbsp / 100 g confectioners' sugar
3 tbsp / 20 g cocoa
3 egg whites

For the kirsch syrup:
(see basic recipes)
$6^{1}/_{2}$ tbsp / 100 g sugar
$^{3}/_{4}$ cup / 200 ml water
$^{2}/_{3}$ cup / 150 ml kirsch

To garnish:
chocolate lattice
sugar wafers

Gluttony (*gourmandise* in French) is one of the seven deadly sins. We should probably renounce gluttony in our everyday lives and do without the pleasures of fine dining and many other earthly delights. But such noble intentions would be surely and swiftly forgotten in face of the irresistible temptation posed by this elegant quark and milk chocolate dessert.

Bernard Proot freely admits his sinful predilection for quark with a high fat content (about 40%). But chocolate also plays a significant role in this dessert. Although its proportion in the dessert is relatively small, it should have a cocoa content of at least 50%.

The success of Les Gourmands is contingent on the ingredients having the correct temperature and consistency when used. Pay particular attention to this when combining the various ingredients for the quark mousse and chocolate mousse, especially when mixing the cooled melted chocolate with the egg and sugar mixture; it must have just the right fluidity to avoid difficulties when doing the decorative work. The gelatin, so important in the quark mousse, must be lukewarm when folded in so that no lumps form.

If you want to save the trouble of making the cigarette batter for the striped sponge cake that encircles each tort, a simple Joconde sponge cake is also sufficient, but do not forgo the chocolate lattice used as decorations.

1. For the quark mousse, beat the egg yolks and half the sugar until foamy. Bring the water and remaining sugar to 250 °F / 121 °C, and pour onto the egg yolks. Stir continuously until the mixture has completely cooled. Add the dissolved gelatin and quark, and finally fold in the whipped cream. To make the chocolate mousse, melt the milk chocolate coating. Beat the egg yolks with the sugar syrup, and add the melted chocolate. Allow to cool, then fold in the whipped cream.

2. Follow the basic recipe for the Joconde sponge cake, spread the mixture thinly onto a tray lined with baking paper, and use a cake comb to draw stripes in it. Freeze. To make the cigarette batter, cream the softened butter and confectioners' sugar and cocoa powder until foamy, then add the unbeaten egg whites. Smooth the mixture onto half of the frozen Joconde sponge cake and bake for ten minutes. Cut out strips 1 in / 2 cm wide and line small tart forms with them. Fill the forms to the height of the sponge cake with quark mousse.

Gourmands

3. From the remaining Joconde sponge cake, cut out circles with a diameter of 2 in / 4 cm. Make the syrup for soaking according to the basic recipe and drench the sponge cake circles with it. Place them on the quark mousse and refrigerate.

4. Turn the gourmands out of the forms. Using a pastry bag with a medium sized star tip, pipe chocolate mousse rosettes onto each tart. Chill until the mousse is firm, then garnish with chocolate decorations and sugar wafers.

Preparation time: 1 hour 30 minutes
Cooking time: 15 minutes
Difficulty: ★

Serves 8

For the dacquoise sponge cake:
20 egg whites
1 cup / 250 g superfine sugar

Almond and sugar mixture:
³/₄ cup plus 3 tbsp / 225 g sugar
1¹/₄ cup / 225 g finely ground almonds
³/₄ cup / 100 g flour
3¹/₂ tbsp / 50 ml cream
¹/₂ cup / 45 g chocolate flakes
macadamia nuts

confectioners' sugar

For the crème anglaise:
1¹/₂ cups / 330 ml milk
7¹/₂ tbsp / 110 g sugar
5 egg yolks

For the chocolate mousse:
1 lb / 500 g crème anglaise
1 lb / 450 g bittersweet chocolate coating
2¹/₂ cups / 600 ml whipping cream

The Macadamia Torte is not, as you might think, an homage to city life or the tarmac (also called "macadam") that paves our cities, immortalizing the name of its inventor, the Scottish engineer J. McAdam. "Macadamia" refers to a type of nut native to Australia that is named for the Australian chemist and naturalist John Macadam.

The macadamia, or Queensland nut, has a taste reminiscent of coconut and is the fruit of a tropical evergreen, a member of the *Proteaceae* family. It should not be confused with the Brazil nut (*Lecythidaceae*) or pecan nut (*Juglandaceae*).

Use very fresh egg whites for the dacquoise sponge cake to ensure that the dessert will have the proper consistency and not collapse. Beyond this, one important thing to keep in mind is to see that the ingredients for the mousse are the correct temperature when combined, which is no more difficult than the preparation of a traditional crème anglaise. Wait to fold in the whipped cream until the mousse has cooled.

When assembling the torte, refrigerate it for a short time after each stage of the work. This allows the various components to achieve the right consistency, and the cake will have the necessary firmness. The chocolate mousse could be replaced with buttercream, though this will not set as firmly.

1. To make the dacquoise sponge cake, beat 15 of the egg whites with the sugar until stiff. Beat the remaining egg whites and blend into them the almond and sugar mixture, flour, cream, and chocolate flakes. Fold the two mixtures together. Place two 1 in / 2 cm high cake rings on a tray lined with baking paper and fill them with the dacquoise mixture. Remove the cake rings, sprinkle macadamia nuts onto the sponge cakes, dust with confectioners' sugar and bake for 15 minutes at 340 °F / 170 °C.

2. To make the chocolate mousse, start by making a crème anglaise: bring the milk to a boil, and beat the egg yolks and sugar until foamy. Combine the egg yolk mixture with the milk and thicken. Stir the chocolate coating into the crème anglaise while still warm. Allow to cool, then fold in the stiffly whipped cream.

Torte

3. Using a pastry bag with a round tip, pipe the chocolate mousse onto one of the sponge cake layers in the form of lamellas.

4. Place the second sponge cake layer on top. Refrigerate the dessert for two hours. Before serving, dust with confectioners' sugar.

Preparation time: 1 hour 30 minutes
Cooking time: 20 minutes
Difficulty: ★★

Serves 8

striped Joconde sponge cake, Duchess sponge
  cake, Italian meringue: (see basic recipes)

For the passion fruit mousse:
1 lb / 500 g passion fruit flesh
3 cups / 750 ml whipping cream
4 sheets of gelatin
7 oz / 200 g Italian meringue

For the syrup for soaking:
(see basic recipes)
12 oz / 375 g passion fruit flesh
6¹/₂ tbsp / 100 ml sugar syrup
2¹/₂ tbsp / 40 ml kirsch

For the raspberry jam:
6¹/₄ cups / 1 kg raspberries
4 cups / 1 kg sugar
³/₄ oz / 20 g pectin

To garnish:
seasonal fruits
passion fruit jelly

The homely fruits of the passion flower, fresh and ripe, can be recognized by their wrinkled, dull, grey-brown peel. Once you get past these first impressions, you will discover a delicate flavor inside. Bernard Proot's clever use of them enhances this flavor even further and will be a true treat for your taste buds. But there are a few things to keep in mind as you prepare this experience.

For example, add the passion fruit very gradually and carefully to the whipped cream. The part of the fruit used is the flesh, or, more precisely, the fleshy aril covering the seeds. Pass the flesh through a sieve to filter out seeds.

The recent growth in demand for passion fruit is not surprising, for it is rich in vitamins, minerals, and other nutrients. By now it is, along with pineapples, the most popular exotic fruit. In this recipe, passion fruit harmonizes beautifully with the raspberry jam spread on the second sponge cake layer.

Assemble the cake from the bottom up to give the mousse a completely smooth surface and help the jelly adhere to it better. The sponge cake layers must be soaked carefully and evenly with the passion fruit punch. Proot suggests using a spray bottle or baby bottle to distribute the liquid evenly over the entire surface of the sponge cake.

1. Prepare the striped Joconde and Duchess sponge cakes according to the basic recipes. Line a cake ring with a strip of the Joconde sponge cake. To make the passion fruit mousse, gently combine the stiffly whipped cream with the passion fruit flesh. Fold the dissolved gelatin into the Italian meringue while it is still slightly warm. Allow to cool and then combine the meringue with the passion fruit whipped cream.

2. Follow the basic recipe for the syrup for soaking. Place a layer of Duchess sponge cake in the cake ring, soak it with passion fruit syrup and cover with a layer of mousse. To make the raspberry jam, heat the raspberries, sugar, and pectin over low heat until the mixture has a syrupy consistency. Remove from the heat and allow to cool.

Fruit Torte

3. Spread the raspberry jam onto the second Duchess sponge cake and place it in the cake ring on top of the passion fruit mousse.

4. Fill the cake ring with the remaining mousse and carefully smooth the surface. Freeze for four hours. Cover the top of the cake with passion fruit jelly and garnish with seasonal fruits.

Preparation time: 1 hour 30 minutes
Cooking time: 15 minutes
Difficulty: ★★★

Makes 12

biscuit (see basic recipes)

For the Chiboust cream with champagne:
$^3/_4$ cup / 190 ml champagne
6 tbsp / 90 ml mandarin juice
$^1/_4$ cup / 60 ml cream
6 egg yolks
1 oz / 30 g pudding powder
5 sheets of gelatin
2 tbsp / 30 ml Napoléon mandarin liqueur
6 egg whites
$^3/_4$ cup plus 3 tbsp / 225 g sugar

For the mandarin mousse with almond milk:
2 egg yolks
$^1/_2$ cup / 120 ml almond milk
2 egg whites
6 tbsp / 90 g sugar
6 sheets of gelatin
1 cup plus 3 tbsp / 280 ml cream
$^3/_4$ cup / 190 ml mandarin juice
2 tbsp / 30 ml Napoléon mandarin liqueur

For the mandarin jelly:
$6^1/_2$ tbsp / 100 ml mandarin concentrate
$1^1/_4$ cups / 300 ml water

For the wood-grain chocolate wafers:
white chocolate ganache (see basic recipes)
chocolate liqueur

This royal composition, created by Bernard Proot, does credit to its name. Contributing elements include its exquisite ingredients; its effective, truly regal presentation; and the renown of the champagne that enhances the Chiboust cream. The refreshing tartness of mandarins, used both as a juice and as a liqueur, predominates the dessert's flavor.

Developed in the mid-19th century by a Belgian, the Napoléon mandarin liqueur is made from Sicilian mandarin oranges marinated in Cognac. Today, the Belgian Georgy Fourcroy, who also awards the annual Prix Mandarine Napoléon to the world's best pastry chefs, is responsible for the continuing high quality of this liqueur.

Creating the chocolate wafers with the distinctive appearance of wood grain can be difficult. First, a fine layer of dark chocolate liqueur, or cocoa mass (left over when cocoa butter is removed from cocoa beans), is spread with a cake comb to yield the wood grain effect. Then it sets in the freezer before a thin coating of white ganache is smoothed over it.

The various components of the cream and mousse should be combined with particular care. With the Chiboust cream, especially, it is important to be aware of the temperature of the different elements when combining them. One final tip: color of the mandarins can be intensified by the addition of a little orange jelly.

1. To make the wood-grain wafers to garnish, prepare the white chocolate ganache according to the basic recipe. Spread the chocolate liqueur thinly over plastic wrap using a cake comb to yield a wood-grain effect. Freeze. When set, smooth white chocolate ganache over it. Refrigerate and allow to set. Follow the basic recipes for the biscuit.

2. For the Chiboust cream, bring the champagne, mandarin juice and cream to a boil. Beat the egg yolks until they are light yellow and slightly thick, then stir in the pudding powder and add to the champagne mixture. Return to a boil, stirring constantly. Remove from the heat and cool slightly, then add the soaked gelatin and the mandarin liqueur. Use the egg whites and sugar to make an Italian meringue, beating until cooled. Combine the two mixtures. Freeze the Chiboust cream in small Flexipan tins for 1–2 hours.

Royal

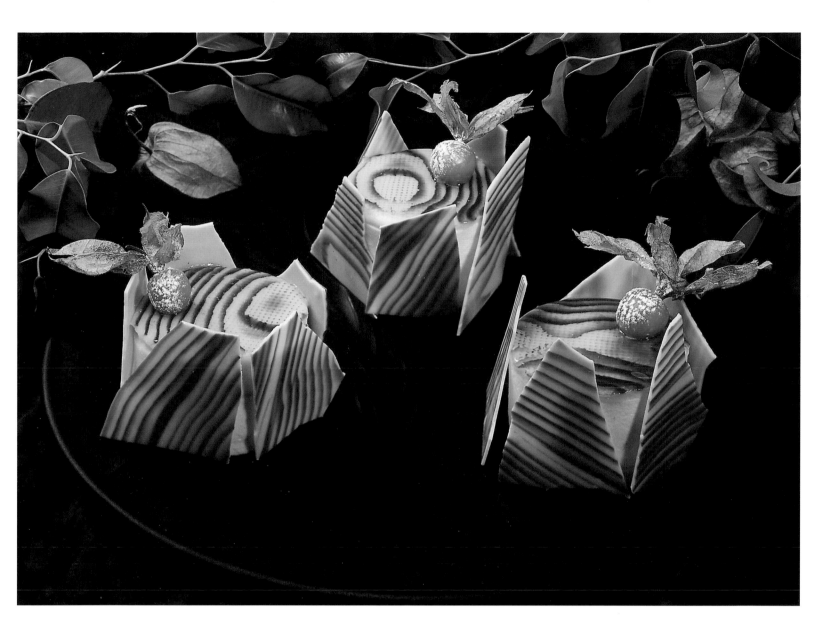

3. Make the mandarin mousse by beating the egg yolks in a double boiler with 3 tbsp / 45 ml almond milk. Again use the egg whites and sugar to prepare an Italian meringue, then fold the soaked gelatin into it. Whip the cream until stiff and then blend in the remaining almond milk, the mandarin juice and mandarin liqueur. Combine the egg yolk, whipped cream and meringue mixtures.

4. To assemble the Royals, divide the mandarin mousse between individual forms similar to those shown below. Press frozen portions of Chiboust cream into the mousse. Cover with circles of biscuit, and refrigerate for 1¹/₂ hours. Turn the desserts out of the forms and cover them with mandarin jelly. Decorate each with wood-grain chocolate wafers and garnish with Cape gooseberries dusted with confectioners' sugar.

Preparation time: 1 hour
Cooking time: 8 minutes
Difficulty: ★★

Serves 12

For the Joconde sponge cake with pistachios:
6 eggs
1¹/₂ oz / 40 g pistachio paste
¹/₂ cup plus 3 tbsp / 170 g sugar
¹/₂ cup plus 2 tbsp / 150 g sugar
³/₄ cup plus 1 tbsp / 150 g finely ground almonds
7 egg whites
¹/₃ cup / 40 g flour
8 tsp / 40 g butter

For the apricot cream:
18 oz / 510 g apricot puree

1¹/₄ cups / 310 ml whipping cream
6 sheets of gelatin
6³/₄ oz / 190 g Italian meringue (see basic recipes)

For the syrup for soaking:
(see basic recipes)
5¹/₄ oz / 150 g apricot puree
1 cup / 250 ml sugar syrup
3¹/₂ tbsp / 50 ml apricot liqueur

For the chocolate cream:
6³/₄ oz / 190 g bittersweet chocolate coating
3 egg yolks
6¹/₂ tbsp / 100 ml sugar syrup
1¹/₂ cups / 375 ml whipping cream

To garnish:
Italian meringue
fresh fruit

The impetus for this torte may have been the reciprocal influence and perfectionism of the Flemish and Florentine schools of Renaissance painting. With this arresting dessert, Bernard Proot leads us into the province of Tuscany, famous for being the birthplace of Chianti, among other things.

The alternation of glistening and matte surfaces recalls the mosaics and facades of the sacred buildings one can admire throughout northern Italy in charming and history-steeped cities like Siena, Florence, Milan, and others. Making this dessert, which actually has a rather simple structure, requires much less effort than the building of the cathedrals, whose construction demanded a staggering amount of manpower and took place over several centuries.

Apricots, the basis of this cake, are used in both the cream and the syrup for soaking. Use fully ripe fruit and, depending on your taste, choose either reddish or orangish fruits. When apricots are out of season, Bernard Proot sees no problem with using apricots that have been frozen when fully ripe, as long as this was done properly.

Spread the pistachio Joconde sponge cake fairly thickly onto the baking sheet so that it is possible to slice it into three useable layers after it has been baked and cooled. There is no reason the sponge cake should be overshadowed by the chocolate or apricot flavors. A delicate apricot coulis is an excellent choice to go with this fragrant dessert.

1. To make the Joconde sponge cake, vigorously beat the eggs, pistachio paste and ¹/₂ cup / 125 g sugar; then add the almond and sugar mixture. Beat the egg whites and remaining sugar until stiff and combine the two mixtures. Finally, fold in the flour and melted butter. Spread the sponge cake mixture thickly on a baking sheet and bake for eight minutes at 465 °F / 240 °C. For the apricot cream, blend the apricots and the whipped cream. Add the dissolved gelatin to the Italian meringue, then carefully combine the two mixtures.

2. To make the chocolate cream, melt the chocolate coating and set aside. Beat the egg yolks and sugar syrup in a warm double boiler, remove from heat and continue stirring until cooled. Add the melted chocolate coating, and finally fold in the whipped cream. Follow the basic recipe for the syrup for soaking. Slice the cooled Joconde sponge cake horizontally into three layers, place one in a square cake pan with hinged sides, and soak it with apricot syrup.

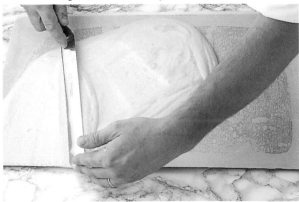

Torte

3. Spread a generous layer of chocolate cream onto the sponge cake. Place the second sponge cake layer on top of the mousse and soak it with apricot syrup. Prepare the Italian meringue for the garnish.

4. Spread apricot cream on the second sponge cake layer, top it with the third layer and soak it with syrup. Freeze the torte. Spread a thin layer of meringue over the surface, remove the cake form, and straighten the edges of the torte with a knife dipped into hot water. Use a salamander to caramelize the meringue and garnish with fresh fruit. Refrigerate for four hours before serving.

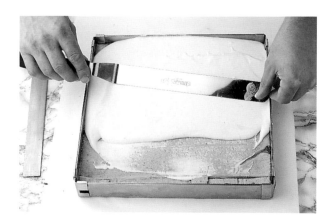

Preparation time: 1 hour
Cooking time: 20 minutes
Difficulty: ★

Serves 7

For the sweet pastry:
1 cup / 250 g butter
6¹/₂ tbsp / 100 g sugar
2 eggs
3¹/₂ tbsp / 50 g sugar
4¹/₂ tbsp / 50 g finely ground almonds
1 tsp / 3 g vanilla
3¹/₂ cups / 450 g flour

For the almond cream:
6¹/₂ tbsp / 100 g butter
2 small eggs
¹/₂ cup / 125 g sugar
²/₃ cup / 125 g finely ground almonds
5 tsp / 12 g cornstarch
2¹/₂ tsp / 12 ml walnut liqueur

For the walnut caramel:
³/₄ cup plus 1 tbsp / 200 g sugar
¹/₂ cup plus 3 tbsp / 160 ml cream
1¹/₂ cups / 140 g walnuts

There are countless varieties of walnuts, many of them excellent, but gourmets often hold the walnuts grown in France in particular esteem. Walnuts are cultivated mainly in the Périgord and Dauphiné regions of France, and there is a strong and lively rivalry between the two on that score. Bernard Proot prefers walnuts from the Dauphiné region and rhapsodizes the nuts harvested in the Grenoble area in November. By that time, they are already well developed and can be used complete with their skins.

Where almonds are concerned, he prefers Italian varieties, even though Californian almonds are more widely available these days. He feels that the aroma, quality, and rounded flavor of Italian almonds simply cannot be equaled. Bernard Proot carefully grinds them himself and folds them into the delicate

almond cream, which is enhanced with concentrated walnut liqueur.

Liqueurs distilled from dried fruits or plants, formerly highly valued as medicines, have fallen out of fashion in recent years, but that is no reason not to use them. Their popularity may even revive in the coming years.

When preparing the sweet pastry for the tart shells, make sure that it does not become too elastic; do not work the ingredients longer than necessary, and let the pastry rest for quite a while in the refrigerator before rolling it out. Bernard Proot makes the sweet pastry as much as a whole week in advance. The dough must not be overbaked and only slightly browned.

1. Prepare the sweet pastry by kneading the butter and sugar together. Add the eggs, and then the almond and sugar mixture, vanilla, and sifted flour. Refrigerate. Roll the pastry out evenly, cut out round pieces slightly larger than the forms in which it will be baked, and line the tart pans with it.

2. Begin the almond cream by creaming the butter until foamy. Add the eggs, almond and sugar mixture and the cornstarch, stirring to combine, and then flavor with the walnut liqueur.

Tarts

3. Fill a pastry bag with almond cream and pipe a thin layer of it onto the tart shells. Bake for 15 minutes at 390 °F / 200 °C.

4. To make the walnut caramel, caramelize the sugar in a saucepan without adding water. Bring the cream to a boil and very carefully and gradually stir it into the caramel. Add the walnuts and stir to coat them. Fill the tart shells with the walnut caramel. Allow to cool before serving.

Preparation time: 1 hour
Cooking time: 20 minutes
Difficulty: ★★

Serves 8

striped Joconde sponge cake, Duchess sponge
cake, Italian meringue (see basic recipes)

For the rhubarb mousse:
³/₄ cup / 170 ml whipping cream
9 oz / 250 g pureed rhubarb
1 oz / 30 g pureed strawberries
4 sheets of gelatin
4¹/₂ oz / 125 g Italian meringue

For the strawberry mousse:
³/₄ cup / 170 ml whipping cream
9 oz / 250 g pureed strawberries
juice of ¹/₂ lemon

6 sheets of gelatin
6 oz / 170 g Italian meringue

For the syrup for soaking:
(see basic recipes)
9 oz / 250 g pureed strawberries
6¹/₂ tbsp / 100 ml strawberry liqueur
³/₄ cup / 200 ml sugar syrup

For the strawberry jelly:
9 oz / 250 g pureed strawberries
1 cup / 250 g sugar
1 tsp / 2 g pectin

To garnish:
wild strawberries
mint leaves

Just as Venice holds an air of mystery, its past an enduring presence in the buildings lining the canals, the outer appearance of this torte, which is known as Le Venise, conceals its true flavors beneath a topping of wild strawberries. Only after his guests have begun to eat it does Bernard Proot tell them, with mischievous glee, that they have been enjoying rhubarb mousse. Due to its beneficial effect on the digestive system, rhubarb has been used medicinally and therefore does not have a terribly exciting reputation in Belgium.

Rhubarb is best eaten in season, usually from May to July but sometimes as late as October. The rhubarb stalks should be nice and red, firm and crunchy. This member of the buckwheat family also freezes well, and is excellent for making purees and jams.

Rhubarb, highly regarded in the United States and England but (according to Proot) misjudged by many in Belgium, cannot really be replaced by any other fruit. If you must, you could try using limes, as long as they are very aromatic; but the results may be disappointing.

The step-by-step assembly of the cake, from the Duchess sponge cake right through to the meringue, should be done as a continuous process. The cake is placed in the freezer periodically so that its components become firm.

Strawberries, by the way, are well-loved in Belgium. The Belgian-cultivated Elsanta variety has a pleasing shape; the ripe berries have an intense flavor and are marvelously fragrant.

1. Follow the basic recipes for the Duchess and striped Joconde sponge cakes. For the rhubarb mousse, mix the whipped cream with the pureed rhubarb and strawberries. Dissolve the gelatin, which has been soaked in cold water, and fold it into the Italian meringue. Combine with the rhubarb and strawberry whipped cream. Prepare the strawberry mousse in the same way.

2. To make the syrup for soaking, bring the sugar syrup and pureed strawberries to a boil, allow to cool, then stir in the strawberry liqueur. Line a cake ring with a strip of the striped Joconde sponge cake, then place a layer of Duchess sponge cake inside. Fill the ring half way with rhubarb mousse.

Rhubarb Torte

3. Top the mousse with a layer of Duchess sponge cake soaked with strawberry syrup, arrange wild strawberries on it. Fill the cake ring with strawberry mousse and smooth the surface. Freeze for about four hours. To make the strawberry jelly bring the pureed strawberries to a boil with the sugar. Remove from the heat, add the pectin and allow to cool.

4. Pipe a garnish of Italian meringue around the perimeter of the torte using a pastry bag with a special Saint-Honoré tip. Brown the meringue with a salamander. Cover the center of the torte with the strawberry jelly and garnish with whole, perfect wild strawberries and mint leaves.

Preparation time: 1 hour
Cooking time: 20 minutes
Difficulty: ★

Serves 8

For the Capuchina sponge cake:
10 egg yolks
1 vanilla bean

For the vanilla syrup:
1 cup / 250 ml water
$^1/_2$ cup / 125 g sugar
$^1/_2$ vanilla bean

To garnish:
confectioners' sugar
fresh sprigs of mint
apricots
vanilla beans (optional)

This Capuchina should not be confused with the torte bearing the same name (see Francisco Torreblanca's recipe for Capuchina Torte in this volume), for there are clear differences. This exceedingly light sponge cake, cooked in a steamer, is impressive because of the simplicity of its ingredients – eggs, vanilla, and sugar – which are enough to make a first-class dessert in and of themselves.

Patience (a virtue of incalculable value) is required for the success of the sponge cake. As soon as the water in the steamer comes to a boil, turn off the heat. Then pour the sponge cake mixture into the cake pan and cook it for 20 minutes in a sealed water bath or steamer. Use this time to prepare a vanilla custard, or perhaps an apricot or raspberry coulis, as an accompaniment for the Capuchina.

Clearly, only the very freshest eggs are suitable for this recipe. In contrast to a meringue-based sponge cake, with the Capuchina one must be careful not to beat the egg yolks too vigorously, as this would introduce too much air into the mixture, causing the sponge cake to collapse like a house of cards (not to mention a castle in the air).

Since this sponge cake gives off very little steam, the vanilla syrup with which it is soaked must be very hot. Afterward, let it rest for at least 12 to 15 hours before serving. Fresh, aromatic mint leaves work well as a garnish for this particularly light delicacy.

1. To make the Capuchina sponge cake, beat the egg yolks with the pulp of the vanilla bean until foamy. Pour the mixture into a 8 in/18 cm round cake pan with a height of 1³/₄ in / 3¹/₂ cm.

2. Place the filled cake pan in a steamer or water bath containing simmering water, but do not continue to heat the water during the cooking period. Seat the pot and steam the sponge cake for 20 minutes. Prepare the vanilla syrup by bringing the water to a boil with the sugar and vanilla bean.

3. After removing the sponge cake from the steamer, immediately soak it with the very hot vanilla syrup, and then refrigerate for at least 12 hours.

4. Take the Capuchina sponge cake out of the refrigerator and place it on a cooling rack. Dust it with confectioners' sugar and caramelize the surface with a salamander. If desired, dry scraped out vanilla beans in the oven, dip them in egg white and roll them in sugar, and then put back in the oven at 355 °F / 180 °C until the sugar crystallizes. Garnish the Capuchina with the vanilla beans or mint leaves and caramelized apricot segments.

Preparation time: 2 hours 15 minutes
Cooking time: 30 minutes
Difficulty: ★★★

Serves 8

For the coffee and caramel cream:
1 cup / 250 g superfine sugar
2 cups / 500 ml cream
4 tsp / 5 g instant coffee
6 egg yolks
6 sheets of gelatin
3 cups / 750 ml whipping cream

For the wafer base:
10¹/₂ oz / 300 g Jijona nougat, liquid
7 oz / 200 g milk chocolate coating

3¹/₂ tbsp / 50 g butter
4 oz / 120 g crisp wafers, crushed

For the hazelnut sponge cake:
7 egg whites
5 tbsp / 75 g sugar
3¹/₂ cups / 375 g roasted hazelnuts, ground

Clear cake glaze:
(see basic recipes)

To garnish:
seasonal red fruits
chocolate lattice

What distinguishes this cake is its crispy wafer base, whose rough texture resembles honeycomb. Its uneven surface could be smoothed over with a thin layer of sugar, cream, jam or other sweet substances of creamy, soft texture that would complement the crunchy base.

Francisco Torreblanca's impetus for this dessert arose when he was eating an ice cream containing chocolate flakes. The contrast inspired him to create this crunchy wafer base, enhanced with butter and milk chocolate coating, and then frozen until it achieves the right consistency.

The torte is filled with a coffee and caramel cream. Begin by making a light, dry caramel. The cream itself must be prepared

with great care and not allowed to boil. Use a particularly mild variety of coffee to flavor it, either very finely ground Colombia beans or highest quality instant coffee. Too intense a coffee flavor will overpower the taste of the caramel.

For the hazelnut sponge cake, Francisco Torreblanca prefers to use the delicious Spanish hazelnuts from Tarragona, but you can also substitute pistachios or walnuts. These are ground complete with their peel and stirred right into the sponge cake mixture.

1. To make the coffee and caramel cream, caramelize the sugar in a saucepan without added liquid. Heat the cream and carefully combine the caramel with the hot cream and instant coffee. Whisk the egg yolks, then combine the two mixtures and thicken like a custard to 185 °F / 85 °C. Add the gelatin, which has been soaked in cold water. Allow to cool and finally fold in the whipped cream.

2. For the wafer base, melt the chocolate coating and combine it with the nougat. Cream the butter and add the chocolate mixture to it. Carefully fold in the crumbled wafers. Pour the mixture to a depth of ¹/₄ in / ¹/₂ cm into a cake ring with a diameter of 7 in / 16 cm. Freeze for four hours.

Caramel Torte

3. Prepare the hazelnut sponge cake: beat the egg whites and sugar until stiff, then gently fold in the ground hazelnuts. Pipe two spirals with a diameter of 7 in/16 cm onto a tray lined with baking paper and bake for 30 minutes at 340 °F / 170 °C. Place a 8 in / 18 cm cake ring that is 1³/₄ in / 3¹/₂ cm high on a cake round and set a sponge cake base inside it. Top with a layer of cream, and then the chilled wafer base. Spread more cream on the wafer base, then place the second sponge cake layer on it and again spread with cream. Freeze.

4. Marble the top surface of the torte with melted caramel, remove it from the cake ring, and cover it with clear cake glaze. Garnish with seasonal fruits and decorate the perimeter with a chocolate lattice.

Preparation time: 1 hour
Cooking time: 12 minutes
Difficulty: ✶✶✶

Serves 8

For the ginger and chocolate cream:
6 tbsp / 90 ml milk
4¹/₂ tbsp / 70 ml crème fraîche
3 egg yolks
4 tsp / 10 g cornstarch

Italian meringue:
4 egg whites
¹/₂ cup / 125 g sugar
6¹/₂ oz / 180 g extra bitter chocolate, melted
2¹/₂ tbsp / 30 g candied ginger

For the sweet pastry:
2¹/₂ cups / 330 g flour
11 tbsp / 165 g butter
1 egg

5¹/₂ tbsp / 85 g superfine sugar
¹/₂ cup / 80 g confectioners' sugar
1 pinch of salt
¹/₂ tsp / 2 g emulsifier

For the lemon cream:
6¹/₂ tbsp / 100 ml lemon juice
6¹/₂ tbsp / 100 g sugar
13 tbsp / 200 g butter
peel of 2 lemons
eggs

To garnish:
superfine sugar
seasonal fruits

Though the Moors have long since left Spain, their influence on Spanish culture is still apparent. In the gastronomic culture, too, the Arabs left their mark: the use of rice as well as saffron, ginger, and many other spices traces back to the Moors. Francisco Torreblanca revels in their inspiration in this mouthwatering ginger and chocolate concoction.

Instead of fresh ginger, with its intense, sharp flavor, Torreblanca uses candied ginger (though candied with only with 10% sugar), which is much gentler, softer, and more easily digestible. In order to candy fresh ginger root, it is first blanched to make its flavor milder, then peeled, cut into slices and steamed with sugar.

The ginger can also be steamed in a microwave oven if it is enveloped in plastic wrap. When it is heated, the steam cooks the ginger until tender, and the sugar caramelizes on the surface. Ginger candied in this way is ideal for this recipe.

Also essential in this torte, of course, is excellent quality chocolate, in this instance one containing little sugar and a high proportion of cocoa, at least 64%. The Criollo variety, composed of an ingenious mixture of cocoa beans from the Ivory Coast and Venezuela, works well. Particularly demanding gourmets choose the so-called "black diamond" of chocolates, the Criollo du Pacifico variety, which is particularly pure and therefore slightly more bitter.

1. For the ginger and chocolate cream, bring the milk and crème fraîche to a boil in a saucepan. Whisk the egg yolks and cornstarch in a bowl. Combine with the milk and continue as for a pastry cream. For the Italian meringue, heat the sugar to 250 °F / 121 °C, beat the egg whites until stiff and pour the hot sugar over them, beating continuously. Mix the pastry cream with the meringue while the latter is still quite warm, then add the melted chocolate and finely diced candied ginger.

2. To prepare the sweet pastry, sift the flour onto a work surface and make a well in the middle. Place the softened butter and other ingredients in it and knead with the flour. Refrigerate the dough; then roll it out and use it to line an 8 in / 18 cm springform pan. Bake blind for 12 minutes at 355 °F / 180 °C. To make the lemon cream, bring the lemon juice to a boil with sugar, butter, and lemon peel. Beat the eggs and remaining sugar until frothy. Combine both mixtures, bring to a boil and pass through a sieve.

Chocolate Torte

3. Place the pastry base in a cake ring that is 2 in / 4 cm high and spread lemon cream on it. Sprinkle superfine sugar on the surface and caramelize. Freeze for two hours.

4. Fill the cake ring with ginger and chocolate cream, then freeze for another two hours. Remove the torte from the cake ring, again sprinkle with superfine sugar, and caramelize the surface. Garnish with seasonal fruits.

Preparation time: 2 hours
Cooking time: 20 minutes
Difficulty: ★★★

Serves 8

shortbread: (see basic recipes)

For the pastry cream:
1 cup / 250 ml milk
6 egg yolks
6 tbsp / 90 g sugar
4 tbsp / 30 g cornstarch

For the saffron cream:
pastry cream
10 saffron threads
3 sheets of gelatin

For the Italian meringue:
5 tsp / 25 ml water
$^{1}/_{2}$ cup / 115 g sugar
2 egg whites

To garnish:
10$^{1}/_{2}$ oz / 300 g apricots
seasonal fruits
chocolate decorations (optional)
Serve with a passion fruit or apricot coulis

The tender hands of the fetching Dulcinéa del Toboso, Don Quixote's beloved, very likely often helped in the harvest of saffron in La Mancha, the adventure playground of bold, wind-mill-tilting heroes in the work of 17th century Spanish author Miguel de Cervantes. Now as then, saffron stigmata are still gathered by hand in the early morning before sunrise, each flower yielding just three threads, just before the purple blossoms of this member of the crocus family close. Francisco Torreblanca uses this understandably expensive spice for his Dulcinéa torte, which he named after the heroine in Cervantes' novel.

Saffron gives food a rich color and distinctive flavor, and should therefore always be used sparingly. It is available either as a powder or as whole stigmas, called threads. The powdered form loses its flavor quickly and threads are defi-nitely preferable.

Before adding the saffron threads to the cream, they can be lightly toasted with a salamander. The slight heat highlights the unique flavor of saffron, a spice that is surprising over and over again, and is certainly not commonplace in a pastry such as this. Since it keeps well in the refrigerator, the saffron cream can be prepared a day in advance.

For the cake to be worthy of its name, decorate it in a manner befitting its class, crowning it with a wreath of ripe, fleshy, golden orange apricots and serve it with an apricot or passion fruit coulis.

1. Follow the basic recipe for the shortbread dough, then refrigerate. Roll it out evently and use it to line a greased springform pan with a diameter of 8 in / 18 cm. Bake it blind for 15 minutes at 355 °F / 180 °C.

2. To make the pastry cream, bring the milk to a boil. Meanwhile beat the egg yolks and sugar, and add the cornstarch. Stir some of the hot milk into the egg yolks, return to the pan with the hot milk and cook for two minutes, stirring continuously so it does not stick to the pan. To make the saffron cream, add the saffron threads and the soaked and wrung-out gelatin to the pastry cream.

Dulcinéa

3. For the Italian meringue, boil the water and 6 tbsp / 90 g sugar to 250 °F / 121 °C. Beat the egg whites with 5 tsp / 25 g sugar until stiff, then slowly pour the hot sugar syrup onto them while stirring. Continue beating at a medium speed until the mixture is completely cooled. Carefully combine the saffron cream and Italian meringue. Pour the mixture into a cake ring with a diameter of 7 in / 16 cm and freeze for four hours.

4. Remove the frozen saffron cream from the freezer and place it on the shortbread base. Caramelize the middle of the frozen saffron cream with a salamander. Cut the apricots into segments, sprinkle with sugar and caramelize with the salamander. Ring the torte with apricot segments and garnish the center with seasonal fruits or chocolate decorations.

Preparation time: 2 hours
Cooking time: 7 minutes
Difficulty: ★★

Serves 8

For the Alhambra sponge cake: 5 eggs
1 cup / 185 g finely ground almonds
³/₄ cup plus 2 tbsp / 210 g sugar
6 egg whites
³/₄ cup plus 2 tbsp / 110 g flour

For the cocoa truffle mixture:
2 cups / 500 ml whipping cream
3¹/₂ tbsp / 50 g sugar
¹/₃ cup / 35 g cocoa powder

For the egg cream:
3 cups / 750 g sugar
1 cup / 225 ml water
¹/₂ vanilla bean
¹/₂ tsp / 2 g cream of tartar
12 egg yolks

For the whipped cream:
2 cups / 500 ml cream
3¹/₂ tbsp / 50 g sugar

To garnish:
chocolate sticks, balls and other ornaments

The Goncourt brothers, famous 19th-century French authors, coined the phrase "alhambresque" to describe a building comparable to the world-famous palace of the Moorish kings in Granada. While this expression is not much used in our day, there is scarcely one more fitting for this visually impressive dessert. As is so often the case in Spain, the name of the torte alludes to its origins in a monastery kitchen.

So this delicate Catalan torte is alhambresque. It is also fairly high in calories and keeps well. Notable is that it is prepared without butter, and contains only the fat of the almonds (which is, of course, extracted for making almond oil).

Francisco Torreblanca has many tips that he is eager to pass on; for instance, you should use pasteurized cream, never sterilized, in this recipe. The cream for the whipped cream filling should be slightly whipped and not overly sweet. For optimal results, all utensils and ingredients should be the same temperature, namely a chilly 32 °F / 0 °C.

To prevent the egg cream from taking on an unappealing dark green color, use the cream of tartar sparingly, or substitute lemon juice. Torreblanca recommends not caramelizing the torte until shortly before it is served, and then serving it with a high-fat crème fraîche.

1. To make the Alhambra sponge cake, combine two of the eggs with the finely ground almonds and ³/₄ cup / 185 g of the sugar, then add the remaining eggs and whisk. Beat the egg whites and the remaining sugar until stiff, then gently blend the two mixtures. Fold in the sifted flour. Spread the sponge cake mixture onto a tray lined with baking paper and bake for seven minutes at 535 °F / 280 °C. When cool, slice through twice to form three layers. Prepare the cocoa truffle mixture by whipping the cream until stiff and adding the sugar and cocoa.

2. For the egg cream, start by making a sugar syrup: boil the sugar, water, vanilla bean, and cream of tartar to 38 °Beaumé. Whisk the egg yolks, add the sugar syrup to them, and pass through a sieve. Stirring constantly, return to the heat and bring to a boil. Allow to cool, and then refrigerate for one hour.

Marcos Torte

3. For the whipped cream filling, whip the cream until stiff with the sugar. Place a layer of Alhambra sponge cake onto a rectangular cake card and spread the cocoa truffle mixture onto it. Cover a second layer of sponge cake with whipped cream, place it on the truffle mixture, and top with the third sponge cake layer. Then freeze for seven hours.

4. Take the torte out of the freezer. Cover the surface with the egg cream, sprinkle it with superfine sugar and caramelize. Straighten the edges of the torte with a knife dipped in hot water. Garnish with chocolate decorations (plain or milk chocolate).

Preparation time: 1 hour 30 minutes
Cooking time: 10 minutes
Difficulty: ★★

Serves 8

For the cinnamon and almond sponge cake:
6 eggs
1 cup / 250 g sugar
1²/₃ cups / 250 g almonds, very finely ground
1 tsp cinnamon

For the apple jelly:
4 cups / 1 l apple juice, made from apple peel
4 cups / 1 kg sugar
³/₄ oz / 20 g pectin
10 sheets of gelatin

For the muscatel jelly:
3 cups / 1 kg apple jelly
³/₄ cup / 200 ml muscatel wine (Moscatel)
¹/₂ cup / 125 ml glucose syrup

For the vanilla cream:
1 vanilla bean
1 cup / 250 ml milk
5 egg yolks
6¹/₂ tbsp / 100 g sugar
9 oz / 250 g white chocolate coating
4 sheets of gelatin
2¹/₂ cups / 600 ml whipping cream

For the white cake glaze:
1¹/₂ cups / 500 g muscatel jelly
11¹/₂ oz / 325 g white chocolate coating

Because of cinnamon's powerful aroma, it should always be used sparingly. Around Valencia, however, a type of intensely flavored cinnamon milk granité (*granizado*) is traditionally enjoyed during the first balmy days of summer. In Francisco Torreblanca's recipe for cinnamon, finding just the right balance between cinnamon and almonds is the key element.

It is best to make the apple jelly for this cake yourself. Place apple peels into a mixture of water and pectin, bring them to a boil, add the glucose and gelatin and freeze the mixture for a while to let it set. This method yields a natural, slightly tart jelly that keeps well.

Moscatel, a muscatel wine from the Jávea region near Alicante, is prized by gourmets for its honey-like aftertaste and gives the jelly an extra, pleasing nuance of flavor. Once you have become adept in making the jelly, you can also flavor it with other muscatels, a Sauternes or champagne.

The first step in preparing the vanilla cream is to allow a carefully scraped-out vanilla bean to infuse in milk for 24 hours. When thickening, the cream should be heated no higher than 185 °F / 85 °C. It will keep for three to four days in the refrigerator and can even be frozen.

1. To prepare the sponge cake, separate the eggs; beat the egg whites and sugar until stiff, then add the lightly whisked egg yolks, ground almonds, and cinnamon. Spread this mixture onto a tray lined with baking paper and bake for seven minutes at 445 °F / 230 °C. To make the apple jelly, boil the apple peels and cores in water, then strain. Add an equal amount of sugar to the resulting juice and bring to a boil. Add the pectin and gelatin, and pass through a sieve.

2. Combine 3 cups / 1 kg of the apple jelly with the wine and glucose, and heat gently to make the muscatel jelly. For the vanilla cream, infuse the vanilla bean in the milk for 24 hours, then bring to a boil. Whisk the egg yolks with the sugar, add to the vanilla milk and thicken like a custard. Add the chopped white chocolate coating and the gelatin, which has been soaked in cold water. Allow to cool and then fold into the stiffly whipped cream.

Torte

3. Assemble the torte from the top down in an 8 in/18 cm cake ring that is 1³/₄ in / 3¹/₂ cm high. Cover a cake round with plastic wrap and place the cake ring on it. Alternate two layers of vanilla cream and two sponge cake layers, beginning with cream. Freeze for about four hours. Make the white cake glaze: heat the muscatel jelly with the white chocolate coating and stir to combine thoroughly.

4. Remove the torte from the freezer, invert it onto a cooling rack, and cover with the white cake glaze. Dry a slit vanilla bean in the oven, dip it in egg white and roll it in sugar, and return it to the oven to crystallize. Edge the cake with chocolate wafers and garnish with the vanilla bean and candied rose petals. Serve with a cherry coulis.

Preparation time: 1 hour 30 minutes
Cooking time: 7 minutes
Difficulty: ★★

Serves 8

For the almond sponge cake:
5 eggs
1 cup / 250 g sugar
1²/₃ cups / 250 g almonds, very finely ground
grated peel of 2 lemons
a little candied ginger

For the lemon cream:
³/₄ cup / 200 ml lemon juice
1²/₃ cups / 400 g sugar

1 cup / 250 g butter
grated peel of 4 lemons
8 eggs

For the lemon syrup:
(see basic recipes)
1 cup / 250 ml water
¹/₂ cup / 125 g sugar
juice of ¹/₂ lemon

To garnish:
clear cake glaze (see basic recipes)
white chocolate decoration
seasonal fruits

In the Spanish province of Alicante, many fruits are grown and are quite rightly renowned. Particularly in the lower Segura valley, a truly idyllic stretch of land peppered with vineyards and orchards, grow countless orange, lemon, and apricot trees. Francisco Torreblanca comes from this fruitful region, and pays it homage in the form of this delicious Lemon Torte recipe, which has been made in the Totel *pasteleria* since 1989.

The basis of this torte is an almond sponge cake made using Marcona almonds, a type of almond that has a very high oil content (store them in the refrigerator to prevent them from becoming rancid). The Marcona almond tree bears copious nuts that only ripen late in the season, in October, and must be eaten within a year.

The almonds must be ground until the almond oil seeps out and the almonds form a homogeneous mixture, rendering it unnecessary to add flour to the sponge cake.

A unique detail of this recipe is the contrast between the fairly acidic lemons from Alicante and the intense flavor of the candied ginger – use it sparingly! You may have to use additional sugar to produce a lemon syrup suitable for soaking the cake, especially if the lemons are fresh. Torreblanca serves the cake with *horchata de chufa*, a refreshing drink made by infusing chufa nuts (also called earth almonds or tiger nuts) in water, which is a specialty of the town of Alboraya near Valencia.

1. To make the almond sponge cake, separate the eggs. Beat the egg whites and sugar until stiff, and gradually add the egg yolks, ground almonds, grated lemon peel, and finely chopped candied ginger. Spread the sponge cake mixture onto a tray lined with baking paper and bake for seven minutes at 445 °F / 230 °C.

2. To prepare the lemon cream, bring the lemon juice to a boil with half of the sugar, the butter, and grated lemon peel. Whisk the eggs with the remaining sugar. Combine the two mixtures and continue to cook for 2–3 minutes. Pass through a sieve and allow to cool. To make the lemon syrup, bring the water to a boil with the sugar and juice of half a lemon.

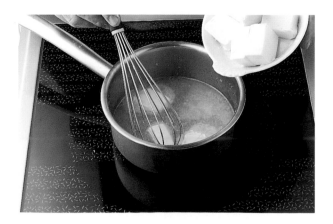

Torte

3. Place a cake ring that is 1³/₄ in / 3¹/₂ cm high and 8 in / 18 cm around on a cake round covered with foil, and line it with a 1¹/₂ in / 3 cm-wide strip of sponge cake that has been sprinkled with cocoa powder. Cut out two sponge cake bases. To assemble the torte, pour some of the lemon cream into the cake ring, top it with a sponge cake layer and soak with lemon syrup. Repeat with the remaining cream, sponge cake, and syrup. Freeze for four hours.

4. Remove the torte from the freezer, invert it onto a cake plate, and remove the cake ring and foil. Cover the top with clear cake glaze. Garnish with a white chocolate cornucopia and seasonal fruits.

Preparation time: *1 hour 30 minutes*
Cooking time: *15 minutes*
Difficulty: ★★

Serves 8

Capuchina sponge cake:
(see Capuchina recipe by Francisco Torreblanca)

For the Malaga sponge cake:
10 egg yolks
1 egg
1 cup / 235 g sugar
6 egg whites
1/4 cup / 35 g flour

1/4 cup / 30 g cocoa powder
1/2 cup / 70 g roasted almonds, very finely ground
5 1/2 tbsp / 85 g butter, melted

For the chocolate cream:
6 tbsp / 90 ml milk
6 1/2 tbsp / 100 ml cream
5 egg yolks
2 tbsp / 30 g sugar
1/3 cup / 50 g confectioners' sugar
9 oz / 250 g chocolate coating (64% cocoa content)
2 cups / 500 ml whipping cream

Chocolate glaze:
(see basic recipes)

The Capuchin, or more precisely the Order of Friars Minor Capuchin, is a branch of the order of St. Francis of Assisi, and was founded in 1529. Particularly characteristic of the Capuchins are their beards and especially their habits, with the typical long cowls. The Capuchina Chocolate Torte is an homage to this monastic order, whose members observe very strict rules; the chocolate glaze covering it is meant to hark back to the Capuchins' brown habits.

In addition to the ethereal Capuchina sponge cake, the torte contains a very fine sponge cake with a high almond content; it keeps for a long time. In keeping with the Franciscan codex, it should not be too sweet, so the chocolate coating used for the glaze must contain a high proportion of cocoa (at least 64%).

Francisco Torreblanca has taken extraordinary care composing his Capuchina Chocolate Torte, much like the Capuchins themselves, who make a first-class chocolate, comparable in that field to the Trappists' skill in making cheese. This is one more example of the important role played by traditions, strongly influenced by centuries-old religious orders, in the art of Spanish baking.

In the old and venerable Spanish monasteries, one finds weighty theological treatises side by side with countless recipes of this kind. This is also true in Portugal and in France; the Carthusians are famed for their sweet liqueurs, the various Trappist orders for their cheeses, and there is even a choux pastry known as "chocolate nuns."

1. Follow steps 1–3 on p. 268 to prepare the Capuchina sponge cake. To make the Malaga sponge cake, whisk the egg yolks, egg and 3/4 cup plus 1 tbsp / 200 g sugar until foamy. Beat the egg whites and remaining 7 tsp / 35 g sugar until stiff. Carefully combine the two mixtures with a spatula. Fold in the flour, cocoa powder, and ground roasted almonds, and finally the melted butter. Pipe the sponge cake mixture onto a tray lined with baking paper and bake for 6–8 minutes at 465 °F / 240 °C.

2. For the chocolate cream, bring the milk and cream to a boil. Beat the egg yolks with the sugar and confectioners' sugar. Combine both mixtures with a whisk and thicken like a custard over medium heat. Remove from the heat and stir in the chopped chocolate coating. Allow to cool to 85 °F / 30 °C. Whip the whipping cream until stiff and fold in the chocolate custard.

Chocolate Torte

3. Assemble the torte from the top down: cover a cake round with plastic wrap and place an 8 in / 18 cm cake ring with a height of 1³/₄ in / 3¹/₂ cm on it. Trim the Capuchina sponge cake to 7 in/16 cm and cut out an 8 in / 18 cm circle of Malaga sponge cake. Pour some chocolate cream into the cake ring, set the Capuchina sponge cake in the center, fill the ring with chocolate cream, and top with the Malaga sponge cake. Freeze for four hours.

4. Make the chocolate glaze according to the basic recipe. Dry a scraped-out vanilla bean in the oven, dip it in egg white and roll it in sugar, then return it to the oven at 355 °F / 180 °C until the sugar crystallizes. Take the torte out of the freezer and invert it onto a cooling rack. Remove the cake ring and cover the torte with chocolate glaze. Garnish with the vanilla bean and candied rose petals.

Preparation time: 1 hour 45 minutes
Cooking time: 20 minutes
Difficulty: ★★

Serves 8

almond sponge cake: (see basic recipes)

For the Jijona cream:
7 oz / 200 g Jijona nougat
3¹/₂ oz / 100 g milk chocolate coating
1 cup / 250 ml cream
5 sheets of gelatin
2 cups / 500 ml whipping cream

For the caramelized almonds:
¹/₄ cup / 65 g superfine sugar
³/₄ cup plus 2 tbsp / 125 g blanched almonds
1 tbsp / 15 g butter

For the chocolate glaze:
³/₄ cup / 180 ml sugar syrup (30 °Beaumé)
¹/₄ cup / 60 ml glucose syrup
¹/₄ cup / 60 ml cream
¹/₃ cup / 40 g cocoa powder
2 sheets of gelatin

To garnish:
candied cherry leaves
chocolate wafers
chocolate decorations

The town of Jijona, in the province of Alicante, is famed for its raisins and Turrón, a light nougat made with almonds and honey, similar to the Nougat de Montélimar. There is even a *denominación origen*, a government-regulated designation of origins, Turrón de Jijona, which guarantees that only rosemary honey and Marcona almonds (a late-ripening Spanish almond) are used to produce nougat bearing this label.

Marcona almonds should also be used for the caramelized almonds, if possible. They are slowly caramelized once the sugar has turned to caramel, and only then is the butter added. The caramel should remain transparent throughout this process.

The almonds used for the classic almond sponge cake should be lightly roasted. For the sponge cake mixture to have an especially soft texture, you can add a little honey, but it must be heated to 140 °F / 60 °C beforehand. The nougat for the Jijona cream should be passed through a large-meshed sieve so that a few crunchy pieces of nut remain.

The sponge cake also contains cinnamon (for which we can thank the Moors, who ruled Spain in the Middle Ages), though only a very small quantity. For this spice to develop its full flavor, use a cinnamon stick that is grated as needed and then passed through a fine sieve, rather than the powdered form.

1. Prepare the almond sponge cake with cinnamon and lemon according to the basic recipe. To make the Jijona cream, pass the Jijona nougat through a large-meshed sieve. Melt the chocolate coating and combine it with the nougat. Bring the cream to a boil and add it to the chocolate-nougat mixture, then the gelatin, which has been soaked in cold water. Allow to cool to 85 °F / 30 °C, then fold in the stiffly whipped cream.

2. For the caramelized almonds, heat the sugar (without liquid) until it melts and caramelizes. Add the blanched almonds and stir to coat them thoroughly, then add the butter. Place the nuts on waxed paper that has been brushed with oil. Retain a few almonds for garnishing the torte, and crush the others.

de Jijona

3. Cover a cake round with plastic and place an 8 in/18 cm cake ring that is 1³/₄ in / 3¹/₂ cm high on it. Cut out two sponge cake bases with the same diameter as the cake ring. Assemble the torte from the top down by alternating two layers of Jijona cream and two sponge cake bases, beginning with the cream. Scatter crushed caramelized almonds on each layer of cream. Freeze for four hours.

4. To make the chocolate glaze, heat the sugar syrup, glucose, cream, and cocoa powder and bring to a boil. Turn off the heat and add the gelatin, which has been soaked in cold water. Cover the torte with the chocolate glaze. Garnish with caramelized almonds, crystallized cherry leaves and fine chocolate rolls, and edge with chocolate wafers.

Basic Recipes

Almond Sponge Cake

Recipes: La Marjolaine by Maurice and Jean-Jacques Bernachons; Tortada de Jijona by Francisco Torreblanca

Ingredients:
5 eggs – 1 cup / 250 g superfine sugar – 1¹/₃ cups / 250 g very finely ground almonds – 1 tsp cinnamon – grated peel of ¹/₂ lemon

Method:
Separate the eggs and beat the egg whites with the sugar until stiff. Gradually add the egg yolks, ground almonds, cinnamon, and lemon peel. Spread the sponge cake mixture thinly onto a tray lined with baking paper and bake for 6–8 minutes at 445 °F / 230 °C.

Angel's Hair Jam

Recipe: El Mediterraneo by Francisco Torreblanca

Ingredients:
6 small spaghetti squash — 2 lemons – sugar to taste – 1 cinnamon stick

Method:
Quarter the squash. Place the quarters in a saucepan, add enough water to cover and simmer until tender (about 1¹/₂ hours). Discard the seeds; remove the angel's hair with a spoon and wash in cold water. Press out the water, then bring to a boil with the two halved lemons, sugar, and cinnamon stick while stirring. Set aside for 12–24 hours. The next day, bring to a boil again, adding half as much sugar as the previous day. Refrigerate in an airtight container.

Apple Jelly

Recipe: Cinnamon Torte by Francisco Torreblanca

Ingredients:
5¹/₂ lb / 2¹/₂ kg acidic apples – 4 cups / 1 kg sugar – ³/₄ cup / 200 ml glucose syrup

Method:
Wash the apples and cut them into 6 segments. Put them in a pan and add enough water to cover. Bring to a boil while stirring, and cook until they are tender and falling apart. Strain and press through a cloth to yield about 4 cups / 1 l of juice. Bring the juice to a boil, then add the sugar and glucose. Stirring constantly, reduce to 32 °Beaumé (35 °Beaumé at most). Cool immediately and store in an airtight container.

Basic Filling

Recipe: Pear Weggli by Eric Baumann

Ingredients:
¹/₂ cup / 100 g sultanas – 1 cup / 200 g dried figs – 2¹/₂ cups / 500 g dried pears – ¹/₂ cup / 100 g prunes – 1¹/₂ cups / 500 g apple jam – 3¹/₂ tbsp / 50 g sugar – 1 oz / 25 g lebuchen spices – 3¹/₂ tbsp / 50 ml fruit schnapps

Method:
Mix all the ingredients together and chop thoroughly.

Baumkuchen

Recipe: Hansa Torte by Adolf Andersen

Ingredients:
1 cup / 250 g butter – 5 eggs – 1 cup / 250 g sugar – 2 cups / 250 g flour – ¹/₂ vanilla bean – ¹/₄ cup / 35 g chopped roasted almonds – 1 cup / 250 ml rum

Method:
Slowly melt the butter. Meanwhile vigorously beat the eggs and sugar until light yellow. Fold in the flour and mix rapidly. Add the vanilla pulp, almonds, rum, and melted butter. Wrap waxed paper around a cone-shaped wooden roller. Make a wood fire. Fasten the wooden roller onto a spit. Rotate the roller and apply a first layer of batter with a ladle. Bake it by turning the spit constantly, catching any batter that falls off in a bowl. Continue ladling batter onto the roller until it has all been used. Allow the baumkuchen to cool on the spit before removing it.

Biscuit

Recipes: Amandine and Torte with Wild Strawberries and Red Currants by Pierre Hermé

Ingredients:
4 small egg whites – ¹/₃ cup / 85 g superfine sugar – 6 egg yolks – ¹/₂ cup / 60 g sifted flour

Method:
Beat the egg whites with 3¹/₂ tbsp / 50 g sugar until stiff. In another bowl, beat the egg yolks and remaining sugar with a whisk until foamy. Carefully blend the two beaten egg mixtures. Finally, use a spatula to fold in the flour.

Amandine: *Spread the biscuit mixture ¹/₂ in / 1 cm thick onto a tray in a rectangular shape, and use a cake comb to draw stripes in it diagonally. Bake without steam at 220–445 °F / 230 °C.*

Torte with Wild Strawberries and Red Currants: *Use a pastry bag with a large tip to pipe two spirals of the biscuit mixture onto a baking sheet. Bake without steam at 220–445 °F / 230 °C.*

Recipe: Le Royal by Bernard Proot and Gunther Van Essche

Ingredients:
4 small eggs – ³/₄ cup / 175 g sugar – almond and sugar mixture: ¹/₂ cup plus 2 tbsp / 112 g finely ground almonds and 7¹/₂ tbsp / 112 g sugar – peel of 1 orange – 5 egg whites – 9 tbsp / 75 g flour – ¹/₂ cup plus 1 tbsp / 100 g ground walnuts – 3¹/₂ tbsp / 50 g melted butter

Method:
Whisk the eggs with 3¹/₂ tbsp / 50 g sugar, the almond and sugar mixture and the grated orange peel. In a separate bowl, beat the egg whites and remaining sugar until stiff. Carefully combine both mixtures, then fold in the flour, walnuts, and melted butter. Spread the biscuit mixture onto a tray lined with baking paper and bake for 10 minutes at 355 °F / 180 °C.

Biscuit Natur

Recipe: Lemon-Lime Torte by Eric Baumann

Ingredients:
10 egg yolks – 6¹/₂ tbsp / 100 ml sugar syrup – 5 tbsp / 75 g superfine sugar – 7 egg whites – 3 tbsp / 45 g sugar – 1 cup / 125 g flour

Method:
Whisk the egg yolks with the sugar syrup and superfine sugar. Beat the egg whites and sugar until stiff. Combine the two mixtures; then fold in the sifted flour with a wooden spatula. Spread the sponge cake mixture onto a tray lined with baking paper or in a cake pan and bake for 20 minutes at 430 °F / 220 °C.

Biscuit Spécial

Recipes: Lemon-Lime Torte, Hazelnut and Chocolate Torte and Caramel Torte à la Baumann by Eric Baumann

Ingredients:
²/₃ cup plus 2 tbsp / 150 g very finely ground almonds – 1 cup / 150 g confectioners' sugar – ¹/₃ cup / 40 g flour – 4 eggs – 2 tbsp / 30 g butter – 4 egg whites – 4 tsp / 20 g sugar

Method:
Whisk the ground almonds, confectioners' sugar, and flour with half of the eggs. Gradually add the remaining eggs and then the melted butter. Beat the egg whites and sugar until stiff. Carefully combine both mixtures with a wooden spatula. Spread half the sponge mixture onto baking paper and make a pattern with a cake comb; color the other half as desired and proceed as for a striped Joconde sponge cake.

Buttercream

Recipe: Hamburg Harbor Torte by Adolf Andersen

Ingredients:
5 eggs – ³/₄ cup plus 1 tbsp / 200 g superfine sugar – a pinch of salt – 2 cups / 500 g butter

Method:
Whisk the eggs, sugar, and salt in a double boiler until frothy. Once they have reached body temperature, remove from the heat and allow to cool while stirring. Cream the butter until it is creamy and white, then gradually add the egg and sugar mixture.

Recipe: Brittle Sponge Ring with Vanilla Cream by Eric Baumann

Ingredients:
¹/₂ cup / 120 ml milk – ¹/₂ cup plus 2 tsp / 130 g sugar – ¹/₂ vanilla bean – 5 egg yolks – 1 large egg white – Sugar syrup: ¹/₃ cup / 80 g sugar and 2 tbsp / 30 ml water – 1²/₃ cups / 400 g butter

Method:
Bring the milk to a boil with ¹/₄ cup / 60 g sugar and the vanilla bean. Beat the egg yolks with the same amount of sugar. Pour a little hot milk over them, combine and pour back into the saucepan. Thicken like a custard, then allow to cool. Beat the egg whites with 2 tsp / 10 g sugar until stiff. Boil the sugar and water to 250 °F / 121 °C, and slowly pour onto the beaten egg whites. Cream the butter and gradually add the custard, finally folding in the Italian meringue.

Recipes: L'Ambassadeur, Strawberry Torte, Grand Marnier Torte, La Marjolaine, Palermo Torte by Maurice and Jean-Jacques Bernachon

Ingredients:
1¹/₄ cup / 300 ml whole milk – ¹/₂ vanilla bean – 1 pinch of salt – 2 egg yolks – 5 tbsp / 75 g superfine sugar – 6¹/₂ tbsp / 50 g flour – 3¹/₂ tbsp / 50 g butter

Method:
In a saucepan, bring 1 cup / 250 ml milk to a boil with the vanilla bean and salt, and boil for 2 minutes. Vigorously beat the egg yolks and sugar in a bowl. Add the flour, then 3¹/₂ tbsp / 50 ml cold milk so that no lumps form. Finally, stir in the boiled milk. Pour everything into the saucepan, return to a boil and allow to boil for 3 minutes, stirring constantly. Allow to cool. When the cream is almost cold, add the softened (not melted) butter.

Recipe: Walnut Mazarin Cake by Michaël Nadell

Ingredients:
1 cup / 250 g sugar – ²/₃ cup / 145 ml water – 3 eggs – 2 cups / 500 g butter – 13 / 4 oz / 50 g walnut compound

Method:
Boil the sugar and water until they reach 250 °F / 121 °C. Beat the eggs until frothy, and slowly pour the sugar syrup over them. Continue to beat until completely cool. Then add the softened butter and walnut compound and continue to beat until the mixture has a light consistency.

Candied Lemon

Recipe: Riviera Torte by Pierre Hermé

Ingredients:
5 oz / 135 g quartered lemons – 1 cup / 250 ml water – ¹/₂ cup / 125 g sugar – ¹/₂ vanilla bean – ¹/₂ star anise – a few Sarawak peppercorns, ground

Method:
Quarter the lemons and blanch three times, using new water each time. In a saucepan, bring the water, sugar, vanilla, star anise, and ground pepper to a boil. Add the blanched lemon quarters and simmer over low heat for 1¹/₂ to 2 hours. Allow to infuse at least overnight.

Caracas Sponge Cake

Recipe: Hansa Torte by Adolf Andersen

Ingredients:
2 tbsp / 30 g butter – 3 tbsp flour – 1 oz / 30 g nougat – 1 / 2 cup / 30 g sponge cake crumbs – 3 egg yolks – 1¹/₄ oz / 35 g marzipan – 4 tsp / 20 g sugar – a pinch of salt – 4 egg whites – 5 tbsp / 75 g superfine sugar

Method:
Melt the butter and let it cool again. Whisk the egg yolks until frothy with the marzipan, sugar and salt. Beat the egg whites and superfine sugar until stiff. Combine a third of the beaten egg whites with the egg yolk mixture, then fold in the remaining egg whites with a wooden spatula. Fold in the flour, sponge cake crumbs, nougat and finally the melted butter, not stirring longer than necessary. Pour the sponge cake batter into a greased and floured cake pan that has been lined with waxed paper. Bake for 12–15 minutes at 340 °F / 170 °C. Invert onto a cooling rack to cool.

Caramel

Recipe: Caramel and Orange Mousse Torte by Pierre Hermé

Ingredients:
$^1/_2$ cup / 130 ml glucose syrup – $^3/_4$ cup plus 1 tbsp / 200 g superfine sugar – 2 tbsp / 30 g butter – 1$^1/_2$ cups / 330 ml stiffly whipped cream

Method:
Dissolve the glucose (but do not boil), add the superfine sugar and heat until it caramelizes. Add the butter, then the whipped cream and reheat to 215°F / 103 °C. Cool completely.

Charlotte Cream

Recipes: Brittle Sponge Ring with Vanilla Cream and Kiwi Torte with Passion Fruit Cream by Eric Baumann

Ingredients:
2 cups / 500 ml milk – $^3/_4$ cup / 180 g sugar – 15 egg yolks – 6$^1/_2$ sheets of gelatin

Method:
Bring the milk to a boil with the sugar. Whisk the egg yolks vigorously, then add them to the milk and thicken while reducing the temperature (to about 180 °F / 82 °C). Fold in the gelatin, which has previously been soaked in cold water. Refrigerate.

Chocolate Génoise

Recipes: Caracao Torte, Palermo Torte by Maurice and Jean-Jacques Bernachon

Ingredients:
3 eggs – 6 tbsp / 90 g superfine sugar – $^3/_4$ cup / 90 g flour – 2 tbsp / 30 g butter – 2 tbsp / 15 g unsweetened cocoa powder – 3 tbsp plus 2 tsp / 25 g ground hazelnuts (optional)

Method:
Beat the eggs and sugar in a double boiler with a whisk, then remove from the heat and allow to cool slightly. Continue to beat with a mixer until the mixture falls from the beaters in long ribbons. Sift the flour and cocoa together; use a wooden spatula to fold first the flour and cocoa, then the ground hazelnuts and finally the hot melted butter into the egg mixture. Turn the batter into a greased and floured cake pan and bake

for 20 minutes in a preheated 390 °F / 200 °C oven. Turn out onto a cooling rack immediately.

Recipes: Birthday Cake and Walnut Mazarin Torte by Michaël Nadell

Ingredients:
6 eggs – $^1/_2$ cup plus 3 tbsp / 170 g superfine sugar – $^1/_2$ cup plus 3 tbsp / 85 g flour – $^1/_3$ cup / 40 g cornstarch – $^1/_3$ cup / 40 g cocoa

Method:
Beat the eggs and sugar in a double boiler until the mixture is firm and frothy. Sift the dry ingredients together and fold them in. Spread the sponge cake mixture $^1/_4$ in / 5 mm thick onto a tray lined with baking paper and bake for about 8 minutes at 445 °F / 230 °C.

Chocolate Glaze

Recipe: Capuchina Chocolate Torte by Francisco Torreblanca

Ingredients:
$^3/_4$ cup / 180 ml sugar syrup (30 °Beaumé) – $^1/_4$ cup / 60 ml glucose syrup – $^1/_4$ cup / 60 ml cream – 5 tbsp / 36 g cocoa powder – 2 sheets of gelatin

Method:
Heat the sugar syrup, glucose syrup, cream, and cocoa powder and bring to a boil. Then remove from the heat and add the gelatin, previously soaked, to the mixture. Cool slightly before glazing the torte.

Chocolate Mousse

Recipe: Riviera Torte by Pierre Hermé

Ingredients:
1 egg – 3 egg yolks – sugar syrup: 5 tbsp / 70 g superfine sugar and 1 tbsp / 15 ml water (boiled to 265 °F / 130 °C) – 6 oz / 172 g Manjari chocolate coating (melted at 115–120 °F / 45–50 °C) – 1 cup / 240 ml cream, stiffly whipped

Method:
Whisk the eggs and egg yolks, and pour the hot sugar syrup over them. Beat at high speed for 5 minutes and continue beating at medium speed until the mixture has completely cooled. Fold a quarter of the whipped cream into the melted chocolate coating, then the remaining whipped cream. Blend in the cooled egg and sugar mixture and combine carefully.

Chocolate Sponge Cake

Recipe: Chocolate Cake with Red Currants, Banana Mousse by Lucas Devriese

Ingredients:
12 eggs – 1$^1/_2$ cups / 360 g sugar – 1$^3/_4$ cups / 225 g flour – 9 tbsp / 75 g cornstarch – $^1/_2$ cup / 54 g cocoa powder

Method:
Whisk the eggs and sugar until the mixture drops from the beaters in long ribbons. Sift the flour with the cornstarch and cocoa powder, and use a spatula to fold them into the eggs. Turn the sponge cake batter into small, greased and floured cake pans. Bake for 25 minutes at 355 °F / 180 °C.

Choux Pastry

Recipe: Saint-Honoré by Christian Cottard

Ingredients:
1 cup / 250 ml milk – 6¹/₂ tbsp / 100 g butter – 1 tsp / 5 g salt – 1 tsp / 5 g sugar – 1¹/₄ cups / 150 g flour – 5 eggs

Method:
Combine the milk, salt, sugar, and small pieces of butter in a saucepan and bring to a boil. Once the butter has melted, add the flour and beat vigorously with a wooden spatula over low heat until the dough is smooth. Continue stirring for 1–2 minutes until the dough separates from the sides of the pan. Once it comes off the spatula easily, remove from the heat. Add the eggs one by one, stirring each one in thoroughly.

Recipe: Nadell's Cappuccino by Michaël Nadell

Ingredients:
1 cup plus 3 tbsp / 285 ml water – 1 cup / 250 g butter – a pinch of salt – 1¹/₂ tsp / 8 g sugar – 1 cup / 125 g flour – 4–5 eggs

Method:
Same as above. Michaël Nadell adds the remark that the dough should fall from the spoon heavily when it is finished.

Cigarette Batter

Recipes: Lemon Tart by Eric Baumann; Torte with Wild Strawberries and Red Currants by Pierre Hermé

Ingredients:
²/₃ cup / 160 g butter – 1 cup / 160 g confectioners' sugar – 5 egg whites – 1¹/₄ cups / 160 g flour

Method:
Cream the butter, then add the confectioners' sugar and half of the egg whites, followed by half of the flour, whisking continuously. Stir in the remaining egg white and flour.

For chocolate cigarette batter, replace a portion of the flour with cocoa powder; for colored cigarette batter, add food coloring as desired.

Clear Cake Glaze

Recipes: Mandarin Torte with Orange Cream, Caramel Torte à la Baumann and Kiwi Torte with Passion Fruit Cream by Eric

Baumann; Roussillon Torte by Christian Cottard; Bavaroise with Tea and Chocolate and White Wine Duchess by Lucas Devriese; Coffee and Caramel Torte by Francisco Torreblanca

Ingredients:
1³/₄ cups / 450 ml water – 1 cup / 225 ml glucose syrup – ¹/₂ oz / 12 g citric acid – ¹/₂ oz / 12 g pectin – 2¹/₂ cups / 570 g superfine sugar

Method:
Bring the water to a boil with the glucose syrup and citric acid. Remove from the heat and add the pectin and part of the sugar. Allow to cool slightly, then gradually add the remaining sugar, stirring until completely dissolved. Refrigerate until needed.

Cocoa Sponge Cake

Recipe: Le Caraïbe by Bernard Proot and Gunther Van Essche

Ingredients:
10 egg yolks – ¹/₂ cup plus 1 tbsp / 135 g sugar – almond and sugar mixture: 6 tbsp / 68 g finely ground almonds and 4¹/₂ tbsp / 68 g sugar – 5 egg whites – ¹/₂ cup plus 1 tbsp / 70 g flour – 6 tbsp / 45 g cocoa – 5 tbsp / 70 g butter

Method:
Thoroughly combine the egg yolks with 5 tbsp / 75 g sugar and the almond and sugar mixture. Beat the egg whites and remaining sugar until stiff. Sift the flour with the cocoa. Pour the egg yolk mixture onto the beaten egg whites, carefully fold in the flour and cocoa, and finally add the melted butter. Spread the mixture onto a tray lined with baking paper and bake for 6 minutes at 465 °F / 240 °C.

Cream for Decorating

Recipe: Amandine by Pierre Hermé

Ingredients:
¹/₂ sheet of gelatin – 1¹/₂ tsp / 7 ml apricot schnapps – 9 oz / 250 g pastry cream – ¹/₄ cup / 60 ml whipping cream

Method:
Soak and dissolve the gelatin; add the apricot schnapps and a quarter of the pastry cream. Combine with the remaining pastry cream and stir thoroughly. Fold in the whipped cream. Refrigerate.

Crème Anglaise

Recipes: Vanilla Kipferl by Franz Augustin; Leaf Torte with Pistachio-Praline Cream by Lucas Devriese

Ingredients:
2 cups / 500 ml milk – ¹/₂ cup plus 2 tbsp / 150 g sugar – 1 vanilla bean – 6 egg yolks

Method:

Bring the milk to a boil with half of the sugar and the slit vanilla bean. Beat the egg yolks and remaining sugar in a bowl until the mixture is light yellow. Stir a little hot milk into the egg yolks, then pour everything into the saucepan and stir with a wooden spoon over low heat. Do not allow to boil! Remove from the heat, and stir continuously until completely cooled. Pass through a sieve.

Duchess Sponge Cake

Recipes: White Wine Duchess, Montblanc and Raspberry Mousse à la Lucas by Lucas Devriese; Passion Fruit Torte, Strawberry and Rhubarb Torte by Bernard Proot and Gunther Van Essche

Ingredients:
4 eggs – 6^1/$_2$ tbsp / 100 g sugar – ^{3}/$_4$ cup / 100 g flour – almond and sugar mixture: 1 tbsp / 10 g finely ground almonds and 2 tsp / 10 g sugar

Method:
Beat the egg whites and sugar until stiff. Carefully fold in the sifted flour and almond and sugar mixture. For a 18 x 27 in / 40 x 60 cm baking tray, 600 g of sponge cake mixture is needed. Bake for 6 minutes at 480 °F / 250 °C.

Flourless Chocolate Sponge Cake

Recipe: Riviera Torte by Pierre Hermé

Ingredients:
13 tbsp / 190 g butter – ^{1}/$_2$ cup plus 1 tbsp / 90 g confectioners' sugar – 5 tsp / 12 g cocoa powder – 5 egg yolks – 2 small eggs – 8 oz / 225 g melted Manjari chocolate coating – 8 egg whites – ^{1}/$_2$ cup / 125 g superfine sugar

Method:
Whisk the butter with the confectioners' sugar and cocoa powder. Add the egg yolks, eggs, and melted chocolate coating to the butter mixture. Beat the egg whites until stiff with the superfine sugar, then fold them in. Use a pastry bag with a large tip to pipe spirals of the sponge cake mixture onto baking paper. Bake for 20–25 minutes at 355 °F / 180 °C.

Ganache

Recipe: Michaël's Stella by Michaël Nadell

Ingredients:
1 cup plus 3 tbsp / 285 ml milk – 3^1/$_2$ cups / 850 ml crème fraîche (40% fat) – 2 lb 12 oz / 1^1/$_4$ kg chocolate coating

Method:
Bring the milk to a boil with the crème fraîche, then remove from heat. Break the chocolate coating into small pieces and stir it into the hot milk. Allow to cool.

Recipes: Bûche de Noël, La Marjolaine, Palermo Torte, Sphinx Torte by Maurice and Jean-Jacques Bernachon

Ingredients:
10^1/$_2$ oz / 300 g cooking or bittersweet chocolate – 1 cup / 250 ml crème fraîche

Method:
Pour the crème fraîche into a saucepan with a thick bottom. Boil for one minute over high heat while stirring with a whisk. Remove from the heat. Break the chocolate into small pieces and add to the hot crème fraîche. Beat the mixture as it cools until it is smooth and homogeneous. Cover and refrigerate for at least 12 hours.

Recipes: Puff Pastry Torte with Stracchin Vanilla Cream and Torta Italiana by Flavio Perbellini

Ingredients:
3^1/$_2$ oz / 100 g baking or bittersweet chocolate – ^{1}/$_2$ cup / 125 ml crème fraîche

Method:
Same as directly above.

Génoise

Recipes: Mandarin Torte with Orange Cream, Caramel Torte à la Baumann, Zug Cherry Torte and Kiwi Torte with Passion Fruit Cream by Eric Baumann

Ingredients:
6 eggs – 5 egg yolks – 1 cup plus 1 tbsp / 260 g sugar – 2 cups plus 2 tbsp / 260 g flour – 1/2 cup/120 g butter

Method:
Beat the eggs, egg yolks and sugar in a double boiler (at 100 °F / 37 °C) until the mixture falls from the whisk or beater in long ribbons. Using a wooden spatula, fold in the sifted flour, and finally add the melted butter. Bake for 20 minutes at 340 °F / 170 °C.

Recipes: Le Canotier and Coffee Mill by Christian Cottard; Amandine and Caramel and Orange Mousse Torte by Pierre Hermé; Meringue Cake with Raspberries and Blueberries, Pistachio Torte, Tiramisu Bianco, Almond Cake, Torta Italiana and Zuppa Inglese by Flavio Perbellini

Ingredients:
4 eggs – ^{1}/$_2$ cup / 125 g sugar – 1 cup / 125 g flour

Method:
In a double boiler over lukewarm water, beat the eggs and sugar at a high speed until foamy, then remove from the heat and continue at medium speed until the mixture has cooled and falls from the beaters in long ribbons. Carefully fold in the sifted flour with a skimmer. Pour the génoise batter into a greased and floured cake pan and bake for 30 minutes at 390 °F / 200 °C.

Note: for Le Canotier, replace 5 tsp / 25 g of the sugar with 1 tbsp / 25 g honey and a little ground vanilla.

Hazelnut Génoise

Recipe: Hazelnut and Chocolate Torte by Eric Baumann

Ingredients:
9 oz / 250 g hazelnut paste – 4 tsp / 20 ml water – 8 egg yolks – 3 egg whites – 3¹/₂ tbsp / 50 g sugar – 9 tbsp / 75 g flour

Method:
Mix the hazelnut paste and water, then stir in the egg yolks one by one. Beat the egg whites and sugar until stiff. Carefully combine both mixtures with a wooden spatula and, finally, fold in the flour. Bake for 20 minutes at 340 °F / 170 °C.

Italian Meringue

Recipes: La Marjolaine aux Saveurs de Provence, Roussillon Torte and Saint-Honoré by Christian Cottard; Puff Pastry Torte with Chiboust Cream and Apples by Lucas Devriese; Amandine and Torte with Wild Strawberries and Red Currants by Pierre Hermé; Hazelnut Cream Torte by Christian Nihoul; Pistachio Torte and Zuppa Inglese by Flavio Perbellini; Passion Fruit Torte, Sienna Torte and Strawberry and Rhubarb Torte by Bernard Proot and Gunther van Essche

Ingredients:
2 cups / 500 g superfine sugar – 1 cup / 250 ml water – 8 egg whites

Method:
In a copper pan, combine the sugar and water and heat to 250 °F / 121 °C. Meanwhile, in a mixer beat the egg whites until stiff, then slowly pour the boiling sugar syrup between the beaters and the side of the bowl while stirring continuously. Beat for three minutes at high speed, then at medium speed until completely cooled.

Japonaise Sponge Cake

Recipe: Zug Cherry Torte by Eric Baumann

Ingredients:
8 egg whites – ³/₄ cup plus 3 tbsp / 225 g superfine sugar – ¹/₄ cup / 35 g flour – 1¹/₄ cups / 190 g very finely ground hazelnuts

Method:
Beat the egg whites and sugar until stiff. Sift the flour with the ground hazelnuts and use a wooden spatula to carefully fold them into the beaten egg whites. Bake the sponge cake mixture for 10 minutes at 300 °F / 150 °C.

Joconde Sponge cake

Recipe: Banana Dessert by Lucas Devriese; Les Gourmands by Bernard Proot and Gunther Van Essche

Ingredients:
4 small eggs – ¹/₂ cup / 125 g superfine sugar – almond and sugar mixture: ¹/₂ cup plus 2 tbsp / 112 g finely ground almonds and 7¹/₂ tbsp / 112 g sugar – grated peel of 1 orange – 6 egg whites – 3¹/₂ tbsp / 50 g sugar – 9 tbsp / 75 g flour – 5 tbsp / 75 g melted butter

Note: for Les Gourmands, use 6 tbsp / 50 g flour and 3¹/₂ tbsp / 50 g butter.

Method:
Beat the eggs with the superfine sugar, the almond and sugar mixture, and the grated orange peel. Beat the egg whites with 31 / 2 tbsp / 50 g sugar until stiff. Combine the egg white and egg yolk mixtures, then carefully fold in the flour and melted butter.

Recipes: Torte with Wild Strawberries and Red Currants and Riviera Torte by Pierre Hermé

Ingredients:
1 egg – ¹/₂ cup plus 2 tbsp / 95 g confectioners' sugar – ¹/₂ cup plus 2 tbsp / 115 g very finely ground almonds – 4 tbsp / 30 g flour – 5 tsp / 25 g butter – 3 egg whites – 4 tsp / 20 g sugar

Method:
Whisk the egg with the confectioners' sugar and ground almonds until the mixture falls from the beaters in long ribbons. Add the flour while mixing at low speed. Melt the butter over minimal heat. Beat the egg whites and sugar until stiff. Combine a third of the almond mixture with the butter, add the remaining almond mixture, then use a spatula to fold in the beaten egg whites. Mix everything thoroughly and then beat a few moments longer so that the sponge cake mixture collapses just slightly. Spread the mixture ¹/₄ in / 3 mm thick on a tray lined with baking paper. Bake 4–5 minutes at 430 °F / 220 °C. (One needs 1 lb / 450 g sponge cake mixture for a 18 x 27 in / 40 x 60 cm tray.)

Recipe: Nadell's Cappuccino by Michaël Nadell

Ingredients:
²/₃ cup / 120 g very finely ground almonds – 1 tbsp almond oil – 3 eggs – ¹/₂ cup plus 5 tsp / 145 g superfine sugar – 8 tsp / 40 g melted butter – 3 egg whites – 3 tbsp / 20 g flour – 3 tbsp / 20 g cornstarch

Method:
Whisk the ground almonds with the almond oil, eggs and ¹/₂ cup / 120 g sugar until the mixture is light yellow. Add the melted butter. Beat the egg whites and remaining 5 tsp / 25 g sugar until stiff. Fold in the flour sifted with the cornstarch, then carefully fold in the beaten egg whites with a wooden spatula.

Marzipan Mixture

Recipe: Riesling Fairy Tale by Adolf Andersen

Ingredients:
1 lb / 450 g marzipan – 3 egg yolks – 1/2 cup plus 1 tbsp / 90 g confectioners' sugar – grated peel and juice of 1 untreated lemon – a pinch of salt

Method:
Stir the marzipan and egg yolks until smooth. Sift the confectioners' sugar with the lemon peel, then add it to the marzipan with the lemon juice and salt. Combine everything thoroughly.

Pastry Cream

Recipes: Bûche de Noël and Brittle Baskets with Cream Puffs by Maurice and Jean-Jacques Bernachon

Ingredients:
2¹/₂ cups / 600 ml milk – a pinch of salt – 1 vanilla bean – 4 egg yolks – ¹/₂ cup plus 2 tbsp / 150 g superfine sugar – 6¹/₂ tbsp / 50 g flour

Method:
In a saucepan, bring 2 cups / 500 ml of milk to a boil with the salt and vanilla bean, which has been slit lengthwise. Boil for 2 minutes. Vigorously beat the egg yolks and sugar in a bowl. Add the flour, then 6¹/₂ tbsp / 100 ml cold milk so that no lumps form. While stirring, pour the boiled milk onto the egg yolk mixture, then pour everything back into the pan and boil for 3 minutes, stirring constantly with a whisk. Allow to cool and refrigerate.

Recipe: Banana Dessert by Lucas Devriese

Ingredients:
4 cups / 1 l milk – 1 vanilla bean – 2¹/₂ tbsp / 20 g dried milk powder – 6 egg yolks – 1 cup / 250 g sugar – 9 tbsp / 75 g cornstarch

Method:
In a large saucepan, bring the milk to a boil with the vanilla bean and dried milk powder. Beat the egg yolks and sugar in a bowl until the mixture is light yellow, then add the cornstarch. Stir in the boiling milk. Pour everything into the saucepan and boil for 2 minutes, stirring constantly so the cream does not stick to the bottom of the pan.

Recipes: Puff Pastry Torte with a Woven Lid and Saint-Honoré by Christian Cottard; Amandine, Macaroons with Aniseed Cream and Raspberries by Pierre Hermé; Dulcinéa Torte and El Mediterraneo by Francisco Torreblanca

Ingredients:
1 cup / 250 ml milk – 1 vanilla bean – 3 egg yolks – ¹/₄ cup / 65 g superfine sugar – 4 tsp / 10 g flour – 2¹/₂ tbsp / 15 g pudding powder – (5 tsp / 25 g butter)

Method:
In a large saucepan, bring the milk to a boil with the vanilla bean, which has been slit lengthwise. Beat the egg yolks and sugar in a bowl until the mixture is light yellow. Sift the flour and pudding powder together, then add to the egg yolks. Stir in the boiling milk. Pour everything into the saucepan and boil for 2 minutes, stirring constantly so the cream does not stick to the bottom of the pan. (When the cream has cooled to 120–130 °F / 50–55 °C, add the butter.)

Note: add the butter to the pastry cream for Pierre Hermé's and Christian Cottard's recipes.

Recipes: Meringue Cake with Raspberries and Blueberries, Almond Cake and Zuppa Inglese by Flavio Perbellini

Ingredients:
1¹/₄ cups / 300 ml milk – 3 egg yolks – 6¹/₂ tsp / 95 g sugar – ¹/₃ cup / 40 g flour – 5 tsp / 13 g cornstarch – confectioners' sugar

Method:
Bring the milk to a boil. Beat the egg yolks and sugar until light yellow. Sift the flour and cornstarch together, then add to the egg yolks. Stir in the boiling milk. Pour everything into the saucepan and boil for 2 minutes, stirring constantly so the cream does not stick to the bottom of the pan. Pour it into a bowl and dust with confectioners' sugar so that no crust forms.

Puff Pastry

Recipe: Puff Pastry Torte with a Woven Lid and Saint-Honoré by Christian Cottard; Pithiviers Torte, Orange and Almond Cream Tart and Alsatian Fruit Tart by Philippe Guignard; Puff Pastry with Spiced Cake, Oranges and Lemons by Pierre Hermé

Ingredients:
4 cups / 500 g flour – 1 tbsp / 15 g salt – 1 cup / 250 ml water
For turning: 2 cups / 500 g butter

Method:
Sift the flour onto a work surface and make a well in the center. Put the salt and water in it and combine with the flour to make a ball of dough without kneading excessively. Allow to rest in the refrigerator for 20 minutes, then on a marble slab roll out the dough into a narrow rectangle. Place the butter in the middle and fold the dough in thirds over the butter to form a square. Immediately, and gently, roll out to form a long strip of dough, without pressing the butter out at the edges. Fold the ends of the strip in to meet at the center, then fold the dough in half and refrigerate for 20 minutes.

Turning (folding and rolling out): Turn six times (three times two turns) at 20-minute intervals, refrigerating the dough in between.

Recipe: Puff Pastry Torte with Chiboust Cream and Apples by Lucas Devriese

Ingredients:
4¹/₃ cups / 540 g flour – 1 tbsp / 13 g salt – ³/₄ cup / 200 ml water
For turning: 13 tbsp / 200 g butter

Method:
See above.

Recipe: Puff Pastry Torte with Stracchin Vanilla Cream by Flavio Perbellini

Ingredients:
4 cups / 500 g flour – 1 tbsp / 15 g salt – 1 cup / 250 ml water – 5 tbsp / 75 g butter
For turning: 1 cup plus 13 tbsp / 450 g butter

Method:
Knead the flour, salt, water and 5 tbsp / 75 g softened butter to form a ball of dough. Allow to rest in the refrigerator for 20 minutes, then on a marble slab roll out the dough into the shape of a star and fold the points of the star over the butter for turning. Continue with three times two turns as above. Refrigerate until ready to use.

Sacher Sponge Cake

Recipes: Hansa Torte and Sacher Torte by Adolf Andersen

Ingredients:
9 tbsp / 140 g butter – 8 tsp / 40 g superfine sugar – a pinch of salt – pulp of 1/2 vanilla bean – 4 egg yolks – 6 oz / 175 g bittersweet chocolate coating, melted – 3 egg whites – 1/3 cup / 80 g sugar – 1/2 cup plus 1 tbsp / 70 g flour

Method:
Cream the butter with the superfine sugar, salt, and vanilla until fluffy and light. Blend in the egg yolks and the melted and cooled chocolate coating. In a separate bowl, beat the egg whites and sugar until stiff. Add a third to the butter mixture, then fold in the remaining beaten egg whites and the flour.

Savoy Sponge Cake

Recipe: Michaël's Stella by Michaël Nadell

Ingredients:
8 egg yolks – 1 1/3 cups / 325 g sugar – 1 1/2 cups / 200 g flour – 1/2 cup / 60 g cornstarch – 8 egg whites
For the cake pan: 5 tsp / 25 g butter – 2 tbsp / 30 g sugar

Method:
Vigorously beat the egg yolks with 3/4 cup plus 1 tbsp / 200 g sugar. Sift the flour and cornstarch together and fold them into the egg yolks. Beat the egg whites with the remaining sugar until stiff. First fold a third of the beaten egg whites into the egg yolk mixture, then use a wooden spatula to fold in the rest. Grease a cake pan with butter and sprinkle it with sugar, pour in the sponge cake mixture and bake for 40 minutes at 355 °F / 180 °C.

Shortbread

Recipe: La Dulcinéa by Francisco Torreblanca

Ingredients:
4 cups / 500 g flour – 1 cup / 250 g butter – 1 tsp / 5 g salt – 3/4 cup plus 2 tbsp / 125 g confectioners' sugar – 1/2 tsp / 2 g emulsifier

Method:
Sift the flour onto a work surface and make a well in the middle. Place the softened butter and the other ingredients into it and knead everything together thoroughly. Refrigerate the dough until needed.

Short Pastry

Recipes: Riesling Fairy Tale, Raspberry Cream Torte, Lübeck Hazelnut Torte and Schöppenstedt Torte by Adolf Andersen

Ingredients:
1 egg yolks – 3 tbsp / 30 g confectioners' sugar – a pinch of salt – 1/4 cup / 60 g butter – pulp of 1/2 vanilla bean – 3/4 cup / 90 g flour

Method:
Using the kneading attachment of a mixer, combine all the ingredients except the flour to produce a smooth dough. Gradually add the flour, and knead thoroughly. Wrap the pastry in a cloth and refrigerate until the next day, so that it is easier to work with.

Simple Génoise

Recipes: L'Ambassadeur, Bûche de Noël, Strawberry Torte and Grand Marnier Torte by Maurice and Jean-Jacques Bernachon

Ingredients:
3 eggs – 6 tbsp / 90 g superfine sugar – 3/4 cup / 90 g flour – 2 tbsp / 30 g butter

Method:
Warm the eggs and sugar in a bowl over a double boiler, then whisk. Remove from the double boiler and continue beating with a mixer until the mixture is light yellow and falls from the beaters in long ribbons. Use a wooden spatula to fold in the flour, then add the hot melted butter. Butter and flour a baking sheet with a high rim, and spread the sponge cake mixture on it 1 1/2 in / 2–3 cm thick, smoothing the top with a spatula. Bake for 10 minutes at 430 °F / 220 °C in a preheated oven. Make a day in advance.

Sphinx Sponge Cake

Recipe: La Marjolaine by Maurice and Jean-Jacques Bernachon

Ingredients:
3/4 cup / 180 g sugar – 1 cup plus 3 tbsp / 180 g blanched almonds – 6 egg whites

Method:
Grind the sugar and almonds in a blender until very fine. Beat the egg whites until stiff. Carefully combine the two mixtures. Use a pastry bag with a large tip to pipe the sponge cake mixture in the desired shape onto a greased and floured baking sheet. Bake for 7–8 minutes at 480 °F / 250 °C in a preheated oven.

Spiced Puff Pastry

Recipe: Puff Pastry with Spiced Cake, Oranges and Lemons by Pierre Hermé

Ingredients:
1 cup plus 2 tbsp / 170 g confectioners' sugar – 3/4 tsp / 1 1/2 g mixed spices (cinnamon or ginger, cloves, nutmeg, allspice) – 1/2 tsp / 1 g ground vanilla

Method:
Mix the confectioners' sugar, mixed spices, and ground vanilla. Roll the puff pastry out very thinly with a rolling pin, using the confectioners'

sugar mixture to dust it instead of flour. Refrigerate the pastry for 30 minutes, then bake at 375 °F / 190 °C. After three-quarters of the baking time, turn the pastry over and dust with the sugar and spice mixture. To caramelize, continue baking at 480 °F / 250 °C. After baking allow to cool and then cut into 2¹/₄ x 4 in / 4.5 x 9 cm rectangles.

Sponge Cake

Recipe: Strawberry Cream Torte by Franz Augustin

Ingredients:
6 eggs – 1 cup / 250 g sugar – 2 cups / 250 g flour – 3¹/₂ tbsp / 50 g butter

Method:
Whisk the eggs and sugar until the mixture falls from the whisk in long ribbons. Use a wooden spatula to fold in the sifted flour, and finally add the lukewarm melted butter.

Recipe: Brittle Sponge Ring with Vanilla Cream by Eric Baumann

Ingredients:
4 small eggs – 1 egg yolk – ¹/₂ cup / 125 g sugar – 9 tbsp / 75 g flour – 9 tbsp / 75 g cornstarch – 6¹/₂ tbsp / 100 g butter

Method:
Heat the eggs, egg yolk, and sugar to 90 °F / 32 °C in a double boiler, then beat thoroughly until it falls from the spoon in long ribbons. Sift the flour and cornstarch together, then blend them in and finally, fold in the lukewarm melted butter.

Strawberry Juice

Recipe: Torte with Wild Strawberries and Red Currants by Pierre Hermé

Ingredients:
1 lb / 500 g strawberries (without stems) – 3¹/₂ tbsp / 50 g sugar

Method:
Put the strawberries and sugar in a metal bowl, cover with plastic wrap and simmer for 1¹/₂ hours over low heat in a double boiler. Strain the juice produced in this way through a sieve and refrigerate so that the solids settle (without squeezing the strawberries). Filter out the solids and use the liquid as the syrup for soaking.

Striped Joconde Sponge Cake

Recipes: Bavaroise with Tea and Chocolate, Banana Mousse and Raspberry Mousse à la Lucas by Lucas Devriese; Sweet Chestnut Tarte by Christian Nihoul; Passion Fruit Torte and Strawberry and Rhubarb Torte by Bernard Proot and Gunther Van Essche

Ingredients:
4 small eggs – ¹/₂ cup / 125 g superfine sugar – almond and sugar mixture: ¹/₂ cup plus 2 tbsp / 112 g finely ground almonds and 7¹/₂ tbsp / 112 g sugar – grated peel of 1 orange – 6 egg whites – 3¹/₂ tbsp / 50 g sugar – 9 tbsp / 75 g flour – 3¹/₂ tbsp / 50 g butter

Method:
Beat the eggs with the superfine sugar, almond and sugar mixture and grated orange peel until foamy. Separately, beat the egg whites and sugar until stiff. Combine the two whipped egg mixtures, then carefully fold in the flour and melted butter.

Raspberry Mousse à la Lucas, Passion Fruit Torte and Strawberry and Rhubarb Torte: *Use half of the sponge cake batter to spread a thin layer onto a tray lined with baking paper. Draw stripes in it with a cake comb and freeze until set. Flavor and color the remaining batter with strawberry or raspberry jelly and spread it thinly over the frozen sponge cake. Bake for 5 minutes at 390 °F / 200 °C.*

Bavaroise with Tea and Chocolate, Banana Mousse and Sweet Chestnut Tarte: *Make chocolate Joconde sponge cake by replacing one-third or more of the flour with cocoa powder, then proceed as above.*

Recipe: Hazelnut Cream Torte by Christian Nihoul

Ingredients:
10¹/₂ oz / 300 g marzipan – 3 small eggs – ¹/₄ cup / 35 g flour – 4 egg whites – 5 tsp / 25 g superfine sugar – 5 tsp / 25 g butter

Method:
Combine the marzipan, eggs, and flour. Beat the egg whites and sugar until stiff. Fold the beaten egg whites into the marzipan mixture, then add the butter. Line a tray with baking paper, spread a thin layer of the sponge cake mixture onto it, and use a cake comb to draw stripes through it. Freeze until set, then spread a layer of chocolate Joconde sponge cake on top of it. Bake for 10 minutes at 355 °F / 180 °C. For chocolate Joconde sponge cake, replace 3 tbsp / 25 g of the flour with cocoa powder.

Sweet Pastry

Recipe: Le Canotier by Christian Cottard

Ingredients:
1 cup / 250 g butter – 1 cup / 150 g confectioners' sugar – 2 eggs – 2 tbsp / 30 ml crème fraîche – 1¹/₂ tsp / 8 g salt – grated peel of ¹/₂ lemon – 4 cups / 500 g flour – 1³/₄ tsp / 10 g baking powder

Method:
Knead the soft butter with the confectioners' sugar. Add the eggs, crème fraîche, salt, grated lemon peel, and, finally, the flour sifted with the baking powder (if using American double-acting baking powder, use one-third less). Shape the dough into a ball and refrigerate.

Syrup for Soaking

Ingredients:
6¹/₂ tbsp / 100 g superfine sugar – 6¹/₂ tbsp / 100 ml water – 6¹/₂ tbsp / 100 ml liqueur, or fruit puree, depending on recipe

Method:
Boil the water and sugar to make a sugar syrup; cool, then add the liqueur or fruit puree. See individual recipes for exact proportions and ingredients.

Vanilla Cream

Recipe: Schöppenstedt Torte by Adolf Andersen

Ingredients:
1¼ cups / 300 ml milk – 8 tsp / 40 g sugar – a pinch of salt – pulp of ½ vanilla bean – 2 egg yolks – 18 g wheat starch

Method:
Bring 1 cup / 250 ml milk to a boil with the sugar, salt and slit vanilla bean. Shortly before it boils, remove the vanilla bean, scrape it out and add the pulp to the milk. Whisk the egg yolks with the remaining milk and wheat starch, and stir into the boiling milk. Bring to a boil and remove from the heat.

Recipe: Brittle Sponge Ring with Vanilla Cream by Eric Baumann

Ingredients:
2 cups / 500 ml milk – 6½ tbsp / 100 g sugar – ½ vanilla bean – 6 egg yolks – 1¼ oz / 35 g pudding powder

Method:
Bring the milk to a boil with half of the sugar and the vanilla bean. Remove the vanilla bean, scrape it out and add the pulp to the milk. Beat the egg yolks and remaining sugar until they are light yellow. Add the pudding powder, and slowly pour in the hot milk. Return everything to the saucepan and bring to a boil again. Refrigerate.

Recipes: Pithiviers Torte and Orange and Almond Cream Tart by Philippe Guignard

Ingredients:
2 cups / 500 ml milk – 6½ tbsp / 100 g sugar – 1 vanilla bean – ½ cup / 55 g cream powder – 1 egg yolk

Method:
Bring the milk to a boil with the sugar and slit vanilla bean. Mix the cream powder and egg yolk. Stir in a little hot milk, pour everything back into the saucepan and bring to a boil. Pour into a bowl and cover with foil until needed.

Vanilla Ice Cream

Recipe: Forest Berries Cake by Christian Nihoul

Ingredients:
4 cups / 1 l milk – 1 vanilla bean – ³⁄₄ cup plus 1 tbsp / 200 g sugar – 12 egg yolks – ½ cup / 125 ml crème fraîche

Method:
Bring the milk to a boil with the vanilla bean and part of the sugar. Beat the egg yolks with the remaining sugar until light yellow. Stir in some of the boiling milk, then pour this into the saucepan with the remaining milk and thicken. Whisk in the crème fraîche, then freeze in an ice cream maker.

Viennese Sponge Cake

Recipes: Riesling Fairy Tale, Raspberry Cream Torte and Lübeck Hazelnut Torte by Adolf Andersen

Ingredients:
3½ tbsp / 50 g butter – 5 eggs – ³⁄₄ cup / 180 g sugar – a pinch of salt – ³⁄₄ cup / 100 g flour – ³⁄₄ cup plus 2 tbsp / 110 g wheat starch

Method:
Melt the butter and allow it to cool again. Beat the eggs, sugar, and salt in a double boiler over low heat until the mixture is frothy and at body temperature (about 95 °F / 36 °C). Remove from the heat and stir constantly until completely cooled. Carefully fold in the flour and wheat starch, then the melted butter. Grease a round 11 in / 24 cm cake pan with butter and line the bottom with baking paper. Pour in the sponge cake batter and bake for 30 minutes at 340 °F / 170 °C. Allow to cool in the cake pan for several hours.

White Ganache

Recipe: Le Royal by Bernard Proot

Ingredients:
4½ tbsp / 70 ml cream – 4½ tbsp / 70 ml milk – 5 tbsp / 75 ml glucose syrup – 1 lb 2½ oz / 525 g white chocolate – 9 tbsp / 135 g butter

Method:
Bring the cream to a boil with the milk and glucose syrup. Remove from the heat and add the white chocolate broken into small pieces and the butter. Mix thoroughly. Allow to cool.

Introducing the Chefs

Adolf Andersen

born August 10, 1936

Konditorei Café Confiserie Andersen
Wandsbeker Markstraße 153
D-22041 Hamburg, Germany
Tel. (0)40-684042; Fax (0)40-680394
Branches: Jungfernstieg 26; Market 16,
Glinde; EKZ Hamburger Straße; Axel-Sprin-
ger-Platz; EKZ Quarree Wandsbek Markt;
Stadtzentrum Schenefeld

Adolf Andersen comes from a family whose
members have been in business as pastry chefs
since 1910; he owns a confectioner's shop with
a number of branches in Hamburg. In his cafés,
visitors can sample his creations based on "old
family recipes, highly modern techniques, and fine discrimination." His personal
style was developed mainly during his apprenticeship in the Voigt confectioner's
shop in Braunschweig. His hobbies are cycling, fishing, and jazz.

Franz Augustin

born April 12, 1954

Demel k.u.k. Hofzuckerbäckerei
Kohlmarkt 14
A-1010 Vienna, Austria
Tel. (0)1-4051717; Fax (0)-405171726

Demel, the court confectioner's – the most
famous of such establishments in the time of the
Austro-Hungarian empire and supplier to the
imperial and royal court – needs no introduction.
Franz Augustin, who received sound training in
the Baumert (1969–74) and Nahodil (1974–89)
confectioneries, has been manager of the
bakery in this renowned establishment since
1994. Besides his great love of classic Viennese delicacies, Franz Augustin is
interested in movies and documentary films. His other hobbies are bowling and
travel.

Eric Baumann

born September 29, 1961

Confiserie Pâtisserie Baumann
Balgriststraße 2
CH-8005 Zürich, Switzerland
Tel. (0)1-3621121; Fax (0)1-3821364

Eric Baumann is a perfectionist. He first trained
at the Kaderschule in Zürich (1988–90) and
then worked in notable establishments in Biel,
St. Gall, and Zürich, as well as a period in
Mulhouse with Gérard Bannwarth. Eric
Baumann maintains excellent contacts with
various pastry chefs' associations, such as the
Cercle des Confiseurs, of which he has been a
member since 1993, and the international society *Relais Desserts*, which he
joined in September 1996. In his free time, Eric Baumann enjoys horseback
riding. He also goes jogging twice a week with his fellow-workers.

Jean-Jacques Bernachon

born October 27, 1944

Chocolaterie Pâtisserie Bernachon
42, Cours Franklin Roosevelt
F-69006 Lyon, France
Tel. (0)4-78243798; Fax: (0)-478526777

After an apprenticeship in the Pâtisserie
Marchand in Bougoin-Jallieu in the French
département of Isère, Jean-Jacques, the son of
Maurice Bernachon, completed several periods
of practical training in Paris at Suchard, in
Amsterdam at Blooker, and at Basle at the
École La Koba. In 1967–8 he worked for
Bocuse, to whose principles he has remained
faithful ever since. In 1969 he returned to Lyon, to work in his father's
establishment. Jean-Jacques Bernachon enjoys team sports, such as soccer
and rugby, and also plays golf. He is also interested in contemporary art,
reading, and travel.

Maurice Bernachon

born January 10, 1919

Chocolaterie Pâtisserie Bernachon
42, Cours Franklin Roosevelt
F-69006 Lyon, France
Tel. (0)4-78243798; Fax: (0)-478526777

The "*roi du chocolat*" (king of chocolate),
Maurice Bernachon, received his training at
Deboges in Pont-de-Bauvoisin and, before the
beginning of World War II, in Lyon at Lauthome
and at Collard. As a result of a war injury, he
returned to Lyon in 1942, and worked at the
Durand establishment. After a brief interlude in
Trévoux, he opened his own confectioner's
shop in Lyon. A close friend and colleague of Paul Bocuse, Maurice Bernachon
has been awarded the Ordre du Mérite Agricole and the Ordre des Arts et
Lettres. His hobbies are flowers, reading, and soccer.

Christian Cottard

born July 17, 1959

Pâtisserie Christian Cottard
49, Rue de la République
F-06600 Antibes, France
Tel. (0)4093340992; Fax (0)4-93340992

Christian Cottard comes from a family of pastry
chefs in Menton. In 1986 and 1989 he reached
the finals for the title of Best Craftsman of
Europe, and in 1989 he became *Champion de
France en Desserts*. In the same year he settled
in Antibes, after demonstrating his abilities at
the Oasis in La Napoule, and the Hôtel de Paris
and the Louis XV in Monaco with Alain
Ducasse. He is "open to all things beautiful" and likes to take part in the
glittering social occasions on the Côte d'Azur. Christian Cottard enjoys skiing
and surfing, is interested in photography, and particularly values family life.

Lucas Devriese

born January 3, 1964

Pâtisserie Lucas
Van Bunnenplein 29
B-8300 Knokke-Heist, Belgium
Tel. (0)50-504885; Fax (0)50-611582

Lucas Devriese trained with Jeff Damme in Ghent in 1985–9. In 1989, in Knokke – where he had gained his first professional experience with Roelens in the Notre-Dame confectionery – he opened his own establishment on the premises of the butcher's shop formerly owned by his parents-in-law. Today he is a member of the association *Top Desserts*. Lucas Devriese's hobbies are motorcycling and cycling in the nearby park, Het Zwin. He also likes dining out. He never forgets to mention how important his wife Hilde is to him in all his personal and professional enterprises.

Philippe Guignard

born March 13, 1963

Maison Guignard Desserts
Grand-Rue 17-19
CH-1350 Orbe (Canton of Waadt), Switzerland Tel. (0)24-4411524;
Fax (0)24-4417969

Since 1989 Philippe Guignard has managed his own bakery and confectionery, to which he added a café-restaurant in 1992. Meeting his friend Albert Bise, a friend with a passion for gastronomy, was decisive in his choice of career. Together with his head pastry chef, Laurent Buet, Philippe Guignard combines "whatever is good and beautiful and goes well together," and he is proud of the constant encouragement he receives from his customers. Philippe Guignard is a nature-lover, enjoys cycling, plays tennis, and is an active member of the Yverdon football club.

Pierre Hermé

born November 20, 1961

Ladurée
16, rue Royale
F-75008 Paris, France
Tel. 49279240; Fax 49279224

Pierre Hermé comes from a family of bakers and pastry chefs and had the privilege of training with Lenôtre. After this he proved his ability in Belgium and Luxembourg and in 1986 he became head pastry chef at Fauchon. In 1994 the Champérard guide gave him the title Best Pastry Chef in France. He has been head of the creative team of Ladurée since 1997. Hermé is an active member of the associations *Croqueurs de Chocolat* and *Relais Desserts*. He is convinced that "one should share one's imagination and creativity." He is interested in contemporary art and describes himself as a hedonist and epicure. His other hobbies are reading and squash.

Helmut Lengauer

born February 1, 1961

Hotel Sacher
Philharmonikerstraße 4
A-1010 Vienna, Austra
Tel. (0)1-4051455; Fax (0)1-4051457810

The genuine Sachertorte is produced in the Hotel Sacher, which is famous far beyond the borders of Austria. This delicious *torte* is named after Metternich's cook Franz Sacher, who created it in the summer of 1815 for the Congress of Vienna. Since 1985 Helmut Lengauer has been head pastry chef at the Hotel Sacher, where he upholds the tradition and renown of this establishment, whose pastries exemplify the European lifestyle. Not surprisingly, Helmut Lengauer is a great lover of classical music. He also loves playing tennis, and in the winter he skis in the mountains.

Michaël Nadell

born December 31, 1946

Nadell Pâtisserie
9, White Lion Street,
Islington,
London N1, England
Tel. (0)171-823 2461: Fax (0)171-713 5036

In Michaël Nadell's life the number seven plays a significant part: after his training at the Westminster Hotel School in London, he worked for seven years at the Mayfair Hotel and for seven years at the Intercontinental. He was awarded seven gold medals in London and Frankfurt for his creations in sugar. His establishment, founded in 1980, today has more than 50 members of staff. In 1994 he received the Catey Award for the Chef of the Year. Nadell's establishment is a member of the Culinary Academy of France. His hobbies are fishing and gardening. He has dedicated one of the recipes for *Eurodélices* to his wife Stella.

Christian Nihoul

born October 8, 1946

Gourmand Gaillard
1–7, Rue J. Jourdaens
B-1000 Brussels
Tel. (0)2-6269030; Fax (0)2-6269033

For 100 years the family Nihoul's confectionery business, which moved into its premises in the Avenue Louise in Brussels, has been a household name, and in particular it enjoys the patronage of the Belgian royal family. Christian Nihoul, who has managed the business since 1964, created a chocolate violin for Queen Fabiola. Moreover, he has set up numerous contacts in other countries (the United States, Korea, the World Exhibition in Seville), and has even opened two branches in Japan. He is a member of the Culinary Academy of France. For a long time Christian Nihoul's hobbies included fencing. He is also interested in Formula 1 racing and comic books.

Flavio Perbellini

born November 8, 1954

Pasticceria Ernesto Perbellini
Via V. Veneto, 46
1-37051 Bovolone (Verona), Italy
Tel. (0)45-7100599; Fax (0)45-7103727

The members of the Perbellini family have worked as pastry chefs for five generations – since the foundation of the firm by Luigi Perbellini in 1862. Flavio Perbellini received his training at the Technical Institute in Forli and then completed his practical training in France, at the Lenôtre School and with Taillevent. In 1986 he won a prize at the confectionery competition in Mestre. He carries on the family tradition with his brothers Giovanni Battista and Enzo. Flavio Perbellini loves his native city of Verona. Other interests are figurative painting – Botticelli is his idol – and swimming.

Bernard Proot

born July 30, 1954

Chocolaterie Pâtisserie Del Rey
Appelmanstraat 5
B-2018 Antwerp, Belgium
Tel. (0)3-2332937; Fax (0)3-2325109

Bernard Proot gained his first professional experience in the Del Rey confectionery, observed by his employer Marchand, who sent him to Lenôtre for several periods of practical training. To avoid "getting out of practice," he then went to Brussels for two years to work with Paul Wittamer. In 1963 he opened his own *chocolaterie-pâtisserie*, which was extended to include a café. He is a member of *Relais Desserts* and the association *Top Desserts*. "One can always exceed one's limits" is Bernard Proot's motto. He values family life, and enjoys good food and going to the cinema. He also likes squash and basketball, especially when his son Jan is playing.